For Peter —

With appreciation for our
joint captivation and
pursuit of true love.

— Michael Nelson

Oct. 20, 2009

HITLER UNMASKED

Hitler unmasked.

(Photo courtesy of John Toland, from *Adolf Hitler,* Doubleday, 1976.)

HITLER UNMASKED

The Romance of Racism and Suicide

Michael Nelken, M.D.

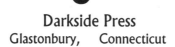

Darkside Press
Glastonbury,   Connecticut

Reader comments will be acknowledged in the second edition from:
Darkside Press-- *"Making the invisible visible"*
P.O. Box 306, Glastonbury CT 06033.
For orders or educational discounts, call:
1-800-DYG-DARK

A brief summary of this material was published in the *Academy Forum* of the American Academy of Psychoanalysis (Spring/Summer 1993) under the title: "Adolf Hitler and Acting-out." A summary of Part Two was presented at Congregation Beth El-Keser Israel, New Haven, Connecticut, in June 1995: "Why Did It Happen to Us?"

Grateful acknowledgement is made to Presidio Press for permission to reprint excerpts from *Lost Victories* by Erich von Manstein, © 1982 Bernard & Graefe Verlag; *Halder War Diary* by Franz Halder, © 1988 by Charles Burdick and Hans-Adolf Jacobsen; and *Inside Hitler's Headquarters* by Walter Warlimont, © 1964 by Weidenfeld & Nicholson; and to Noontide Press, P.O.Box 2739, Newport Beach CA 92659, for permission to reprint excerpts from *Panzer Leader* by Heinz Guderian. Excerpts from *The Young Hitler I Knew* by August Kubizek. Copyright, 1954, by Paul Popper & Co. Copyright © renewed 1983 by Paula Kubizek and William Guttmann. Reprinted by permission of Houghton Mifflin Co. All rights reserved. Special thanks are offered John Toland for permission to use photographs from *Adolf Hitler* by John Toland, published by Doubleday & Co., © 1976 by John Toland. Photo production: Bruce Ackland.

Printed in the United States of America.
10 9 8 7 6 5 4 3 2 1

Publisher's Cataloging in Publication (by Quality Books Inc.)
Nelken, Michael
  Hitler unmasked: the romance of racism and suicide / Michael Nelken.
  p. cm.
  Includes bibliographical references and index.
  LCCN: 95-83613
  ISBN 0-9649979-0-8

  1. Hitler, Adolf, 1889-1945--Psychology. 2. Heads of state--Germany--Biography. 3. Germany--History--1933-1945. 4. World war, 1939-1945. I. Title.

DD247.H5N35 1996   943.086'092
                          QBI96-20242

This work is dedicated to Harry S. Truman.

He desegregated the United States Army and recognized the State of Israel in its first minutes. Like Lincoln and Wilson before him, Truman saw that, in a democracy, the evil of war has to buy something decent, to balance and justify the eruption from the dark side of human nature.

This work is also dedicated to the best of my teachers:
(alphabetically)

E. James Anthony, Mehadin Arafeh,
Jules Victor Coleman, Jean F. Delord,
Joe Freeman, Doris Gilpin*, Marcel Heiman*,
Dori Laub, Turk Murphy*, Steve Ramsey,
Benjamin Sachs, Norman Schwemberger,
Carl Whitaker*.

And was also inspired by:

Sam and Zoila* Nelken, Alonzo Ensenat* and Steve Farber*

* *in memoriam*

ACKNOWLEDGEMENTS

I was extremely fortunate to attract the diligent efforts and superb advice of Leonard Rosenman, whose hand is as steady and deft with the editorial pen, in his ninth decade, as ever it was with a scalpel. He was kind enough to review this work in detail, although its faults and peculiarities remain, necessarily, my responsibility. In addition, C. E. Poverman generously enlarged his academic year with a very helpful critique.

Another kind of sturdiness is needed to worry through earlier and rougher versions of a work. This labor was generously offered by Larry Greenberg, Charles Goetsch and Brian Holmes. Brian also supplied the title for this book. Additional and very valuable comments were offered by S. T. Parker, Sandy Clark Festa, Mary and Lew diSibio, Paul and Frances Raymer, Kevin Miller, John Keyes, Stuart Sugarman, Jack Barrack, Jon-Jay Tilsen, David Lesser, Eric Beller, Larry Fiquette, Francesca Cancian and Ronald Lee. Gale Cooper gave important early support, as did Bob Mann. Many others were kind enough to listen attentively to wide-ranging discussions, especially Sharon Ives Lawson, Charlotte Pinto and Henni Schwartz. The advice of David Kovel was particularly useful. For their authoritative nods of early encouragement, I wish to thank John Updike, Fritz Redlich, Elie Wiesel and Joseph Lieberman; however, they have not seen or endorsed this work, for which no one bears any responsibility except myself. Ultimately, the one person who endured most patiently across the years of preparation was my wife, Susan, to whom I am grateful beyond telling for her steadying influence as well as her unfailing support.

EDITOR'S NOTE

I would be very conscious that I was putting forth a daring set of hypotheses to explain the phenomenon of Hitler. You began with what had puzzled you: What (not who) was Hitler? How can we understand that phenomenon (not why can we detest him and why must we fear recrudescences of his like)? You sought and found new information which were your clues, which generated your new insights. You integrated and you analyzed in your own fashion as an experienced analyzer....You assembled and set in order the bases for your interesting conjectures, which you expounded and explained. You offered your evidence pari passu.

Nevertheless....you cannot convince your reader by Decrying. If the conjectures really are credible and stimulating and fruitful, you weaken them by displaying hatred. You cannot allow yourself to vilify Hitler if ever you wish to destroy the historical personifaction of that evil phenomenon. He was an evil man, nevertheless, a man with all his evils exposed for you to illuminate....an arch-fiend, a contemptible rabble-rouser, or whatever. But don't diminish him in his greatness of evil, by making him less than a whole person.

You seek to explain his very own varieties of lust and exultation, indeed, Hitlerian. You share your horror but you must accept the fact that Hitler was human. I will recite, again, what Terence wrote about three centuries B.C.: "Being human, nothing human seems strange to me." And part of your thesis is the exemplification of another quote: "Power corrupts and absolute power corrupts totally."

You have tried to discover why Hitler's corruption and Germany's (that blanket generality...) was different from the poker player who wins one pot after another by bluffing, and then seeks to overwhelm all the others at the table with a last Grand Bluff. Why did Hitler's exultations and why did his successes lead to his downfall? Were they wired together? Whether he recognized that or not was not your task to discover. It is enough that you connected the beginnings with the end. But was that kind of connection different in Hector and Achilles, in Darius II and Xerxes, in Alexander and Julius Caesar, in Caliph Omar and Ghinghis, in Robespierre and Napoleon and Pasha Mehmet and Ibrahim? You have a lot to say and you challenge your reader.

--Leonard Rosenman, M.D.
San Francisco, California

A LESSON

1924: *"The great crime the German people committed against itself in 1918 [surrender] can be expiated only by prodigious efforts, perhaps by very great and cruel sufferings...better die, die at once [than live in shame]."*

1933-38: Takes power, defies his generals, risks war.

1937: *"It is not my way to issue a direct challenge....I use my intelligence to help me to maneuver him into a tight corner, so that he cannot strike back, and then I deliver the fatal blow."*

1939: Begins war.

1939: *"It is no longer a question of justice or injustice, but of life or death for [Germany's] eighty million human beings."*

1940-41: Expands war until forced to retreat.

1942: *"If the German people are not ready to fight for their survival, well, then they have to disappear."*

1942-44: Throws away armies in Stalingrad, Tunis, Normandy.

1944: *"[Germany] must have been too weak; it had failed to prove its mettle before history and was destined only to destruction."*

1945: Destruction and partition of Germany; suicide.

--Adolf Hitler

A PLEA

1995: "This [now] is a sensible government

that makes sensible decisions."

--*Chancellor Helmut Kohl*

defending the first foreign adventure
of the Luftwaffe since Hitler:
peace-keeping in Bosnia.

TABLE of CONTENTS

TABLE OF CONTENTS, continued

Photographs

Hitler unmasked: the Führer wriggles for an aide and some
Bavarian schoolgirls:

frontispiece

Hitler ecstatic in February 1945 as the Red Army nears Berlin.
He reviews plans to destroy his hometown, Linz, to improve it:

p. 27

Hitler throbbing in February 1942 as he tells new SS officers
that in Russia, they can die as heroes:

p. 78

[Photos from John Toland: *Adolf Hitler*, Doubleday, 1976, by
courtesy of John Toland.]

Maps

Author's Preface

Perhaps Hitler lost the war because he became distracted or reckless sometime between 1938 and 1943. And he created the Holocaust-Shoah in 1941 because he suddenly realized he could. However, these concepts are not supported by the evidence. What if Hitler did things his way only and dedicated himself to answering boldly any restriction, no matter what the cost. 'Defy and avenge' were his watchwords.

Perhaps Hitler had long planned the Holocaust because he hated Jews. In this circular reasoning, he murdered therefore he hated, and he hated therefore he murdered. Few ask why Hitler would hate Jews, and the answers have been desperately weak, such as: his dying mother's doctor was one. If a part-Jewish Hitler had mixed feelings about Jews and about racism, his final solution could be both to order the Holocaust and to condemn himself for it.

Whatever cautions it provides for the future, to examine Hitler's outlook does not change history. He remains a monster even if we name the pieces. We are all his victims; the dead were our cousins. So were the killers. The most significant lesson Hitler taught was the insanity of trying to split a nation, calling one part good and one bad. Did he plan his lesson?

It cannot be emphasized too much that Hitler did not visit any of the concentration camps. He spent most of the war hiding in the woods. He hurt no one by his own hand and never watched a killing. He permitted no discussion of the roundups of Jews. The systematic murder of civilians never took place, as far as he personally witnessed. All he saw were typewritten body counts. In the pristine temple of his own mind, he kept genocide purely an abstract idea.

With five chimneys spewing the ashes of ten thousand people a day at Auschwitz, Hitler signed nothing and saw nothing. Furthermore, Hitler often claimed death to be a good choice. His notion of the Holocaust-Shoah could have been both abstract and equivocal.

The new concepts fit together better. However, many prefer a simpler Hitler, so to promote World War II as a morality play about good ultimately conquering evil. It did. But Hitler was never the cardboard caricature boogey man of popular lore.

Part One of this book shows that Hitler played by his own rules; Part Two defines those rules, and shows how his early life shaped them. He started life as a tiny, helpless child, not as the monster he became. This peculiar boy even had reason to hate Germans and to love Jews. Later, in his agony of confusion, he shrieked that the world was black-and-white.

Almost nothing about Adolf Hitler is what it at first seems. A dozen years ago I started what I thought would be a dry, academic inquiry into Hitler's family ties. It turned into a shocking, surreal adventure as I saw that an obstinate, withdrawn teen-age dreamer grew up to set the world on fire, destroy his chosen country and gas civilians.

We all still live with the fifty million people who were not erased, but immortalized by their deaths in the war. But Hitler's motives have remained obscure--no ordinary reason could explain unthinkable acts. To investigate the author of this carnage, I start with the courtship of his parents and weigh his formative years. Later, the fervent nationalist and rabid anti-Semite would ruin Germany and revive Israel. Call these accidents of history due to miscalculations and circumstances beyond his control. Yet he once seemed so shrewd.

Hitler found reasons to wage war, to its bitter end. Some dismiss Hitler as a madman. Twenty years in psychiatry have taught me that even madness has a kind of logic. Hitler got away with doing terrible things. We swear that he was from

Mars, or a mutant, but our fascination with his evil signals some kinship. Could buried envy make us curious? Kind as we may try to be, we are all descended from creatures that roamed hungry, hunting and killing to survive. We too know how to rip and tear, but we belong to a more civil world, so we hold back. Hitler achieved a terrible combination of power and isolation that left him empty, and freed him of restraint.

The facts have all been published before. I try to show what kind of man must have lived these facts. Countering the distraction of his violence, to emphasize Adolf Hitler as a person, I put his statements *in italics*. Take none at face value. He gave many reasons for his actions, much propaganda. With time and distance, and by comparing him to similar people, we can estimate the root sources of Hitler's frenzy. Psychiatrists need lengthy personal interviews to penetrate the ordinary surface of an ordinary life, but a man of action leaves many marks of his character and outlook, and many witnesses. The first American psychiatrist to study Hitler thoroughly, Walter Langer, predicted Hitler's suicide years in advance, without ever meeting him. The wealth of material that came to light after the war lets us say much more about Hitler now.

Since he first won and then did not, some authors present two Hitlers, one smart and one dumb. I integrate the early with the late Hitler. To the end, he held Germany loyal. The string of diplomatic and military victories that made him seem so cunning and terrifying came from the same mind that produced years of muleheaded posturing in defeat.

I have long avoided this ugly subject. When I was a boy in Connecticut we closed black window shades at night so the Germans would not see lights and bomb us. Later I saw German prisoners of war chained together, wearing stripes and pounding rocks alongside a road in Louisiana. They looked surprisingly ordinary. Who would bother to gather and ship people to be killed? Why start a war? They had to be savages. I was past forty before I could stand to read about Hitler.

Calling him human brings a shiver of embarrassment; it seems far too kind. We boys feared German bombers even in New Orleans, whenever a low-flying airplane rumbled. DP's (Displaced Persons) arrived from Europe numb, alone and still shaking from their escape. Hitler made his name a curse word, yet he has to be examined, as would any devastating virus. When we were medical school professors, Stuart Sugarman told me Helm Stierlin had written that Hitler was wrapped up with his mother. Marion Gilliam-Lederman said Hitler's father abused him brutally, according to Alice Miller. My investigation started then.

Hitler ordered death for everyone, friend and foe, but those who hope evil is a genetic flaw avoid discussing him; the only sins of his first thirty years of life were arguing and loafing. Finding the roots of his attitude requires patient digging. We must scrutinize his path through childhood to avoid it.

Could anyone have fixed the anguished twenty-year-old who later became Führer of Germany? Part Three takes up the challenge of what almost happened.

Clausewitz called war an extension of diplomacy, but the Second World War was an extension of Hitler's personality. He was author, producer, director and star. Psychological studies of him have slighted the details of the war, while military studies gloss over Hitler's mental workings and family tensions. This autopsy draws on both sources.

The racist mythology Hitler sold Germany proved to be a Trojan Horse that destroyed her. Her resulting arrogance set the world at her throat. She then added ridicule and loathing for her contradictory claim: that genocide was needed to protect herself. With hindsight, Germany may one day decide her Viennese lover was an impostor.

PART ONE

HITLER'S

CONFUSIONS

His war for and against Germany.

INTRODUCTION

Deceptively ordinary, a couch and chairs stand guard against chaos. A man's body sprawls over a low table. Blood pours from a hole torn in his head. Bone, brains and blood have spattered a cushion. The loose fleshiness of his long face shows him to be much older than the woman lying alongside. Her trim, athletic figure twitches feebly, and a bitter almond smell seeps from her blue-tinged nostrils. Pistols lie cooling on the floor, his and hers, flung or dropped. On an iron clothes rack hang a coat, a hat, soft deerskin gloves and a dog leash. A door opens, and men enter wearing uniforms of the National Socialist Party, the Hitler Youth and the *Schutzstaffel*. This is Germany, or a hideous fairy tale about Germany, a tale which came to life, but has now ended.

For his final paradox, the sorcerer has laid himself out in his concrete cell with his own 7.65 mm. Walther pistol. Russian artillery pounds the ruins of Berlin far above, on the surface of the earth. By choice, Hitler crept into this dungeon twelve years after becoming Germany's Chancellor. The men in pretty suits--Hitler's own designs--disappear instantly, but the damage is done. The illusion was that one people would master all others. Despite Hitler's promises, Germany will have no thousand-year *Reich*, no *Lebensraum* of conquered land to settle, and no tidal wave of military glory. She has hunger, rubble and shame.

Incredibly, it all hung on him. After six years of war, one shot from the Walther puts Europe at peace. Except for her Leader, Germany has long been ready to surrender. Finally, on April 30, 1945, Hitler and his virgin mistress kill themselves. They pretended to marry the day before, under the ground. Suicide was the only pledge they kept. Refusing to flee Berlin,

Hitler boasted: *"At her own request she goes to her death with me."* Did he also mean Germany? He had long claimed: *"My only bride is my Motherland."* His corpse, lying in front of his mother's picture, is his first victim as Chancellor and Führer: he has not killed anyone himself, nor even watched. [Note: Hitler's words are *emphasized* throughout this work.]

One hundred fifty miles from the capitol, three weeks earlier: Dwight Eisenhower leads the British and American armies into the German heartland. He marches the citizens of Gotha to its zone of barbed wire, guntowers and extremely thin men in striped uniforms. The shaven-headed men in stripes stare silently; they move slowly, as if they were underwater. From thousands of stacked cadavers the stench stretches for miles. The people of Gotha deny having noticed. Their mayor and his wife hang themselves. In the countryside near Cracow, Soviet troops find barbed wire protecting large public showers in a building full of ovens and ash at the end of a railroad spur. A massive wrought-iron gate spells out *Arbeit macht frei*: work will make you free. Orderly ledgers have counted by country and race, up to ten thousand people a day. Contracts to build the ovens and the gassing chambers were awarded only after competitive bidding by responsible firms. Some Germans merely watched sealed cattle-cars roll by, but Hitler made his death factories a permanent obligation for all Germans. Even the German-American Eisenhower leaves the *Lager* shouting at his sentry: "Still having trouble hating them?"

Flashback: 1905.

Any explanation of Hitler's life must tell why he cut it short. He left a physically devastated Germany and the crisis of faith her barbarism forced on the world. But even as an adolescent, Hitler had planned for a notorious suicide. The young Hitler had told his only friend two versions of his suicide plan. Both versions revolved around the blind loyalty of a woman.

The first plan was to jump into the Danube River along with Stefanie, a girl Adolf worshipped from afar. He had never spoken to her; she was to perish for attracting him--Hitler would always limit his contact with women. His second plan was to be a Leader of the People like the operatic hero Rienzi. But Rienzi, refusing to flee, dies next to his sister, who joins him when the ungrateful People set fire to his palace. Forty years after he first saw *Rienzi*, the Leader had Berlin in flames and brought Eva Braun to join him in his bunker. He died cursing the German People for being unworthy of him and failing *"to prove its mettle before history."*

Hitler had always kept himself ready for death. All his life he stayed on the fringes of human society, a man apart. A childless bachelor, he had little contact with women. A brief domestic arrangement with a niece ended with her suicide. Eva Braun he largely avoided until their last act. His closest male associates say they hardly knew him--he was friendless as well. As a youth, he called his constraint devotion to art. As a politician, he called it devotion to his adopted country. He was a man of few pleasures: opera, dogs, architecture and chocolate cake. He neither drank nor smoked, apart from the occasional beer that ceremony demanded. His social relationships amounted to lectures.

A Peculiar Career.

Hitler strenuously advocated German nationalism. However, he kept taking bigger chances, even after Germany began losing. When she was retreating on all fronts, he still refused surrender. Over six million German Christians were killed, with twice that many wounded. Nearly all of these twenty million casualties came during the pointless years of retreat. Famous for killing Jews, Hitler also wilfully devastated the Christians, after his luck seemed to change.

Most of the human race stands ashamed of what he was able

to get Germany to do. For years no one could stand against his armies, yet it is Hitler's murder factories which have eclipsed Napoleon's victories in fame. Not the Ardennes, Tobruk or Kiev, but Dachau and Auschwitz have replaced Austerlitz, Marengo and Jena as universally recognized place names.

For nine years, the apocalypse loomed over those in Hitler's path. From his ascent to power January 30, 1933, until the Soviet counterattack December 6, 1941, he seemed unstoppable, an inhuman evil force spewing hatred and magically triumphing against all odds. Throughout the years of success his motives seemed clear enough: to conquer foreign land and to shame the people who still used old religious rituals. However, the 1941 invasion of Russia marked a turning point. He insisted on grinding up the German Army thereafter. This confused his generals; he fired those who complained. At the same time he began systematically murdering Jews. The murders were thus a kind of riotous extravagance of Hitler's decline, and were pursued with greater urgency the worse the war went. Chapter Nine begins an examination of Hitler's use of certain people, those called Jewish, as targets, weapons, and alter egos. Yet beside the Jew when Hitler finished lay Germany herself, demolished, conquered, occupied, cut in half and despised.

Hitler's Trap.

German Christians died alongside the Jews in Hitler's opus, an eye for an eye. Six million Jewish civilians he gassed or shot. But also among the German Christians, half were civilians. Germany has excused Hitler her fallen Christian millions as the inevitable casualties of war. Many of her citizens still take pride in his years of triumph. In reputation, the astonishing consistency of his initial winning has overshadowed the puzzling consistency of Hitler's maelstrom of losses. But in reality, the losses prevailed.

During forty-five years of imprisonment by foreign armies, Germany forgot nothing. Today again roving bands of Nazi thugs beat and murder the weak while bystanders watch in silence or applaud. The politicians speak cautiously. No matter how dreadful Germany's punishment by Hitler, some Germans still believe his sinister enticements and beg for one more kiss. The President of the German legislature notices: "The past cannot be pushed aside. What we repress and lie about always returns to us." "Germany for the Germans," scream the street gangs again--but who is German enough? Hitler seduced Germany into a negative identity: non-Jewish, non-Gypsy, non-Communist, non-homosexual, non-dark-skinned, non-Slav, non-disabled.

Identity built on hatred and persecution of the supposedly imperfect is poisonous, because such logic ultimately reaches everyone. Under a Hitler, all must live warily. Each feels pressure to accuse his neighbor, if only to save himself. Today, Hitler's negative identity surfaces, intact. In Germany, echoing the murderous thugs in the streets, a state Interior Minister declares: "We have to decide as a society whether we want an unlimited number of foreigners....If we want to reduce the number...we have to carry through with the deportation." But amidst the rattling of the cattle cars, a German diplomat now protests:

> To believe that nonsense these neo-Nazi groups spread--Germany for the Germans--is, to put it bluntly, suicide....We will cope with our problems, because a society does not commit suicide.

Once it was different. Hitler's headlong rush towards world conquest trapped him--or else he trapped in his war the whole world, beginning and ending with Germany. He shot himself only because finally he could not deny his defeat and the ruin of all his plans; Germany had no hope left. But a far different interpretation beckons: he could finally shoot himself when Germany had no hope left, if that completed his deeply buried plan. Seeming an arch-racist, Hitler at least used racism as a hypnotic lure to gain power over Germany. He camouflaged his purposes with numbing horrors that glare and confuse. Yet Hitler may have worn other colors underneath the layer marked racism and fanaticism. Hitler, who compared himself to a sleepwalker, blindly acted as a saboteur--a mole. Unwitting as he may have been at first, by the end he openly labored to destroy not just the Jews and the European world, but Germany herself, in a ghastly, nihilistic burlesque. According to him, all the world had proved unfit. He shamed Germany with another lost war and with killing her own citizens. He made Germany ridiculous when she pretended that killing could be orderly. He was still laughing when the Russians came for him, as seen in the photograph facing. Was this *Schadenfreude*, malicious gloating? Germany may awaken [*Deutschland erwache!*] to see cruel mockery in his work. Grateful for his ultimate defeat and death, the Allies did not much question how these came about, nor did the Germans, stunned by their total reversal of fortune.

The world paid too much for his lesson not to extract from it every insight possible. No one, German, Jew or conqueror, should forgive Hitler, but to dismiss him as just bad luck--a monster or an accident of history--wastes fifty million lives. His list of victims begins to grow again. We need to learn his secret. Look beyond Auschwitz, Lidice, Guernica, Rotterdam, Coventry and Leningrad. To see better the shape of the man behind them all, look at the facts that do not fit Hitler's reputation as an insatiable conqueror. To find causes, not effects, focus on Hitler's ominous agony more than his endless sadism. No one could doubt the viciousness of the prince of ashes. Not his evil, but its source has been eluding us. Only the study of the rabies virus has made mad dogs rare. Similarly, we need the key to Hitler's nightmare passions and his barren life.

Exultant as the Soviet Army nears Berlin, Hitler, buried in his bunker, still plans to destroy his hometown, saying he wants to improve it; he reviews a model. February 1945.

(Photo courtesy of John Toland, from *Adolf Hitler*.)

Not to be turned to stone like Lot's wife, many have refused to look back at the frightening message Hitler forced on an unwilling world. The domesticity of post-war America in the nineteen-fifties ignored and denied Hitler's teachings, as if to say: Humans are not vicious; we want nothing more than family life and bland suburban routine. When Hitler was active, it had taken a certain bravery to get up in the morning. As romanticized in the classic film, *Casablanca,* depression, cigarettes, suicide and whiskey then had a patina of respectability and poetic meaning that have been totally reversed. Today's pill-driven morality is that no one should waste time on sadness. It has been branded as vestigial and old-fashioned. In place of sadness and duty, we honor homicide and rage; we call them assertive. This change is Hitler's most significant legacy. Orphaned (at eighteen) but forever refusing to mourn, he proved that any death could be obliterated by another, newer death. When he had exhausted his ability to kill others, he killed himself. The war ended then, being of no use to anyone else.

A red thread of betrayal runs through Hitler's work. The outrage of Germany's professional soldiers challenges Hitler's claims of nationalism. Shakespeare might think he protested too much. Tainting generations of Germans with loathing and remorse, he conquered the small and the weak, and hapless France, but went on to pit Germany, virtually alone, against the united strength of the three greatest powers of the western world. We leave for Part Two what plagued his mind. Review now Hitler's loyalty to German interests. Just as whispering Iago led Othello to destroy himself, breast-beating Hitler led Germany back into a war of one-against-all and held her to it. He made his name a curse. Why did he lose, and why the Jews?

Chapter One

WINNING BY LOSING
[Overview of the War]

Hitler's significance rests on what he did, not what he claimed or believed. His stunning initial success made him infamous for shrewd daring, but he stretched the German forces thin in every direction while he scoured up enemies who could grind them into crowbait. His steady stream of military blunders, large and small, amounted to an insidious betrayal which, coming from the depths of him and papered over with vehement slogans, fooled even Hitler. This chapter lists the major puzzles of Hitler's war strategy; the details divide by campaign into eight additional chapters. Afterwards, Part Two works towards solving the puzzles, using as clues the knots of love and hate that bound Hitler. Part One presents facts, many not given full weight in other works; Part Two offers explanations.

Hitler's reputation endures for ferocious mastery and rapid, brutal triumphs, but he lost almost every battle in his final two years, as he systematically registered, corralled, shipped and killed millions of civilians. He avoided having a personal life; he did not marry until his last day.

War always offers a theater for our unyielding viciousness, but Hitler's strategy stands out as bizarre, a strangling web of errors, each of which taken alone has been excused as merely foolish, inept or overzealous. Not Stalingrad nor Dunkirk, Moscow, Tunis or Normandy, nor any other one uniquely unlucky blunder, but his insistent sacrifice of advantage, over and over, day after day, guaranteed defeat. The human family has winked at the debacle, honoring Germany as a rapacious aggressor, but simply unlucky. The harsher truth is that, lacing seduction with shame, Hitler got Germany to commit suicide along with him.

Hitler as Politician.

Like other promises from politicians, Hitler's claims of racism and patriotism work: true or not, they put him in power. With his Viennese wiles, Hitler pretends love for Germany and offers four popular lies: that the idea of "race" has a clear meaning, that Germans make up a race, that the German race is the best, and that this gives them the right or even the duty to trample others.

When pushed, Hitler announces that true Germans are the residents in 1914 (he arrived in 1913), minus Jewish residents of however many centuries, plus relatives abroad, German-speaking people, those whose ancestors spoke German, and children of these. Minus Gypsies, homosexuals, the mentally retarded and mentally ill, as variously identified. Minus social-ists and communists anyone accuses. Minus the *Sturmabteilung* (SA), his now-surplus private army. Jews are those who have at least two Jewish grandparents (Hitler worries he had one), and Jewish children can become Germans if they look German (Hitler has blue eyes and a straight nose), or if they marry a German (as his father did). Relatives abroad sometimes include the inhabitants of Scandinavia and Britain, sometimes not. Hit-ler announces degrees of purity, but no one laughs at his sar-donic joke: the middle-sized, pudgy, dark-haired Leader praises tall, lean blonds. No member of the Nazi élite looks the part.

By this hideous but conclusive demonstration, Hitler proves no one can define a race. He says nothing of the importance for him of his enormous exertion. Because of this secrecy, many agree with Oxford historian Alan Bullock that: "[Hitler had] no personal experience [to explain] hatred of the Jews." In any case, Hitler wins total control over Germany, and Germany declares herself racist, by letting him.

In her guilty downward spiral, she alone breaks the international conspiracy of official denial and silent understandings about anti-Semitism. Hitler's hectoring oratory and simple slogans reap thirteen million votes (more than a third of those cast) in the July 1932 election, revealing his Nazis as by far the strongest party in Germany. Named Chancellor January 30, 1933, Hitler demands dictatorial powers, crushes all opposition and makes Germany a prison.

The German people, groaning from the agonies of a ghastly war, a bad peace and a deep economic depression, stumble into the arms of the angry young politician. Hard and ruthless, he tells lusty fairy tales of a vindictive, victorious warrior Germany that was and will be again. This promised land is shrouded by the mists of indefinitely remote times, but the legends give distraction from the present dejection and deprivation. Hitler sings of Germany colonizing the world to offer the joys of order and correct living, and the example of German blood, purified for the occasion. No one asks what *"pure blood"* means; hecklers are beaten. Now scolding, now cajoling, Hitler offers to show the way and says he will take all burdens on himself. He will be their sole and complete Leader, their savior. Some sense a trick and draw back, try to stand back from the swelling hysteria, get pulled under.

With perverse artistry Hitler shames Germany. He screams that the *"master race"* must get started on running the world. He rages against: *"the November criminals* [and] *the great crime the German people committed against itself* [by surrendering in November 1918]." Hitler insists that war is normal, not peace, and that Germany has shirked her destiny. Once given command, he abuses Germany scornfully. *"I follow my course with the precision and security of a sleepwalker,"* Hitler boasts. He takes Germany wherever he likes; moreover, he implies or pretends that he ignores the consequences. His vanity, wrapped in patriotic bombast, and in so many spoken words, turns out to be recklessness and a fascination with death. Some Germans worship the Führer who brought them years of glory, yet the same man broke them. Famous as a conqueror, he was more unusual in defeat, giving macabre praise alongside his menacing prediction:

> The German people...will make every sacrifice which is human-
> ly possible....The nation acts as well as anybody could expect.
> There are no better people than our Germans.

In the time of his ascent, Hitler swears he will rescue Germany from surrender. His methods prove extreme: his generals complain when, after resuming the First World War on exactly the original, losing terms, Hitler sabotages their work, then keeps Germany fighting until there is nothing left to surrender. In March 1945 Hitler vainly orders the destruction of all pro-ductive structures such as power stations and factories. The next month his Political Testament hints at a permanent waste-land: *"Centuries will go by, but from the ruins of our towns and monuments...."* Yet Hitler never acknowledges any gaps in his patriotism. Those who do are shouted down, or shot down. He finally has to scream at his Chief of Staff:

> *Don't you think I'm fighting for Germany? My whole life has been one long struggle for Germany.*

The Chief, General Heinz Guderian, already fired once and brought back, had again objected to senseless orders, as had Field Marshal Erwin Rommel, former Chief of Staff Franz Halder and Field Marshal Erich von Manstein. One after another, Hitler fires them, Germany's most skillful soldiers of the Second World War. Halder is jailed; Rommel forced to commit suicide. Hitler will never face what he is doing.

General Walter Warlimont worked directly for Hitler at his headquarters; he too is finally fired for speaking bad news. All these career officers, whatever their military exploits--or because of those exploits--seem dangerous rebels to Hitler. Their memoirs are quoted extensively below. The soldiers write to absolve themselves (among Germans) of the defeat and to cleanse themselves (before the victors) of any suspicion of Nazi politics. And hindsight is always sharp. However, these particular generals, Halder, Manstein, Guderian and Warlimont, have special credibility: they were all sacked by Hitler for criticizing him--during the war.

Manstein and Guderian have much to say about battlefield tactics; Halder and Warlimont focus on life at headquarters. All criticize Hitler's military decisions and policies. However, the generals make excuses for Hitler himself. Either they still believe in his earnestness, or they fear to offend believers. Manstein does not call Hitler disloyal, although he questions Hitler's goals in certain battles. Guderian concludes Hitler tried his utmost despite advancing physical illness. Halder, in diary entries at the time, excused Hitler's blunders as stubbornness and lack of training. Having read Halder, Warlimont adopts the same position. No one questions Hitler's patriotism. Actually, no one seems much concerned with Adolf Hitler, the man. All show anger over the ways in which he steadily interfered with their doing their jobs.

Hitler as Warlord.

Bold in defeat, fearful in victory, Hitler took a path that amazes military analysts, and German generals most of all. Even the stunningly successful invasion of France raises questions. Hitler's insistence on the Manstein plan for the invasion seems brilliant in retrospect. However, when the plan worked, Hitler balked, as discussed below. Furthermore, his original reasons for choosing the plan remain unclear. At every step forward and backward Hitler defied the Army General Staff; his insistence on Manstein's unusual idea seems part of this struggle, since the General Staff strongly opposed the upstart Manstein. Indeed, the German General Staff opposed each invasion: the Rhineland, Austria, Czechoslovakia, Poland, France and Russia. Hitler always insisted there would be no response. He was right each time, yet Germany still lost. Something interfered--as discussed in Part Two. The General Staff simply tried to avoid war, then wanted to surrender when defeated; Hitler refused both pleas. When he started losing, rather than ask advice, he listened even less. His precipitous fall from the heights smacks of treachery. Hitler noticed this, but he blamed others: *"I want them to write on my tombstone: 'He was the victim of his generals!'"*

SNAPSHOT: in 1938 Hitler threatens Czechoslovakia; his Army is unprepared, and Chief of Staff Halder arranges to arrest Hitler, but Britain suddenly gives in to him. In 1939 Britain warns against taking Poland, declares war, does nothing. Hitler takes Poland in a month, then fires the winning generals. Hitler stalls the whirlwind 1940 French campaign several times, the longest at Dunkirk, where he personally rescues the British from the Germans. He arranges to forfeit the fight with Britain for air superiority. In 1941, he traps three million German soldiers in endless Russia. The rush to Moscow is repeatedly deflected--by Hitler. He shuffles his goals until the Russians and the winter take charge.

In 1942, Hitler takes the Crimea, but disbands the German Eleventh Army the moment they win. He sacrifices one hundred seventy thousand green troops en masse, then he pins down the highly mobile German Sixth Army in Stalingrad to be destroyed. He curses its commander, Field Marshal Friedrich Paulus, for refusing to make *"a heroic ending."* Hitler insists Paulus should shoot himself.

In 1943 Hitler proclaims national mourning for the Sixth's two hundred thousand soldiers, then drops three hundred thousand in Tunis. In 1944 Hitler scatters his tanks and immobilizes his battalions in Normandy. One German division counterattacks successfully: Hitler traps them at Falaise, and kills them all. As the war grinds to the conclusion Hitler had arranged, he refuses to interrupt by surrendering. In July 1944, a month after D-Day, many officers join in a violent revolt that fails. Hitler alone keeps Germany bleeding nine more months before making *"a heroic ending"* for himself.

This extraordinary record shows confusion and/or sabotage. It is hard to imagine what Hitler could have been thinking. But Germany continued to take him at his word. Coating terror with shame and pride kept her loyal to the bitter end. Yet looking at the military events in more detail only raises further questions.

HITLER AT WORK

POLAND: Hitler Begins His Finale.

Only deft handling can lure Germany into war again after just twenty years. Beginning in 1933, the new Chancellor provokes piecemeal. Germany holds her breath. No military response comes, but each step is bolder. On the one hand, Hitler succeeds in getting the German generals to act warlike, in the belief there will be no war. However, he gradually forces the West also to act warlike, in the belief there will be no war. The result is well known.

This dazzling sideshow distracts Hitler's prisoners--that is, the Germans--and also the world at large. He plays on at statesmanship, win or lose. The 1933 boycott of Jewish-owned shops fails, but the non-aggression treaty with Poland wins. In 1934, the murder of the Austrian Chancellor, Engelbert Dollfuss, buys nothing. Then a weekend of murders of a hundred political rivals secures Hitler's power and signals his ruthlessness.

Hitler wins with the 1936 march into the Rhineland under the French guns and sends Luftwaffe squadrons to bomb the Spanish government. March 1938 sees him invade Austria without a shot. That September British Prime Minister Neville Chamberlain comes to Munich to hand Hitler half of Czechoslovakia; Hitler takes the rest in March 1939. The West had created Poland in 1919 by taking the German city of Danzig and a corridor of land around it. Britain and France now threaten war should Hitler reclaim any of this. Field Marshal von Manstein remembers the military view:

> Everyone among us [was] disquieted by the number of emergencies through which the Fatherland had passed since [Hitler took power]....The British guarantee to Poland convinced [us] there would in the end be no war....[Hitler] had explicitly assured [us] that he was not idiot enough to bungle his way into a world war for the sake of Danzig or the Polish Corridor....[Besides] it was preferable to keep Poland between us and the Soviet Union.

Regardless, Hitler sets a surprise attack on Poland for August 26, 1939. Chief of Staff Halder, believing it another bluff, this year says nothing and positions the troops. Braced by an agreement with the Soviet Union signed August 23, Hitler on the 25th confirms the attack. However, that evening he cancels it. "How could any man reach such a decision and then cancel it again in the space of a few hours?" asks Manstein. In between, Hitler learned that British resistance had at last stiffened, and so had Italian. But Hitler promises to protect the British Empire [*sic*]. He tells his generals this promise will keep Britain neutral. Refusing an international conference that might again hand him what he asks, Hitler instead attacks on September 1.

After six years building a destitute and chaotic Germany into a world power Hitler, entirely on his own, shoves her and Europe back into war. However extraordinary this feat, no one thinks his odds are good--including Hitler. When Britain and France declare war, he portrays amazement, asking his retinue: *"What happens next?"* He then makes four separate proclamations of innocence over German radio, blaming *"our Jewish*

democratic global enemy" for the new war. However, neither
Britain nor France moves, and Germany easily crushes the
Poles, who formally surrender September 27. Hitler's reaction
to the cheap and rapid victory is to fire the planners and take
direct personal command of all German troops. Manstein thun-
ders: "The elimination [from authority] of OKH, or the General Staff of the Army [came] just after [OKH] had conducted
one of the most brilliant campaigns in German history!"

FRANCE: Hitler Again Fails to Lose.
   A man who knows no rest and no pleasure, Hitler rushes past
victory towards danger. On the fall of Poland, the German General Staff defends the border with France; they can hold off
any attack long enough to make peace attractive. But Hitler
instead orders them to invade France immediately, despite being
outdone in tanks and guns. Hitler does not mention these military realities. Relying on seduction and shame, he emphasizes
abstractions like duty, triumph and hatred. He meets the panic
among his generals with excuses:

> [1.] *I am convinced of the powers of my intellect....*[2.] *No one
> has ever achieved what I have achieved...I have led the German
> people to a great height, even if the world does hate us now....*
> [3.] *One might accuse me of wanting to fight and fight again....*
> *Nobody can avoid fighting if he does not want to go under....*
> *The decision to strike was always in me....*[4.] *We can oppose
> Russia only when we are free in the West.*

No one dares question the need to *"oppose Russia."* The great
German heroes, Bismarck and Moltke, Hitler brashly criticizes
for *"insufficient hardness,"* but he says nothing about surviving
or winning.
   Hitler repeatedly delays his attack on France--but waiting only
on the weather. His Stuka divebombers need sunshine. The
Leader [*Il Duce*] of Italy, Benito Mussolini, once Hitler's idol,
pleads with him to make peace. In March, still waiting for

clear skies, Hitler suddenly endorses an unprecedented proposal by a junior officer to send massed tanks through a forest, all at one spot. Aghast at the risks, the senior staff transfer Manstein, the plan's author, to a reserve unit far in the rear.

However, the plan works. Like the German General Staff, the French think the Ardennes forest an impenetrable barrier, so they do not defend it. The truth is, neither side had ever seen a tank attack. Victorious Hitler claims joy, but seems "worried over his own success," according to Halder's diary. A military man, Halder does not consider that Hitler might fight for goals other than military "success," but he will get more evidence.

DUNKIRK: Hitler Rescues Britain.

Hitler now saves the British army: motive obscure. Germany invaded France May 10, 1940. By May 20, Guderian crosses to the English Channel with his tanks, cutting off the British and French armies in the north. Yet Hitler stalls and disrupts him and prevents victory, says Guderian:

> Nobody had reckoned on our appearance that day [the 20th]....
> [Lamentably] the 21st of May was wasted while we waited for orders...I wanted the Tenth Panzer [tank] Division to advance on Dunkirk [trapping the British]....[but the] Division was withdrawn from my command....On the 24th of May....Hitler ordered [us] to stop....We were utterly speechless....On the 26th of May...we attempted once again to attack towards Dunkirk and to close the ring....But renewed orders to halt arrived. We were stopped within sight of Dunkirk!

Over three hundred thousand British and French soldiers sail away. British military college professor John Keegan calls Dunkirk a blink, one: "strategically decisive for the outcome of the Second World War....[Hitler's most] severe attack of indecision [*sic*]." More explicit about Britain's near-defeat, West Point teaches that Dunkirk was "incredible...a grave mistake.... [Hitler] seemed almost frightened by the magnitude of his success....[Britain] would have had few options other than a [peace] settlement." With undisguised contempt, Field Marshal Manstein says: "[Hitler wanted to] throw a golden bridge across the Channel for the British Army....Dunkirk was one of Hitler's most decisive mistakes."

BRITAIN: Hitler Prods the Lion.

Hitler, the new ruler of Europe, remains opposed by Great Britain. The Royal artillery, tanks and trucks lie abandoned in Flanders after June 1, but Hitler does not move. The French surrender on June 21; still he waits. Finally he says: *"I can see no reason why this war must go on."* He publically demands that Britain beg for terms. The new Prime Minister, Winston Churchill, offers to fight to the last. Hitler now demands an invasion plan, and German staff officers scramble to make one. Ten months after declaring war on Britain, no such plan exists. Hitler invaded France with no hope of winning.

Years before, Hitler ruled: *"A war against England is quite out of the question!"* Now loath to proceed, Hitler gives an unusually timid order: *"I have decided to prepare* [sic] *a landing operation against England, and if necessary to carry it out."* He signals his staff that he will not invade: *"If it is not certain that preparations can be completed by the beginning of September* [in six weeks], *other plans must be considered."*

Only two weeks later Hitler turns to *"other plans."* Before any bombs fall on Britain, before the Royal Air Force can rise to its hour of testing, Hitler concludes: *"Russia must be liquidated. Spring 1941."* Hitler often repeats the claim that Moscow connects to London: *"If Russia is smashed, Britain's last hope will be shattered."* Through 1941, he will focus on Russia. But this implies Britain and her hopes are to be set aside. The British do not know it, but the wolf has passed their door.

While waiting for Spring, Hitler puts on a terrifying show. Its victims find it real enough, although Hitler carefully limits the damage. He gathers troop transports at English Channel ports. Seventy-five days after Dunkirk, on August 15, 1940, Hitler at last strikes against Britain, sending the *Luftwaffe* to fight the Royal Air Force and bomb air bases and aircraft factories. Churchill reports British casualties: "out of a total pilot strength of about a thousand, nearly a quarter had been lost." Luftwaffe high command hears even higher numbers from their staff: "The RAF since August 8th has lost 1,115 fighters....During September...the enemy's fighter defense will be [ruined]."

Reichmarshal Hermann Göring hears this on September 1; by September 7 Hitler stops bombing air bases and factories. Churchill shudders: "If the enemy had persisted...the whole intricate organization of Fighter Command might have been broken down." Instead, Hitler wears down the Luftwaffe with bombing civilian London. The Royal Air Force he has just rescued hits enough German ships and planes by September 17 to permit Hitler to officially abandon the invasion of Britain. He will not have to risk an embarrassing defeat. However, as at Dunkirk four months before, Hitler also evades the danger of a complete victory. He keeps Britain largely off-limits, according to those who know him best.

BRITAIN via RUSSIA: Hess to the Rescue.

Hitler will eventually coerce a show of enthusiasm from his captive generals for a "six-week campaign," but in July 1940 an invasion of Russia seems wrong to Chief of Staff Halder, who writes secretly: "Purpose is not clear. We do not hit the British that way. Risk in the west must not be underestimated....If [when attacked there] we are then tied up in Russia, a bad situation will be made worse."

Looking back on the campaign, West Point is more emphatic: "In any prolonged war, the superior human resources of the British Empire (and potentially of the United States and Russia, as well) would doom Hitler to failure. [Therefore] Hitler had assured the German generals time and again that the Kaiser's main mistake was that he had permitted the development of a two-front war." Sir Stafford Cripps, the 1940 British ambassador to Moscow, tells Downing Street "with absolute certainty" that Russia will not attack first. On his own, Hitler demands the two-front war.

Hitler schedules the invasion for May 1941. His principal German biographer, Joachim Fest, declares: "[Hitler was] showing a continual process of self-persuasion [and] magical self-reassurance....[Russia] was the last and most serious example of his suicidal impulse to double his stake once the game was going against him."

Fest records that the Führer showed "depression and nervousness" that were contagious. Out the back door, Hitler sends Hess in an eleventh-hour attempt to secure peace with Britain. In utter secrecy, flying alone with extra fuel tanks on his fourth try, May 10, 1941, Deputy Führer Rudolf Hess parachutes into rural Scotland to make contact with the British government. This Hess calls: "A mission of humanity [undertaken because] the Führer did not want to defeat England and wished to stop the fighting."

Churchill imprisons Hess without meeting him. Hitler denies any knowledge of the failed mission. "The Führer was taken completely by surprise," according to Halder. Hitler salutes Britain; he says Hess has cracked: "[due to] *inner conflict growing out of his personal attitude toward England and his grief over the fratricidal struggle between the two Germanic nations.*"

Hitler apparently feared Russia. Either he used Hess in hopes of freeing his hands for the new task, or in hopes a British truce would let him stay home. The half-hearted and ill-conceived stunt flight also gets rid of Hess, a family man who dreamed of peace, and a conscience who was too close to Hitler for him to ignore. As the date for the invasion approaches, Hitler admits:

"I feel as if I am pushing open the door to a dark room never seen before, without knowing what lies behind the door." Hess spends the rest of his long life in jail. On June 22, 1941, Hitler invades.

RUSSIA: Napoleon's Shadow.

Lecturing about Napoleon's errors, Hitler throws away the German Army where Napoleon's died. At first, German tanks cut off hundreds of thousands of the Red Army, and Halder writes: "The Russian Campaign has been won in the space of two weeks." One hundred twenty German divisions tear eastward, but the Russians field three hundred sixty divisions, twice what Hitler says he expected. To make matters worse, he continually shifts his goals. By the sixth week of fighting, Halder's optimism dies: "Our command function is exhausted in details ....[without] a clear idea of what [Hitler] regards as the prime objectives....A revised assessment[:]...the plain truth is that [we] are exhausted and have suffered heavy losses."

Similarly, West Point criticizes: "Hitler had the worst effect on planning." The Americans search for excuses: "[Hitler] lacked the intelligence to combine political, economic and military considerations into a clear strategy....[He was] undisciplined....arrogant....fumbling and uncertain....[an] emotionally unbalanced amateur....like a greedy child....relentless, illogical ....[and] haphazard." Both friends and foes search for any explanation for Hitler other than the insidious hints of disloyalty that shame both sides. To silence military objections, Hitler often scoffs: *"My generals know nothing about the economic aspects of war."* However, by calling his own plans *"economic,"* he points out that they stand distinct from military victory.

Russia

miles

0   100   200

N

- - - LINE OF DEEPEST '41-'42
GERMAN ADVANCE

FINLAND

Baltic Sea

LENINGRAD

ESTONIA

LATVIA

LITHUANIA

DVINSK

E. PRUSSIA

POLAND

SMOLENSK

DNIEPER RIVER

UKRAINE

KIEV

CHERKASSY

VINNITSA

KHARKOV

VOLGA RIVER

MOSCOW

VOLGA RIVER

DON RIVER

STALINGRAD

VOLGA RIVER

DON RIVER

DNIEPER RIVER

CRIMEA

ROMANIA

SEVASTOPOL

BULGARIA

TURKEY

Black Sea

MOSCOW: the Road Not Taken.

The German Army does not take Moscow because Hitler will not let them try. He keeps them circling and bleeding for three grueling months. Warlimont very politely calls this: "an almost classic instance of the basic fault in Hitler's leadership, the desire to command in detail without having studied." Halder privately screams: "This perpetual interference by the Führer ...is becoming a scourge which will eventually be intolerable.... [Hitler shows] a willingness to throw away the opportunities offered us....Representations stressing the importance of Moscow are brushed aside without any valid counterevidence.... Moscow comes last."

"Hitler had forgotten [*sic*] that it was he himself who had ordered a rapid offensive": protests Guderian, making excuses for his Leader. But, as in France, Guderian resents interruptions: "On July 26th [we] succeeded in closing the pocket [on] ten Russian divisions....On July 27th....I expected to...push on towards Moscow...[but] Hitler had ordered...that my Panzer Group [of tanks] would be swung around and would be advancing in a south-westerly direction, that is to say towards Germany....August 4th...Hitler...designated the industrial area about Leningrad as his primary objective....[but said] he hoped to be in possession of Moscow and Kharkov [as well]....No decisions were reached." By August 7th a demoralized Halder drops the plural pronoun, worrying: "can he [*sic*] afford not to reduce Moscow before winter sets in?" On one point, Guderian has to confront Hitler: "As for splitting up the Panzer Group that, I said, would be criminal folly." "On August 23rd...Hitler had now decided that neither the Leningrad nor the Moscow operations would be carried out....a strange decision": mildly offers Guderian. But Manstein remembers with anger: "one could make neither head nor tail of all this chopping and changing....No one was clear any longer what the actual aim of our strategy was."

The British Army concludes: "[It is] the nineteen day inter-regnum (4-24 August) which may well have spared Stalin defeat in 1941." Hitler finally orders a drive on Moscow to start October 2, as snow begins. He had often boasted he could be harsh and ice-cold. Germans soldiers in summer uniforms meet temperatures of sixty-eight degrees below zero. Guns and engines jam. Rallies in Germany seek donations of warm clothing. Supplies cannot move, and the soldiers go on half-rations. Nonetheless, winning many battles, the Wehrmacht advances within fourteen miles of Moscow. Russia counterattacks with one hundred divisions, including fresh troops trained in Siberia with clothes and tanks all white, like the snow.

The Soviets turn the Wehrmacht around. The next day, December 7, Japan attacks Pearl Harbor. Although neither consulted nor warned by his ally, and with his army exhausted and caught, Hitler immediately declares war on yet another great industrial power, the United States. As before, Hitler tells his generals not to worry because he will win the current fight before the new opponent can move.

The Russians force back the German Army. Hitler fires six Field Marshals and Generals, even Guderian, the tank master, who had asked for a strategic withdrawal to prepared positions. Freed from objections, Hitler names himself Commander-in-Chief of the Army. Having so far lost in Russia eight hundred thirty-one thousand killed and wounded, the new C-in-C gives his winter orders for those remaining: *They must dig into the ground where they are and hold every square yard of land!...I believe that I, too, [like Frederick the Great] am entitled to ask any German soldier to lay down his life."* Hitler's apologists credit this order with preventing a repetition of Napoleon's disastrous retreat. Warlimont objects: "exaggerated insistence on this principle, to which Hitler clung against all good sense, led to immense losses which could never be made good."

STALINGRAD: *Hitler Tips His Hand.*

Having at terrible cost held on near Moscow through the vicious winter, in the spring of 1942 Hitler heads south instead. Once again: "The objectives assigned were beyond the power of the troops...[and], from a military point of view, were nonsensical," according to Guderian, sent home to watch. To brace up the generals still in action, Hitler lists reasons why Russia might abruptly surrender. New victories do come: attacking southward catches the Russians off-guard. Burdened by military and political convention, they thought Hitler would still want to take their capital. Manstein, steadily edging towards Leningrad, is suddenly sent off to take command of the Eleventh Army. By July they take the Crimea and the fortress at Sevastopol, a great military feat. Hitler immediately breaks up the Eleventh Army and scatters the parts. Some other armies he urges south, some east. Manstein murmurs: "This dismemberment [of my Army]...was deplorable....[Besides,] the duality of Hitler's objective--Stalingrad and the Caucasus--would split the offensive in two directions....Halder made it quite clear that he completely disagreed [with Hitler]...but said that Hitler had insisted."

The Führer fires Halder. September 1942 finds German casualties one million six hundred thousand, half the initial force. Hitler also fires Field Marshal Sigmund List and takes direct command of a wide sector of the southern front. He remains Commander-in-Chief, Minister of Defense and Führer. Notwithstanding the burden of his titles, he spends much of his time in the woods, either at his headquarters in East Prussia or at his mountain home in Berchtesgaden, a thousand miles west of the front. His generals must go to him to make requests.

Manstein, transferred again, asks to use in central Russia one hundred seventy thousand Luftwaffe reservists, since they have no airplanes. Refusing to answer, Hitler instead hints to Manstein about a possible promotion and talks of invading the Near

East, right after mopping up Russia. With Germany strapped for manpower, the Luftwaffe reservists do eventually see action. Instead of using these trainees as replacements in seasoned units as Manstein urged, Hitler throws them into battle on their own, with equally green officers. The Russians destroy them.

Hitler fetters the highly mobile Sixth Army within the streets and buildings of Stalingrad, far to the east. Manstein calls this a "fatal mistake." Hitler, as Commander-in-Chief, assigns a chain of Hungarian, Romanian and Italian armies to connect German Army headquarters with the Germans on the Volga. Manstein succumbs to doubt: "Hitler must have known that... the [borrowed] armies could not stand up to a strong Soviet attack."

"I won't leave the Volga!" shouts Hitler when the Russians hit the Sixth Army's supply line; he insists retreat would damage his personal prestige. Instead, twenty divisions (two hundred thousand men) are cut off. The Luftwaffe can fly in only a trickle of supplies. When a hasty relief attempt fails, Hitler sentences its commander, General Heim, to death. For the rest, Hitler orders suicide: *"Surrender is forbidden. Sixth Army will hold their positions to the last man and the last round."*

At last Hitler uses Manstein, who fights within thirty miles of the Sixth Army. Hitler still does not allow the Sixth to leave the city and break out. After two months of shelling, on February 2, 1943, Sixth Army fires its last round. Its commander, Field Marshal Friedrich Paulus, and the remaining ninety-one thousand ragged, half-starved Germans surrender; almost all will die in captivity. Manstein rages: "[Hitler was] guilty of dire irresponsibility...[He] ignore[d] all factual considerations....[Once] I sent Hitler a detailed appraisal [and] it was [five days] before we received a reply....This tug-of-war continued until the very last chance of saving Sixth Army had been thrown away."

The Führer sees a different opportunity lost. He lists the justifications for suicide that Paulus had ignored: "[1.] *What cowardice to be afraid of that! Ha!...*[2.] *He knows well enough that his death would set the example....*[3.] *When one's nerves break down there is nothing to do but say 'I can't go on' and shoot oneself. In fact you could say that the man ought to shoot himself....*[4.] *One had to assume that there would be a heroic ending.*"

AFRICA and ITALY: Starving the Fox.

In North Africa Hitler for two years ignores every opportunity to win, then, while withdrawing, creates a hopeless and ruinous defense. Africa at first promised to be a great feat of German arms. Early in 1941 Hitler rescues Mussolini's retreating army in Libya. Rommel's tank division goes on the offensive as soon as it lands, earning him the nickname, "Desert Fox," and the rank of Field Marshal. However, ignoring the pleas of the German Navy, Hitler does not cut into Britain by taking Egypt and closing the Suez Canal. He steadily refuses reinforcements for the *Afrika Korps* until the British and Americans have time to invade North Africa. The invasion comes on November 8, 1942. Then Hitler sends two hundred fifty thousand German and Italian soldiers to Tunis. Rommel's small force escapes there from the east, pursued by a large British army. Hitler withdraws only Rommel himself. When Tunis falls in May 1943, Germany loses one hundred twenty-five thousand soldiers.

For the subsequent retreat through Italy Hitler gives the bizarre orders that have become routine: hold every yard--but make no defensive preparation. American and British forces invade Sicily July 10. Mussolini resigns and flees on July 25, and Hitler takes over the battlefield. He holds Rome until June 1944. He refuses to allow any organized withdrawal. The Allies gradually grind up the Germans.

Hitler also manages the home front strangely; he prevents women from working in factories. In the United States and England, a great number work. Hitler insists: *"The sacrifice of our most cherished ideals is too great a price."* Instead, one million five hundred thousand German domestic servants remain at their duties throughout the war, eight times the tiny number of German women included in war production. The English have two million women working in factories. As late as 1943, despite the defeats at Stalingrad and Tunis, Hitler works German factories only one shift daily and continues full production of civilian goods.

BERLIN: "A Heroic Ending."

Two years after Stalingrad, the Russians arrive at Berlin, where Hitler waits with his Walther pistol. During the retreat, he never allows his generals to mass any useful force. Manstein often tries; however, he finds: "It was quite futile to attempt to refute Hitler's arguments, since he would merely retort...that I *lacked an overall perspective."* Warlimont recalls: "Discussion would be drowned in [Hitler's] ceaseless repetitive torrent of words in which matters old and new, important and unimportant were jumbled up together."

Göring's second-in-command, Luftwaffe General Hans Jeschonnek, commits suicide "to spotlight a mortal danger," as he writes. His warning concerns the danger to the German homeland, bombed steadily since May 1942. Fighter plane production under the miraculous Albert Speer reaches 7,477 in the first eight months of 1943; however, the Luftwaffe finds the new planes scattered far and wide: "By Hitler's express command absolute priority was given to the [Russian] front and ...the Mediterranean...in a hopeless battle against overwhelming odds....[At 485] the number of serviceable day-fighters available for the defense of Germany...reached its all-time 'high.'"

In March 1944, Hitler traps another German army, the First Panzer. Manstein reports: "the Führer...[says] *continue to hold* [on]....Hitler declared that *according to the Luftwaffe there were very few enemy tanks to be seen, but that whole German units were running away from them.*" Nonetheless, Manstein, for several hours, presses the issue of rescuing the stranded men. An angry Hitler relieves them, but fires Manstein, giving him some parting advice: *"All that counted now,* [Hitler] said, *was to cling stubbornly to what we held."*

Coming Clean.
After the D-Day landings in Normandy June 6, 1944, Germany faces invasion from both east and west. Hitler becomes openly threatening:

> The question is...whether Germany has the will to remain in existence or whether it will be destroyed....The loss of this war will destroy the German people....I have never learned to know the word 'capitulation'....Nothing will make the slightest change in my decision to fight on.

Willing to fight to the last German, Hitler alone keeps them at war. A group of generals try to kill him, but fail. The American and British air forces destroy the Luftwaffe and Germany's largest cities. *"[Germany] must have been too weak; it had failed to prove its mettle before history and was destined only to destruction,"* sneers Hitler. He arranged for Germany to face the combined might of three industrial giants. To the last, he denies any responsibility: *"It is untrue that I or anybody else in Germany wanted war in 1939. It was wanted and provoked exclusively by those international statesmen who either were of Jewish origin or worked for Jewish interests."*

Summary.

A stream of evidence shows that Hitler fooled himself and many others with patriotic shouting, but consistently sabotaged the German Army. He started by provoking mighty enemies. Although he beat the French by a clever stroke, their army by itself had equalled Hitler's in size and had been better armed. Personally and willfully, without provocation, Hitler pitted the eighty million Germans also against the British Empire, and then Russia as well, and then America as well. Such a betrayal, had it been done on behalf of a foreign country, would have made Hitler the most effective mole in the history of espionage. If he did it unknowingly, it becomes a stunning example of sleepwalking. In any case, through his deceptions and his actions, he made war against Germany.

Did Hitler--ruthless, demonically shrewd and coldly efficient as he was--simply decorate his suicide with the destruction by fire of Germany and the Jews? Such ideas are the stuff of opera, not world affairs. The dignity of death in battle depends on not noticing what stupid motives led to the battle. (Were Göring's fantastic uniforms a prancing mockery of the Nazi mystique?) This view of Hitler causes embarrassment; the world hungers for purely virtuous heroes and purely evil villains, not romantic necrophiles embroidering their exits.

Working against that wish for purity, additional chapters now present in greater detail Hitler's infidelity during his war. He lured Germany deeper, campaign by campaign. Readers impatient with the currents of war might turn to Chapter Nine, which examines Hitler's use of the Jews as weapons.

Chapter Two

STARTING THE DYING
[POLAND]

Prologue.

The details of Hitler's efforts follow the lines of the broad-brush picture in the previous chapter: he repeatedly pitted Germany against hard odds, then ruined her chances. At the end, he kept her from any surrender that would cheat Armageddon. In these seven chapters, examine more closely Hitler's leadership. Did he greedily overshoot and blindly persevere, as has been commonly assumed, or did he hobble his horse as he rode her?

Focus on actions and results, not Hitler's explanations. He kept Germany obedient by claiming fanatical nationalism whenever he courted disaster. He spoke of duty when the issue was defeat; he shouted about honor when the issue was survival. He was an isolated bachelor with nothing to lose. The deceptions of few politicians endure so long, but Hitler asserted a purity of motive that both his supporters and his enemies wanted to believe. In all likelihood, he believed it himself. No antidote is known for his poisonous seduction. Germany is still reeling.

In war, Hitler led from behind. Although he called himself a front-line soldier of World War One, he had actually been a messenger, running between units behind the lines, in the days before radio. The Leader chose to avoid World War Two. For the most part, he hid in the woods, at the remote headquarters he built in Bavaria, East Prussia and elsewhere. The last months he spent beneath the ruins of Berlin. Throughout, he rarely visited any battlefront and never visited the *Lagers* where he killed civilians. This delicacy contrasts with the grim fervor he showed in getting war started.

No one wanted to take public responsibility for renewing the pointless butchery of the 1914-1918 war. Britain and France several times backed away from confronting Hitler. They did not know how heavily the odds weighed in their favor, they saw some legitimacy in his complaints and, most of all, they hoped he could be bought off. The Allies gave Hitler victories without war. He would not accept.

Inventing the War.

Trumpeting President Woodrow Wilson's Fourteen Points, Hitler demanded the new virtue, self-determination: the map should put every person of German heritage within the Nazi state. This approach took six years to get war started. His bloodless expansions along the way are usually listed as glittering triumphs, but they were seen by the German military as foolhardy. Hitler's reputation for shrewd diplomatic bluffing and military genius rests on the fact that his provocations went unpunished until the Russian counterattack of December 1941. In 1936 Hitler was still bragging about the risks he ran:

> *The forty-eight hours after the march into the Rhineland were the most nerve-racking in my life. If the French had then marched into the Rhineland, we would have had to withdraw with our tails between our legs...[and] a retreat on our part would have spelled collapse [for our government]....What would have happened if anybody other than myself had been at the head of the Reich! Anyone you care to mention would have lost his nerve.*

"The French covering army could have blown us to pieces," agrees General Alfred Jodl, Hitler's personal advisor. Hitler sends just one division to the French border, enough to provoke, but not enough to survive attack. Germany's generals recoil in horror: the Chief of the General Staff urges concessions; the Minister of Defense urges retreat. But neither Britain nor

France does anything, and Hitler boasts of working a miracle.

Hitler sends his bombers against the Spanish government, for the training. By November 1937 Hitler talks of aggressive war, only to have the Minister of Defense report: "[There is] total inadequacy of the *Wehrmacht*'s war potential." Hitler fires him, takes over his job and again risks war--without mustering the warriors. General Walter Warlimont, Jodl's assistant, recalls German haste and alarm preceding the takeover of Austria in March 1938: "When preparations for the Austrian Anschluss were begun, [Hitler] created complete confusion....[His Chief of Staff] reported to Hitler that the Army was in no way prepared....Nevertheless within five hours improvised orders had to be got out....[Hitler's advisor, Field Marshal Wilhelm] Keitel's own description [was:] 'the next night was hell for me. There was telephone call after telephone call from the Army General Staff...all imploring me to work on the Führer to give up the move into Austria.'"

Hitler presses Germany's luck, but not a shot is fired. Even the underground Austrian Socialist Army simply disbands, including Sergeant Bruno Bettelheim. Nonetheless, with Hitler's next defiance, the Army panics. Warlimont says: "Preparations for a surprise attack on Czechoslovakia...led to the most serious upheavals in the...OKH [Army High Command]." Hitler's advisor, Jodl, contends: "we were by no means ready." The Chief of Staff, General Ludwig Beck, organizes opposition, so Hitler fires him in favor of General Franz Halder. However, Halder continues the organizing. Hitler lectures for three hours, only to have his generals renew their complaints. A group of them prepares to arrest Hitler. Halder recalls:

> By the beginning of September [1938], we had taken the necessary steps to immunize Germany from this madman....We had taken this action only because we were convinced [Germany was] being led to certain disaster.

A tank division waits to take control of Berlin. They will imprison Hitler and the entire Nazi government. September 10 Halder and his Commander-in-Chief, Field Marshal Walther von Brauchitsch, argue with Hitler until four in the morning. Nonetheless, Hitler publicly threatens a *"great day of reckoning with Czechoslovakia."* Halder readies his men, but holds off, dumbfounded, when British Prime Minister Neville Chamberlain flies to Munich for talks. By month's end, for "peace in our time," Chamberlain (and France) agree to give Hitler half of Czechoslovakia, including the line of forts that had protected her. Yet Hitler had only: "five fighting divisions and seven reserve divisions...against one hundred French divisions," testifies General Jodl. Czechoslovakia herself had thirty-five divisions waiting to march.

Yet Hitler complains: "[Chamberlain's concession] *spoiled my entry into Prague* [as a conqueror]!" Hitler immediately devises a sharper goading: *"the liquidation of the remainder of Czechoslovakia [and] the occupation of the Memel district* [in Lithuania]." He takes these in March 1939. No bullets answer, but Chamberlain threatens war, and Germany's ambassador reports a "fundamental change" in Britain's temper. Carrying France along with him, Chamberlain swears to defend Poland if Hitler attacks her. Hitler toys with the potential ruin of his adopted country. More than this, he seduces her, waltzing her along the edge.

POLAND: War at Last.

Hitler insists he can act with impunity as before. He schedules an invasion of Poland and agrees with Russia on a division of Polish territory. Guderian recalls thinking that would not be enough: "[In] August, 1939....illusions were still being cherished [by Hitler] concerning the probable [lack of] reaction of the Western Powers; [others thought] they would declare war ....The attitude of the army was very grave indeed." Manstein confirms the anxiety of the generals, as noted in the previous chapter. France has 90 divisions, superior artillery of 1,600 guns, and 55 tank battalions. Left facing these during the Polish campaign will be only 36 divisions with 300 guns and no tanks whatever--every German tank will be in Poland. Halder anxiously sketches reactions to some of the possible French attacks. Mussolini pleads for peace; he has a wife, children and a mistress.

Hitler spends an entire day seducing his generals with scorn for Britain and France: *"There is nothing to force them into a war. The men of Munich will not take the risk....The last weeks have brought increasing conviction of [Poland's] isolation."* Hitler speaks only of his own conviction. A week later, he blithely reverses himself, says war with Britain and France is certain, but schedules them to wait their turn. Saying nothing of peace, Hitler offers a smorgasbord of excuses for war. His reasons will be similar for each invasion; they say more about Hitler than about his targets. His impudent foolishness shows that no one remains who dares confront him. The seventh reason falsely suggests the backing of Brauchitsch. He claims that war is inevitable, but the eighth reason admits he prefers it:

[1.] *Poland would be sure to take advantage of any difficult situation to attack us in the back. It has therefore become necessary to dispose of the eastern problem before tackling the west* ....[2.] *[The] Army must see actual battle before the big final showdown in the west....*[3.] *We have nothing to lose; we have everything to gain....Our economic situation is such that we can only hold out for a few more years. Göring can confirm this....* [4.] *No one knows how much longer I shall live. Therefore, better a conflict now....*[5.] *We are faced with the harsh alternatives of striking or of certain annihilation sooner or later....*[6.] *I have always taken a great risk....*[7.] *No one is counting on a long war. If* [Commander-in-Chief] *Herr von Brauchitsch had told me that I would have replied: "Then it cannot be done"....* [8.] *Our enemies are small fry....I am only afraid that at the last moment some swine or other will yet submit to me a plan for mediation.*

Hitler openly declares the odds based on population and industrial strength: just his first enemies will already be half again larger than the German Reich in population, one hundred twenty-five million vs. eighty million. The Army fears worse odds: another two-front war. Hitler sardonically challenges their heroism and demands a *"resolution to fight on all sides."* Before firing a single shot, Hitler hints of a dark hour coming for Germany: "[I demand] *iron steadfastness of all responsible authorities.... [and] As long as I am alive, there will be no talk of capitulation."*

"The great drama now is approaching its climax," notes a now-passive Halder, one year after his aborted revolt. His language implies that even the very reserved Halder finds an operatic motif in Hitler's behavior. On August 11 Mussolini's Foreign Minister, Count Galeazzo Ciano, visits Germany, then looks deeply at Hitler: "War at this time would be folly....It would be impossible to localize it in Poland....[But] the German decision to fight is implacable. Even if they were given more than they ask, they would attack just the same, because they are possessed by the demon of destruction."

On the eve of the scheduled invasion, Hitler falters, as discussed in the preceding chapter, then presses on. Opposed by Britain and Italy, he insists without clarification: *"[Italy's neutrality] serves our best interests."* In what proves to be a set excuse, Hitler promises to crush Poland so fast, he can turn on France and Britain before they mobilize. Only hours from war, Mussolini and *Luftwaffe* Chief Hermann Göring plead in vain for caution and consultations. Despite his Leader's public ferocity, Halder finds Hitler "worn, haggard, [with a] creaking voice, preoccupied." The nation also gets hints of Hitler's darker thoughts. As he announces war to his captive Reichstag, he twice warns of the potential difficulties he envisions for Germany and himself, then wagers his life:

> *If I am pushed to it, I shall wage even a two-front war...[and] I have once more put on that [soldier's] coat that was most sacred and dear to me. I will not take it off again until victory is secured, or I will not survive the outcome.*

Hitler then feels forced to insist: *"My whole life has been nothing but one long struggle for my people, for its restoration, and for Germany."* This motto he will repeat to Guderian five years later, almost verbatim, as noted in a prior chapter. He concludes his speech with sombre references:

> *One word I have never learned: that is, surrender....we are facing a hard time...with a ridiculously small state....a November 1918 [surrender] will never be repeated...[I] stake my life--anyone can take it...so I ask the same of all others....It is quite unimportant whether we ourselves live....The sacrifice that is demanded....resolved never to surrender...hardship and difficulty....hardship and suffering.*

As the German Army heads east, Hitler names successors in the event of his death: Göring first, then Hess. He recommends they be accorded: *"the same blind loyalty and obedience as to myself."* Hitler then makes a "sudden departure for the front [with]....his photographers and his doctors,"--leaving the Army High Command behind. The cautious Warlimont calls this merely eccentric: "another example of Hitler's predilection for working in an atmosphere of disorder and snap decisions." As a further example, Warlimont recalls how Hitler's closest military advisors learned of the secret clauses in the August 23, 1939, Nazi-Soviet pact: "On 16-17 September I [heard]...of the imminent entry of Russian formations into Eastern Poland....I was completely without knowledge of any agreements. Even Keitel and Jodl knew nothing about it. One of them, on first hearing the news that the Russians were on the move, replied with the horrified question 'whom against?'" The Russians move but the French do not. Later General Jodl testifies on Hitler's preparations: "If we did not collapse in 1939, that was [because]...the approximately one hundred ten French and British divisions in the West were held completely inactive against the twenty-three German divisions [left there]."

Left alone, Hitler quickly overruns Poland. Still the Wehrmacht trembles, as Warlimont recalls: "The declaration of war by the Western powers on 3 September had had a shattering effect upon senior [German] officers...aware of the unpreparedness of the German armed forces....[Hoping] the war could somehow be brought to an end by political means.... the Army Staff had already issued initial instructions for...defensive [preparations]." Army Commander-in-Chief Walter von Brauchitsch tries frantically to head off further aggression. He begs for rumors from Hitler's aides and fears the worst: "You know we cannot do that; we cannot attack the [French] Maginot Line. You must let me know at once if ideas of this sort come up even in the course of conversation." As noted earlier, the day Poland surrenders Hitler demands the immediate invasion of France. Warlimont recalls: "all [present], including even Göring, were clearly entirely taken aback." Despite Hitler's manifest determination to make war, his victory speech talks of defeat: *"Italy will give up its nonparticipatory attitude and participate. That is possible in three weeks! If we can't bring that off, we will deserve to be beaten."*

Epilogue.

On May 23, 1939, Hitler had treated his generals to a look at his long-range strategy: *"There will be war. Our task is to isolate Poland [diplomatically]. If this is impossible, then it will be better to attack in the West and settle Poland at the same time ....The idea that we can get off cheaply is dangerous; there is no such possibility. We must burn our boats, and it is no long-er a question of justice or injustice, but of life or death for [Germany's] eighty million human beings.*" Germany lay de-molished and occupied by foreign troops six years later. Yet in the "Political Testament" he wrote just before his suicide, Hit-ler appears only as a victim:

It is untrue that I or anybody else in Germany wanted war in 1939....I have made too many offers...for responsibility for the outbreak of this war to be placed on me. Further, I have never wished that after the appalling First World War there should be a second one....The ruling clique in England wanted war.

However, it was victory Hitler did not want, as he would prove again in France.

Chapter Three

PURSUED BY VICTORY
[FRANCE]

Prologue.

Hitler, insisting he was an indignant patriot, had for years been seeking war. His carefully measured provocations let him claim innocence; they seemed justified to Germans and credible elsewhere. At last Prime Minister Chamberlain awarded Hitler a declaration of war, but neither Britain nor France budged. In weeks, Poland went the way of Czechoslovakia and Austria. Fighting ceased, except for isolated encounters at sea. Pacifists on both sides, including the German General Staff, hoped to avoid any larger conflict. Hitler could not get the German Army to invade France immediately--they pleaded the weather. Through the fall and winter, he grew desperate.

FRANCE: A Headlong Plunge Fails.

France falls in forty-three days. This result seems to shock Hitler as much as the Allies. Despite being the invader, apparently he had expected to lose. Either way, through the eight months from September 1939 to May 1940 Hitler postpones the invasion of France fourteen times waiting for good flying weather. At the start he gave a variety of reasons for attacking, some already familiar from his invasion of Poland:

> [1.] *All historical successes come to nothing when they are not continued....*[2.] *Time does not work against the enemy....In six to eight months they will be better....*[3.] *We would be too late in a counterattack....Therefore, no delay until the enemy arrives,*

but, should peaceful efforts fail, direct assault in the West. [4.]
The sooner, the better....We cannot wait.

The Army promises to defend. Hitler demands attack; he cites
moral and esthetic benefits, although he seems to expect defeat:
*"We must not wait....Even if we fall short of the original ob-
jectives....even if we do not gain a decisive victory...there
would be little danger that we fritter away our strength in
defensive warfare."*

"[Hitler] knew that the Army was strongly opposed": notes
Warlimont. Offensive or defensive, Germany is not ready.
The air force alone used up in Poland two full weeks of the total
national fuel production; steel reserves dwindle. Halder and
von Brauchitsch insist: "[The] techniques of the Polish campaign [will be] no good against a well-knit army." They again
plot to remove Hitler, but Hitler shouts down von Brauchitsch
and sets the attack for the following week, November 12, 1939.
He treats objections as a morale problem and focuses instead on
the difficulties for the French: *"Of paramount importance is
the will to smash the enemy....Enemy forces are limited. The
French cannot replace losses....Manpower losses pose a difficult
problem for them."* Hitler's strategy regarding scarce supplies
is simple: *"Save ammunition!"* He plans to attack through
Holland and Belgium, north of the French forts. The Allies
will expect this, and Halder grimly writes his diary: "None of
the higher headquarters [of the Army, OKH] thinks that the offensive ordered by OKW [Hitler's staff] has any prospect of
success."

Manstein Snatches Victory from the Jaws of Defeat.

"[Hitler's plan] contained no clear-cut intention of fighting the
campaign to a victorious conclusion....OKH [the Army head-
quarters] regarded the chances of achieving decisive results in
the French theater of war as extremely slender, if not non-exis-

tent," recalls Manstein. In February 1940 he suggests the novel plan previously noted: send massed tanks through the hilly Ardennes forest at the French center. Hitler adopts this risky idea in March, long after he had first scheduled an invasion.

May 10 Hitler sends his 2,200 tanks against a total of 4,000 heavier French ones. But the French have spread their tanks out. General Guderian leads the concentrated German armor through the French lines to the English Channel in ten days, cutting off much of the French Army and all of the British. The attack offers a stunning triumph, yet Hitler takes fright.

Hitler Snatches Defeat from the Jaws of Victory.

"Nobody at that time actually believed [in tanks], with the exception of Hitler, Manstein and myself": claims Guderian. Hitler adopts Manstein's plan to risk everything on one bold jab that tempts catastrophe: if the French show up, they can knock off one by one the tanks lumbering in line through the forest--a turkey shoot. For seducing the Führer with a pipe-dream, Manstein's superiors banish him to a reserve unit, far to the rear. Guderian scares Hitler by making the plan work.

Hitler bridles. May 16 could hardly have gone better for him: "Our breakthrough wedge is developing in a positively classic manner...," writes Halder, "Our advance is sweeping on, smashing tank counterattacks in its path. Superb marching performance of the infantry." Then the tanks roll through their first British units. Halder reports to Hitler: "Regrouping for continuance of drive westward offers no difficulties." The telling day of May 17th starts favorably: "[The] enemy has not taken any serious steps to close the breakthrough gap." Hitler's reaction stuns his Chief of Staff: "The Führer insists that main threat is from the south. (I see no threat at all at present!)....
[This is] an unpleasant day. The Führer is terribly nervous. Frightened by his own success, he is afraid to take any chance and so would rather pull the reins on us. [He] puts forward the

excuse that it is all because of his concern for the left flank!"

Halder sneers at the "excuse" Hitler gives for telling Guderian to halt. Guderian howls: "Our [March] conference with Hitler [determined]...not to stop until we had reached the English Channel. It certainly never occurred to me that Hitler himself...would now be the one to be frightened...and would order our advance to be stopped at once. I asked that I might be relieved of my command." On second thought, Guderian continues his advance, but lays a telephone wire behind him so that his radio signal still comes from his assigned position. Manstein recalls the halt order with disgust: "The reason given was...morale....[Hitler] risked losing the chance to destroy the very enemy forces in northern Belgium which the Panzer [tank] Group was supposed to take....Twelfth Army [also] was to go over to the defensive....[but] there was no reason."

"[May 18 again] shows the enemy making an orderly withdrawal...," writes Halder; "No concentrations foreshadowing a counterdrive can be discerned....The Allies are evacuating Belgium [to the north]...[and] frantically trying to improvise a front." It is a rout, yet Halder sees panic also on the winning side: "The Führer unaccountably keeps worrying about the south flank. He rages and screams....He won't have any part of continuing the operation."

DUNKIRK: Hitler's Mercy.

Hitler pleads for: *"agreement with Britain [and a way] to make peace with Britain."* This astonishes his generals. As stated before, Guderian, on reaching the Channel, turns north to encircle completely the British and French forces he has cut off, but Hitler again stops him. Halder fumes over the lost victory: "A very unpleasant interview with Führer....The left wing, consisting of armor and motorized forces, which has no enemy before it, will so be stopped dead in its tracks....The encircled enemy army is to be left to [the] air force!!" Acting the courtier, Göring matches his Führer's twisting logic, saying: "My *Luftwaffe* will do it alone!" Out of earshot, Göring's Chief of Staff Hans Jeschonnek sneers: "The Führer wishes to spare the British a too crushing defeat."

Britain ferries 337,000 men out of Dunkirk to fight again. Winston Churchill, made Prime Minister by the May 10 invasion, is relieved and encouraged: "We shall fight on the beaches, we shall fight on the landing grounds, we shall fight in the fields and in the streets, we shall fight in the hills; we shall never surrender." Guderian criticizes cautiously: "The opportunity was wasted owing to Hitler's nervousness." Warlimont reaches a harsh conclusion: "The army officers [under me] were flabbergasted by Hitler's orders....They seemed entirely incomprehensible....The influence [Hitler] exerted at this moment was decisive for the outcome of the campaign, perhaps even for that of the entire war, and it was not to the benefit of Germany."

DUNKIRK: Hitler's Choice.

Churchill's memoirs portray Hitler as an innocent bystander at Dunkirk. "Halder....[and] other German generals have told much the same story, [implicating Hitler]": Churchill admits, then dismisses their testimonies on the basis of a single piece of "authentic documentary evidence," purportedly the diary of an anonymous German staff officer. The former Prime Minister tries to rescue the reputation of Hitler, the man he has just beaten. Churchill says General Gerd von Rundstedt halted the tanks on his own and even disobeyed a direct order to renew their attack. Nonetheless, both the American and British military colleges credit Hitler with the decision, as noted in the previous chapter.

Accusing Hitler alone, Guderian and Halder are quoted above; Manstein, in the previous chapter. Warlimont assays thinking at OKW, Hitler's personal headquarters: "Jodl made not a single reference to...von Rundstedt [yet] there could have been no better argument." Warlimont quotes a post-war, 1949 letter from von Rundstedt: "[The halt was] solely and exclusively on an explicit order from Hitler....[who] stated that he *had hoped to come to some rapid agreement with England [by this]."* Had a disobedient von Rundstedt been responsible for Dunkirk, he would have been hanging from a lamppost by morning. Instead, the next day finds Hitler indirectly apologizing for Dunkirk. The town lies in the part of Belgium called Flanders. Hitler invokes esthetics again, telling Halder: *"The battle of decision must not be fought on Flemish soil."*

BRITAIN: Keeping Hope Alive.

Demoralized France soon falls, catching the new master of Europe at a loss. Warlimont recalls: "When the Western [French] campaign was brought to a successful conclusion after barely six weeks, Supreme Headquarters [OKW] had no plans for and had done no preliminary work on any further operations ....Looking back on all this, such lack of foresight seems almost incomprehensible."

Yet Hitler still holds back. When he first ran into English troops, he tried to stop his tanks. He talked of making peace when he reached the English Channel. Then came Dunkirk. Now Hitler bewilders Count Ciano of Italy with talk of keeping Britain *"a factor in world equilibrium,"* and tells his generals Britain's defeat *"would not benefit Germany."* France gives up June 21. Not until July 2 does Hitler order Wehrmacht staff even to plan an invasion of England. His order cautions: *"[this is] only a plan [that] has not yet been decided upon."* In pungent language unusual for him, Manstein objects: "We threw away our best chance of taking immediate advantage of Britain's weakness. The preparations that were only now put in train used up so much time that the success of any landing became doubtful for reasons of weather alone. This...gave Hitler his grounds--or rather his pretext--for dropping the invasion project and turning right away from Britain to strike at the Soviet Union. The outcome is well known. "

With or without a "pretext," Hitler prefers to invade Russia. Warlimont heard that: "As early as...2 June 1940 [a day after Dunkirk]...Hitler said that *now that he imagined England was ready for peace, he would begin to settle the account with Bolshevism.*" It suited Hitler to proclaim that Germany had an *"account with Bolshevism."*

Not eager to invade Britain, Hitler instead stimulates British resistance. His only peace offer comes July 19, as an aside in a long speech, as quoted earlier: *"I can see no reason why this war must go on."* He prefaces even this small opening with insults: *"I am not the vanquished begging favors."* Two days after this sneering offer and its prompt rejection, Hitler turns eastward instead. He formally orders General von Brauchitsch to attack Russia, possibly by that fall, and to expect to face no more than *"seventy-five good divisions."* Hitler announces: *"Stalin is flirting with Britain to keep her in the war."* The Army reels in disbelief, as Warlimont recalls: "The most urgent representations from Keitel and Jodl...had been necessary to convince the Supreme Commander that...this [fall] plan [was] totally impracticable....[Others began] to range themselves against this ghastly development....[But] how to counter Hitler's fresh intentions, how to avoid this new and apparently limitless extension of the war."

Weeks later, on August 15, Hitler starts a battle in the airspace over the English Channel. While claiming to prepare England for invasion, Hitler sends twelve divisions to eastern Poland August 26. No soldiers ever go to England. Hitler constructs a remarkable excuse for avoiding Britain: *"We could never attempt a second landing....So long as the attack has not taken place however, the British must always take into account the possibility of it."*

Looking back, Field Marshal Keitel, Hitler's advisor, observes: ".Although the Führer appeared to be throwing himself into all the preparations with great enthusiasm...[when] actually executing the operation, he was in the grip of doubts and inhibitions." "Hitler always wished to *avoid a contest with Britain....* [He] did not *want to land in Britain"*: so concludes Manstein [emphasis in original]. Churchill believes the Royal Air Force made the difference: "Never...was so much owed by so many to so few." However, Hitler's deference towards Britain shows up other times as well. He occupies Crete in May 1941. At that point even the U.S. Navy secretly concludes that the British fleet can be driven from the Mediterranean and Britain might sue for peace. On his own, the head of the German Navy, Grand Admiral Erich Raeder, urges Hitler to try exactly that, calling it "a deadlier blow than the taking of London." Hitler files the idea--accepted, but postponed until Russia is cleaned up. Warlimont says: "All [Hitler] was worried about was...the opening of the Russian campaign." Hitler sells it as a religious duty: *"the anti-Bolshevik crusade."* He also insists that Russia links to Britain. Warlimont notes: "In June 1941, the draft of [the Russian invasion plan] *Directive No. 32* [read] *'once the Russian armed forces had been smashed'*...the lifeline of the [British] Empire [the Mediterrranean link] was to be cut and as soon as a *'collapse'* of the British Isles appeared imminent, an end was to be brought about *'through a landing, in England.'"*

Summary: France.
France fell swiftly to Hitler, for which he took full credit. However, the victory was not entirely of his making. Had the French guarded the Ardennes or responded promptly, they could have decimated Germany's armor. In any case, Hitler first scheduled the invasion of France for November 1939, long before Manstein had a plan. The November invasion through

Belgium and Holland would have met the main Anglo-French force head on. When Manstein's risky, make-or-break scheme actually worked, Hitler balked, several times. When France fell anyway, Hitler seemed unprepared to win.

Perhaps Hitler meant to win, then was overwhelmed by the actual event. He seemed shocked by success (said Halder), then fended off victory (as Guderian and Manstein conclude), spared the British to be his assassins later (Jeschonnek's interpretation), or simply froze in confusion (as Warlimont assumed).

Hitler's handling of Britain worked to maintain her will and her ability to fight. Before dropping his first bomb, he had shied away from invading. France fell before Hitler could avoid it; with Britain he pulled his punches. Finally, he alone declared Russia a threat, a priority and a path to Britain. Now consider the eastward march of the three million grenadiers.

Chapter Four

INTO THE ABYSS
[RUSSIA]

Prologue.
Master of Europe, Hitler in July 1940 sets England aside. He will invade Russia instead. As his bow to tradition--the military tradition of finishing one battle before starting another--Hitler proclaims it one battle, against a *"Soviet Russian-Anglo-Saxon plot."* He targets the one available nation still able to withstand the full power of German arms. The next year, on the eve of the fatal invasion Hitler writes Mussolini; Hitler does not emphasize practical constraints of transport or supply: *"Months of anxious deliberation and continuous nerve-racking waiting are ending in the hardest decision of my life.....I again feel spiritually free....I am happy now."* Avoiding anyone who might disagree with him, Hitler drags along lame-legged Goebbels to "pace up and down in his salon for three hours" until "Führer seems to lose his fear." Hitler's public statement twice demands a *"final relief of tension."*

Calling Russia a stunning blunder, Joachim Fest thinks Hitler was tempted beyond reason: "Rule of the world was, as he saw it, within his grasp." Others find substance in Hitler's alternating claims: *"The possibility of Russian intervention sustains the British....*[and:] *Russia has to be beaten in any case."* Fest claims: "There can be no doubt that Hitler saw and considered the many drawbacks of his new design." But the historian Alan Bullock disagrees: "[Russia was] so reckless....[simply] the biggest gamble of his career." The German Army finally produces optimistic estimates to support their Führer's call for rapid victory. (Separately, the 1941 American military also mocks the possibilities of a communist army, but does not have to pay for its politics.)

Hitler corners his generals. He implies that anyone who objects to the invasion lacks the appetites of a true soldier. Ignoring the Red Army, Hitler speaks of Russia as simply a bread basket to provision endless strife: *"Germany will have the means for waging war even against continents at some future date. Nobody will then be able to defeat her anymore. If this operation is carried out, Europe will hold its breath."*

Foreign Minister Joachim von Ribbentrop shouts at Hitler not to invade. Never outdone at dramatics, Hitler clutches his chest, moaning: *"I thought I was going to have a heart attack. You must never again oppose me in this manner!"* Ribbentrop, who negotiated the 1939 pact, protests that the Soviets have faithfully kept it. Hitler changes the subject.

Waiting for the Russian spring, Hitler sends troops to halt the Italian retreats in the Balkans and in North Africa. He reaches the Mediterranean both ways, then stops. He avoids cutting a wedge out of the British Empire. The Germans return to the Russian border with no winter clothing, ready to whisk away Bolshevism. Hitler warns that he has staked everything: *"I therefore decided today again to lay the fate and future of the German Reich and our people in the hands of our soldiers."*

As it happens, Josef Stalin, the Soviet Premier, discounts all warnings of the German attack. To him, the secret advice from the British and others is part of a plot to have him provoke Germany. He refuses to alert Soviet armies at the border. This passivity guarantees Hitler great initial success. But Russia's size guarantees time to recover. As the Soviet Foreign Minister tells his Naval Commander: "Only a fool would attack us." Hitler's proclamation of war (after the fact) admits Germany will face *"Soviet Russian Armies...together with England and supported by American supplies,"* but assures his adopted country she faces a Red Army of only one hundred sixty divisions.

RUSSIA: Staging Götterdämmerung.

The trap opens with an inviting rush. On the anniversary of Napoleon's invasion, June 22, 1941, three million Germans begin to march, shoot, bomb, shell and strafe. However, they have no specific target. Warlimont recalls in amazement: "As soon as the Soviet Armies in White Russia had been broken, Army Group Center was to divert [tanks] northwards...The advance towards Moscow was to be continued only when Leningrad [now St. Petersburg] and Kronstadt had been captured.... As so often before and even more later, [Hitler] disregarded the invariable first principle of all strategy, the destruction of the enemy forces."

Hitler's next instructions bring further chaos. The sabotage is disguised as greed: *"The annihilation of the Russian Army, the seizure of the most important industrial areas, and the destruction of the remainder will be the objective* [sic] *of the operation --and the area of Baku must also be occupied."*

As in France the year before, success upsets Hitler. Manstein recalls: "Exactly four days and five hours after the zero hour, we had actually completed, as the crow flies, a non-stop dash through two hundred miles of enemy territory." Guderian exults: "We had managed to take the enemy by surprise along the entire Panzer Group Front." The result, says Guderian: "Hitler had become nervous....He wanted to halt the panzer groups....Fortunately, we [panzers] were unaware."

On the fifth day, Hitler did manage to stop the tanks. Manstein recalls frustration and confusion: "Was the objective to be Leningrad or should we turn towards Moscow? The Panzer Group Commander...could tell us nothing....We were to wait [although] the safety of a tank formation operating in the enemy's rear largely depends on its ability to keep moving....

Finally, on 2nd July [the eleventh day], we were able to move off again....Six days had elapsed since the corps' surprise dash to Dvinsk. The enemy had had time to recover."

Stalin revives from a week of nervous prostration that had prevented a Russian response. Not knowing that Stalin had been sick, Hitler claims: *"To all intents and purposes the Russians have lost the war."* Hitler's reaction on July 23 is to halt his main army and to widen its mission. Says Warlimont: "The objectives in the south were now to be, not only Kiev, but Kharkov and the lower Don, Caucasia and the Crimea; [however,] as soon as Army Group North had reached its objectives...OKH was told to send *'considerable forces, including Armored Group 3 [tanks] back to Germany!'* Similarly, as soon as action in the Smolensk area was completed, the *Luftwaffe* was ordered to send a number of dive bomber groups to Finland." A shocked Halder writes: "This means that [Field Marshal Fedor] von Bock will have to give up his armored groups and advance on Moscow with infantry alone....In any case, the Führer takes no interest in Moscow at the moment, only in Leningrad....[due to his] stubbornness." Halder believes Hitler stubborn. With that camouflage, Hitler keeps Army Group Center out of Moscow, but Army Group North steadily approaches Leningrad.

LENINGRAD: The Manstein Affair.

Manstein moves toward Leningrad until, with two hundred miles to go, Hitler splits the offensive and pulls the best tank division out entirely. The Reds cut the division off, and the Germans must stop to rescue it. Manstein's tone remains mild: "We still had no success with our proposal that the forces of the Panzer Group be at long last concentrated." A preliminary directive says that the two tank armies would combine for an assault on Leningrad but, says Manstein: "On 16th August, we [were] moved back." An entire month passes. Manstein proudly recalls: "Nine enemy divisions were considered to have been destroyed and nine more badly battered....We still failed to find any real satisfaction in these achievements, however, for no one was clear any longer what the actual aim of our strategy was."

Hitler takes this moment to transfer Manstein one thousand miles south. The Germans never reach Leningrad. History records that the city withstood a seige of years at terrible human cost. However, in truth, Hitler turned away. His only profit was the city's agony.

At his new command, Manstein discovers: "The task assigned to Eleventh Army by [Hitler] inevitably committed it in two divergent directions....The dual role...was unrealistic." As in France, Manstein revises. He recalls: "[Hitler] made not the least effort to interfere in our plans [for Eleventh Army] or, as was so often the case later on, to ramble off into endless recitation of production figures."

Manstein proceeds to conquer the Crimea and its stronghold, Sevastopol, which falls July 1, 1942. Hitler makes Manstein a Field Marshal, but then breaks up the Eleventh Army and scatters the pieces, including Manstein, who comments quietly: "What was undoubtedly a mistake, however, was the [decision] to withdraw Eleventh Army....The Stalingrad tragedy might then have been averted....The duality of Hitler's objective-- Stalingrad and the Caucasus--would split the offensive." At headquarters, Manstein finds: "Halder made it quite clear that he completely disagreed with Hitler's proposal...but said that Hitler had insisted." The three of them meet: "Hitler took this as an occasion for indulging in a tirade...Halder emphatically contradicted him [which] provoked an outburst of fury." As noted, Hitler then fires Halder and loses Stalingrad.

To concern over Leningrad, Hitler suggests more punishment. Manstein comments: "As for Hitler's belief that the city could be compelled to surrender through terror raids by Eighth

Air Corps, we had no more faith in this than had Colonel-General von Richtofen, the force's own experienced commander." Manstein grows increasingly disillusioned, as discussed later. Meanwhile, the Moscow problem festers.

MOSCOW: The Road Not Taken.

Hitler avoids Moscow. The British military describe the results when Hitler, as in France, stops his tanks: "Guderian was outraged....His leading elements, which had already advanced four hundred forty miles in six weeks, stood only two hundred twenty miles from Moscow [and] might certainly be led to reach the capital." The West Point text comments: "The direction of the war became fumbling and uncertain because Hitler, although he had no clear strategy in mind, refused to let his generals make their own decisions....Apparently, Hitler's decision to make Leningrad a primary objective was irrational." Hitler's shell game proceeds for the better part of August. Warlimont remembers that even Hitler's dutiful lackey, General Jodl, got his back up: "On 10 August...Jodl submitted to Hitler an appreciation [that] the most important objective was the annihilation of this [central] enemy grouping, followed by the capture of Moscow....A last attempt was made, via General Guderian, to see whether Hitler could possibly be made to change his mind...on 23 August."

At the meeting with Guderian, Hitler demands the capture of Kiev, five hundred miles in a different direction. This surprises everyone, including the Russians. In consequence, the Germans take six hundred sixty-five thousand prisoners. However, as the U.S. Army text notes: "In his restless, illogical way, Hitler neglected the Ukraine following the Kiev encirclement." One result does endure: the side-trip to Kiev decimates the German tanks. One regiment has only four good ones left, says Guderian, who adds: "Our tank engines had become very worn....Hitler promised to supply three hundred new tank engines for the

whole Eastern Front, a figure which I described as totally inade-
quate. As for new tanks, we were not to get any." The West
Point text notes a bizarre production picture: "Germany lolled
along on a one-shift economy for another two years....The Germans produced few tracked prime movers, and their production
of heavy infantry weapons and field artillery even declined during 1941."

Moscow finally beckons to Hitler. Jodl, in his diary, excuses
the delay: "[Hitler] has an intuitive aversion from treading the
same path as Napoleon; Moscow gives him a sinister feeling."
Strange undertones sound in Hitler's *Directive No. 35*, which
suggests the Army merely: *"begin* [sic] *the advance on Moscow."* Then Hitler sneers that the drive would have to be completed: *"in the limited time which remains available before the
onset of the winter weather."* West Point's text comments:
"The generals' thinking is clear, but Hitler's motives are hard
to define." Indeed, Hitler sets the attack for October 1; the
winter snows begin five days later.

"The [German] Army which set off on the last stage of the
road to Moscow in late September was greatly different....
Battle deaths, wounds and sickness had reduced its strength by
half a million....All ranks were filthy and bearded, with dirty,
rotting and verminous underclothing; typhus was shortly to follow." So notes the British Army textbook. Nonetheless, the
Germans get within sight of the Kremlin, from fourteen miles
out. As West Point puts it: "Hitler's haphazard direction of the
war had one advantage: the Soviets were caught off balance because they had ceased expecting...offensive operations [against
Moscow]." Winter freezes the grease in the German guns and
tanks. German soldiers go on half rations wearing summer uniforms, pulling sleds by hand. More die of cold than of bullet
wounds. The Russians counterattack on December 6. Guderian
grieves: "I would never have believed that a really brilliant
military position could be so fucked up in two months."

Hitler admits only one error: *"I haven't convinced that man [Guderian]!"* Within days of Pearl Harbor, Hitler declares war against the United States. "We [in overall command] have never even considered a war against the United States," laments Warlimont. He continues: "We had merely improvised decisions by Hitler....He [would] tamper with [his advisory staff] ...to make it a completely pliable tool of his will....[and] spread chaos in this field as in all others."

Hitler now fires von Brauchitsch and names himself Commander-in-Chief of the Army. Joseph Goebbels, the sly Minister of Propaganda, insists: "[Brauchitsch] spoiled the entire plan for the eastern campaign as it was designed with crystal clarity by the Führer." However, General Heusinger, the Chief of Operations, complains: "The chaos at the head of affairs is becoming greater every moment." Warlimont first takes a mild view: "Hitler did not want unity; he preferred diversity." But Warlimont gains intensity: "Hitler's flow of speech however must have been the worst, well-nigh physically intolerable burden....The urgent questions and proposals under discussion would be drowned in this ceaseless repetitive torrent of words in which matters old and new, important and unimportant were jumbled up together."

Hitler simply insists: *"I am in command and everybody must obey me without question."* He dismisses six more generals, blaming them for the defeat at Moscow. Hitler halts the retreat; men freeze in the open. A hundred thousand German soldiers require treatment for frostbite. In an astonishing speech over dinner, Hitler now openly discusses extermination--of the Germans:

> *As long as there is one stouthearted man to hold up the banner, nothing has been lost....If the German people are not prepared to give everything for the sake of their self-preservation, very well! Then let them disappear!*

However, the fruit of this tenacity is not the fall of the Russian capital. On January 3, 1942, without apology, Hitler turns south: *"The object is to resume the offensive towards the Caucasus as soon as the weather allows. This is the most important direction...[to gain] oil fields...[and] freedom of movement in the Arab world. Naturally we shall also do all we can to obliterate Moscow and Leningrad."*

This speech demonstrates Hitler's methods for blunting any potential criticism. He does not acknowledge retreating from Moscow; instead, he calls for victory there even as he withdraws. Furthermore, he increases the violence of his language, calling on the Army *"to obliterate Moscow."* Finally, he offers new goals (oil and movement) which sound attractive, even though they are not military objectives. Hearing Hitler's speech, Guderian mildly calls it "eccentric" and calls Hitler "erratic....a paradoxical man." And yet, as seen on the following page, in February, with his army snow-bound, the spellbinder brings the hall to its feet when he promises new SS officers that in Russia, they can die as heroes. By March, Army Operations Chief Adolf Heusinger feels: "Further offensive operations seemed to be beyond our strength. But it is impossible even to mention this to Hitler." By then, "Moscow did not figure as an objective at all," says Warlimont. The Russian invasion had ended; all that follows comes in retreat.

Sabotage Backfires at Home.

Whatever his wishes, Hitler cannot entirely control the resourcefulness of others, once he appoints them to high office. This is in no case more evident than with Albert Speer. The reversals of the winter of 1941-42 for Germany include the accidental death in a plane crash of her skillful minister for weapons and munitions, Fritz Todt. Hitler replaces him with a courtier having no executive or manufacturing experience whatsoever, Speer. However, Speer single-handedly prolongs the

Hitler, in February 1942,
promises new SS officers that in Russia,
they can die as heroes.

[Photo courtesy of John Toland from *Adolf Hitler*.]

war, perhaps by years. West Point comments: "In a typical gesture, Hitler made his personal architect the top industrial planner in February 1942. By a lucky chance, Albert Speer happened to be a highly intelligent and able manager, who used Hitler's authority to initiate full war production. As a result the Germans produced in 1944, under difficult circumstances, about five times as many armored vehicles as they had in 1941."

Hitler's 1942 Strategy.

Abandoning Moscow after terrible sacrifices, Hitler as Commander-in-Chief appears nonchalant, says Warlimont: "[Hitler] seemed to find this [command responsibility] compatible with spending weeks and months in the Berghof [a thousand miles away]....He proved incapable of taking even the most urgent decisions in good time....Decisions were almost invariably late and therefore disastrously overtaken by events."

His generals betray him--they win anyway. Hitler begins to interfere more actively, especially after the July 1 fall of Sevastopol. Warlimont recalls one subterfuge: "He considered that we must reckon on landing attempts by the Allies in the West....[By July 9, 1942] Hitler's apprehensions had as usual so far increased that he gave categorical orders for...reinforcements to be moved to the West...[He] ordered...one of the élite formations of the army to halt in the midst of its attack and prepare to move to the West." Hitler's biographer, Fest, describes the unique features of Hitler's next strategy:

> On July 23 [Hitler] gave orders to divide the offensive into two simultaneous, separating operations....The forces that at the beginning of the offensive had occupied a front of about 500 miles would, at the end of the operations, have to cover a line more than 2,500 miles long against an enemy whom they had been unable to engage in battle, let alone defeat.

"Those on the spot, where victory is within their grasp, are furious with [Hitler's] High Command and reproach it bitterly," writes Halder. The prize-winning American biographer, John Toland, comments: "It was another revealing example of Hitler's dangerous dispersion of forces." By August Halder advises withdrawing, because the troops are exhausted from the summer campaign. Using the same technique he used on von Ribbentrop before the invasion, Hitler forbids advice as if it were an attack on him personally: *"How dare you use language like that in front of me! Do you think you can teach me what the man at the front is thinking?...I won't stand that! It's outrageous."*

Hitler also blunts the effectiveness of his major new weapon, a tank heavy enough at last to beat the Russian T-34. Guderian recalls watching from exile: "In September of 1942 the first Tiger [tanks] went into action [but only piecemeal]....[and] in a terrain that was utterly unsuitable....The results were not only heavy, unnecessary casualties, but also the loss of secrecy." Hitler devises a frenzied torrent of design changes which reduce tank production to twenty-five per month. Returning after his layoff, Guderian forcibly intervenes, fearing: "This [production snafu] would certainly have led to the defeat of the German Army in the very near future."

September 9 Hitler fires another Field Marshal and himself takes over command of Army Group A. Halder is dismissed September 24, as Hitler bluntly dismisses military logic: *"In view of the tasks now facing the Army, rather than relying upon technical competence, it must be inspired by the fervor of belief in National-Socialism."*

Summary.

Against military advice and without provocation, Hitler decided to invade the Soviet Union. He flattered and shamed reluctant generals with talk of a six-week campaign. The June 1941 invasion began with the Russians unprepared and leaderless; Hitler's prediction of easy victory seemed possible. Then he brought the army to a halt. His further directives, although brilliantly executed by the Army, lacked an objective. As a result, the Germans were exhausted by Pyrrhic victories, and the Russians saved their major bases: Moscow, Leningrad and the oil fields at Baku.

Nonetheless, Hitler repeated his disastrous tactics in 1942. Again, brilliant victories spread the Army far and wide until the troops were exhausted and vulnerable. Hitler neither sought nor accepted anyone's advice. In the words of Germany's revered historian Walter Goerlitz, Hitler had set the stage for "certainly the greatest defeat that a German army had ever undergone." Its name is Stalingrad.

Chapter Five

STALINGRAD and SUICIDE

Prologue.
"I alone bear the responsibility for Stalingrad!" Hitler tells Manstein. "The cause of [the] Sixth Army's destruction at Stalingrad is obviously to be found in Hitler's refusal...to give up the city," agrees Manstein. Stalingrad casts doubt on Hitler's sanity and on his loyalty. West Point observes: "Hitler gave the German Army impossible missions and abandoned it shamefully when it failed to accomplish them....He had no real sympathy or affection for the soldiers whose lives he recklessly sacrificed. Probably no strategy could have brought decisive German success in 1942, but only a strategy as inane as Hitler's could have brought a disaster."

Hitler sent two hundred thousand German soldiers to the city now once again called Volgograd. Five thousand would eventually straggle home. Hitler's coldness shook Manstein, who agrees with the Americans: "[Hitler seemed] deeply affected by this tragedy [and] deeply depressed in a purely personal sense by the fate of the soldiers....Yet later on I came to doubt whether Hitler had any place whatever in his heart for the soldiers."

Hitler's Trap Shuts on the Wehrmacht.
"The moment at which the strategic initiative really passed out of Hitler's hands was...November 1942, the month of doom in modern German history, when the enemy struck both in East and West," concludes Warlimont. Under fierce attack in North Africa on November 2 Rommel still lacks reinforcements. He

had wanted to finish off Egypt and the Suez, but he gives up El
Alamein. Hitler orders suicide:

> *You can have no thought other than to hold on, not to give way
> an inch and to throw every man and every weapon into the battle
> ....You must show your troops that they have no alternative
> other than to triumph or to die.*

Hitler tries to confuse Rommel: *"In spite of his superiority the
enemy must now be at the end of his tether."* Rommel halts,
suffers new losses and again falls back. One day Hitler will
have his head.

Meeting only French forces, on November 8 English and
American armies land in Morocco and Algeria. The French
had been cooperating with Hitler during the two years since
France fell, but they offer little resistance. Hitler holds back
any German response until the Allies have time to take over.
Warlimont recalls: "Although there was a major concentration
of shipping in Gibraltar, although he had recently received
warnings from Mussolini referring to French North Africa and
finally although by 7 November it was known that the [Allied
naval] armada was on the move....Hitler [ordered] that all defensive preparations should be made in Tripoli [Libya]....[and]
ordered reinforcements to Crete [both] at the other end of the
Mediterranean." Hitler then put himself out of reach as well.
Warlimont notes: "As tension reached its height Hitler left [in]
his train to travel right across Germany."

American and British landings go almost unopposed at
Casablanca, Oran and Algiers, a thousand miles and more from
Hitler's Tripoli preparations. Warlimont says: "on the German side nothing was available to meet them except a few U-
boats and air squadrons." The Allied armies converge on Tunis
from east and west, pushing Rommel ahead of them. Faced
with the imminent loss of Africa, Hitler prevents any coherent
or timely response. Warlimont reports the vacuum of leader-

ship without comment: "On 8 November....I was ordered to... Munich where the 'Führer Special' [command train] was standing on one of the tracks of the main station in the midst of the normal traffic...empty. I finally came across Jodl....The [advisory] staff had meanwhile been summoned from East Prussia but could not arrive for another forty-eight hours....Hitler now wished to think over the new situation in the solitude of the Berghof [his mountain home]." Warlimont believes as he is told: "[Hitler's] every thought and action became increasingly centered on holding what had been won." Warlimont does not, however, ignore facts: "The result was to tie ourselves down until it was too late....[Hitler's] division of command responsibility meant that the OKW [advisory staff]....was no more than a spectator [because of] the shapeless confusion which Hitler spread around him."

Having sent no one to help Rommel conquer Africa, Hitler now throws in two hundred fifty thousand Italian and German soldiers to help him lose it. November 22 the Russians cut off two hundred thousand more at Stalingrad while Hitler, overlooking the Alps from his far-away mountain home, drains off additional men elsewhere: "The Balkans [Hitler] now figured suddenly as the main target of Anglo-Saxon strategy....[This] enormous area...started to swallow up forces," recalls an incredulous Warlimont. For Stalingrad, Hitler repeated his ominous standard order, suicide:

> The army should fight to the last man....The pocket must be held to the last man....[must] under all circumstances be held.

When Manstein fights his way close, the new Chief of Staff, General Kurt Zeitzler, recommends that the Sixth Army break out of Stalingrad to link up with Manstein. The escape is crisply forbidden by Hitler: *"When we withdraw I am always afraid of equipment being left behind. That means you've got men but*

no equipment.   Can't start anything--quite apart from the mo-
rale aspect. "

"Who could suppose that he would accept the loss of a whole
army?" asks Manstein, then scornfully recalls: "While not dis-
puting the number of enemy formations [Hitler] nonetheless
contended that *the[ir] strength...had been reduced and that the*
enemy command would have trouble in maintaining supplies
and proper control as a result of its unexpected successes....
mere hypothesis." Hitler offers to airlift supplies. The flow
proves meager, and on December 12, Manstein asks for tanks.
Taking no action, Hitler instead recites the number of tanks
available at various times in Sixth Army's twenty divisions.
The stenographic notes show Hitler makes no direct references
to the trapped men. When he mentions the situation, it is only
to repeat his decision to change nothing:

> *Looking at the big picture...under no circumstances must we*
> *give [Stalingrad] up; we should never get it back again....It's*
> *ridiculous to imagine that we can do it a second time after having*
> *withdrawn and abandoned our equipment....We can never re-*
> *place what we have there. If we give it up we in fact give up the*
> *whole object of this campaign.   It's ridiculous to think that I*
> *could get there a second time....We shall never get this far*
> *again.   Anyway we've shed too much blood getting there....The*
> *important thing is to hold on to this place....It's quite clear that*
> *this is not the best imaginable situation.   But it must be an abso-*
> *lute principle that we do not withdraw from here.   We mustn't let*
> *this attack* [sic] *get bogged down.   Time is pressing....The main*
> *thing is that we should then go all out to re-establish this front.*

Hitler argues with Zeitzler, his third Chief of Staff, over the
smallest details of command, and keeps everything fatally stall-
ed: *"When has the [troop] decision got to be taken?"* Zeitzler
says: "The sooner the better." Hearing this, Hitler puts on the
brakes: *"Is it good enough if we take the decision during the*
course of the day, so that at least we can wait and see how the

attacks get on? If they go well and if the front holds, then I would say that we don't need to use [that] brigade up here but we may well be able to hold it in readiness down there [pointing at map]. *Then I would be prepared to take a chance and use it.*"

"[Hitler] did nothing but put spokes in our wheel," Zeitzler said later. In agony Manstein recalls the following week: "On 19th December...the race with death on either side of the Don [River] had entered its final and decisive phase!...[The] Sixth Army...could only [escape] if not a single hour were wasted!... [Hitler] continued to insist that it should hold its...fronts....Hitler's reasons...were unrealistic."

The Operations Staff War Diary for December 21 states with striking frankness: "As before no decisions were taken; it looks as if the Führer is no longer capable of making them." Manstein again asks for the Sixth to retreat. Tucked away in the East Prussian forest, a thousand miles away, Hitler telephones: *"I fail to see what you are driving at. Paulus has only enough gasoline for 15 to 20 miles at the most."* Hitler condemns the plan because it saves only men, not trucks and tanks. Manstein notes for December 26, fourteen days after his original request: "Although Hitler now promised to let the Army Group have 7th Panzer Division [tank support], it was bound to arrive too late for the relief operation."

A Twin Disaster Threatens.

"Unless you order a withdrawal from the Caucasus now, we shall soon have a second Stalingrad on our hands," Zeitzler tells Hitler. By splitting the offensive, Hitler is losing both ways. "Hitler, however, would not admit this possibility at the time, although...even if we could get Sixth Army out, it would not be possible to hold the Caucasus front permanently," concludes Manstein. January 1943 nearly ends the First Panzer Army as well, he says: "A wide gap opened up....Hitler was still not disposed to give up the Caucasus region....It was impossible to get a quick decision from Hitler....On 24th January Hitler [finally] decided that if possible the whole of First Panzer Army should be withdrawn....Thanks to Hitler's hesitation [two] divisions were withheld from the crucial battleground [at Stalingrad] while some four hundred thousand men lay virtually paralyzed in the Kuban [area]."

February comes. "The only question now was whether to abandon the Donetz area by itself or to lose [my] Don Army Group along with it," says Manstein. Hitler does save the Army Group--it is still the month of Stalingrad, and deniability still the watchword. There is a limit to the amount of German blood Hitler is prepared to pour out on the ground within a thirty-day period.

Suicide and Stalingrad.

To stave off outrage, Hitler manifests outrage. General Paulus surrenders to the Russians February 1. Hitler then makes a florid speech about suicide and begs for sympathy by referring to a personal tragedy. He says everyone should show the courage to kill themselves in a timely manner, as did his niece and mistress, Geli Raubal, after a spat:

[Sixth Army] have finally and formally surrendered there. Otherwise they'd have concentrated, formed square and shot it out using their last bullet on themselves. When you think that a woman's got sufficient pride just because someone's made a few insulting remarks to go and lock herself in and shoot herself right off, then I've no respect for a soldier [Paulus] who's afraid to do that but would rather be taken prisoner....

A man who hasn't got the courage at a time like this to take the road that every man has to take one day won't have the strength to stand up to [interrogation]....In peace-time in Germany about eighteen thousand or twenty thousand people a year choose to commit suicide although none of them are in a situation like this, and here's a man [Paulus] who sees forty-five

thousand to sixty thousand of his soldiers die defending them-
selves bravely to the end--how can he give himself up to the Bol-
shevists? God!...

Hitler stands alone among national leaders in his belief that suicide is *"the road that every man has to take one day."* The next
moments would have startled the world, had they become public
knowledge. Hitler praises two former officials for shooting
themselves, then falls into a maudlin reverie:

> *A revolver--makes it easy. What cowardice to be afraid of that!*
> *Ha! Better be buried alive!...When one's nerves break down*
> *there is nothing to do but say "I can't go on" and shoot oneself.*
> *In fact you could say that the man ought to shoot himself. Just*
> *as in the old days commanders who saw that all was lost used to*
> *fall on their swords. That goes without saying. Even [the*
> *Roman general] Varus told his slave: "now kill me"....[For*
> *Stalingrad] one had to assume that there would be a heroic*
> *ending.*

The Führer leads into the subject of heroism and away from the
problem of survival. Drawing a veil over his authorship, he
shames and mocks his generals into shrugging off the catastrophe as a mysterious quirk of fate: *"I must say: how heroi-*
cally they--there's no arguing about that. Of course many
fought like Germans!--and yet we can't manage [victory], al-
though our commanders are so intelligent and our soldiers so
well trained and finally our equipment is so superior to that of
the Russians. Yet apart from Stalingrad we were always supe-
rior."

To give his strategy time to work, Hitler has to keep not just
the generals, but also the German people docile: *"As soon as I*
heard [of the surrender] last night I asked...whether the news
was out. If it hadn't already been given out on the radio I'd
have stopped it straight away." Hitler rambles on in search of
moral leverage to stem the outrage of his generals: *"Character*

is the first essential with soldiers and if we can't teach that, if all we can do is to bring up intellectual and mental acrobats and athletes, then we shall never get a race capable of standing up to the heavy blows of fortune. That's decisive." Hitler has tipped his hand, talking about the *"heavy blows"* he anticipates for Germany. He quickly reverts to the topic of the day, suicide: *"How can anyone be afraid of this moment which sets him free from this vale of misery, unless the call of duty keeps him in this vale of tears!"*

Hitler tries to expand the disaster with his orders for the soldiers still fighting, having been cut off from Paulus: *"We must let the commander in the northern pocket have something that he is to hold the pocket under all circumstances. The pocket must be held to the last man."* Here inspiration seizes the Führer: *"We must make out that the staffs fought to the last man and that they were only taken prisoner when they were wounded, overwhelmed and faced by superior forces....We must say that there was no surrender but that they were overwhelmed."* To all intents shameless, Hitler elaborates: *"Say that they've been without rations for months and that the Russians were able to overwhelm many of them."* Having scripted the melodrama to be played out for the masses, Hitler returns to begging for pity, referring to Geli again and to fame:

I can't understand how a man like Paulus wouldn't rather die. The heroism of so many tens of thousands of men, officers and generals is cancelled out by a man like this who hasn't got the character when the moment comes, to do what a weakling of a woman can do....He could have got out of this vale of tears and into eternity and been immortalized by the nation and he'd rather go to Moscow. How can he even think of that as an alternative. It's crazy.

Summary.

Hitler's dark mood fit the punctuation he had given Germany's military history, but neither the mood nor the disaster were accidents. Suicide had always held great appeal for Hitler, as will be discussed in Part Two. The flowering of those ideas in speech at the climax of the Stalingrad affair has an eerie and sinister aspect. The excuse is evenhandedly made that Stalingrad took on a symbolic value for both Hitler and Stalin. But Stalin needs no excuse for his watershed victory. What dirge was Hitler whistling under his breath for the uncovered German bones still bleaching in the sun fifty years later in the flat, open fields that gave no hiding place, around that town.

Hitler's one apology is the sentence quoted at the beginning of this chapter and spoken to Manstein, who alone demands an apology. No one else cares to confront the Führer. All now see the war as lost, if not yet over. The Allies have Manstein and Speer still to contend with, and Hitler has much left to do to prostrate Germany. He soon shows he has learned nothing from his experience at Stalingrad. Or is it that he holds to his strategy because it works--not in furtherance of military goals, but in aid of a hidden plan, deeper and stranger, in his private mind.

Chapter Six

THE DOWNWARD TRAIL

[1943]

Prologue.

The fall of Stalingrad brought no change in Hitler. To his hand-picked circle of compliant generals he offered several reasons for standing pat. Yet all understood that the overwhelming Soviet strength made holding still impossible. Hitler himself probably did not know why he kept the path of defeat. He tried out several excuses:

[1.] *I cannot turn back now. Any change in my attitude would certainly be misunderstood as giving in, the military situation being what it is, and would bring a landslide....*[2.] *I have a duty to think of tomorrow, and the day after tomorrow. I cannot forget the future for the sake of a few momentary successes....*[3.] *Policy is made not with illusions but with facts.* [4.] *Space is the deciding question for me in the East!*

From Stalingrad to Berlin, throughout the last two years of the war, Hitler denies the Wehrmacht even any *"momentary successes."* He says he makes his decisions based on considerations of *"space."* In any case, he fails to pursue military victory.

TUNIS: the Other Shoe Drops.

In February 1943 Warlimont reports pessimistically after a trip to Rome and Tunis. Apparently unperturbed, Hitler regales his dinner guests with his rosy plans for retirement: *"After the war, I'll hang [my uniform] on the hook....Then, as an old man, I'll write my memoirs and will only have around me bright, gifted people."* This fantasy of the chaste salon is virtually the same one he had at fifteen, as will be discussed in Part Two. Says Warlimont: "Between 10 and 13 May the catastrophe occurred [at Tunis]. Two German-Italian armies went into captivity; they totalled about 300,000 men--the same number [*sic*] as the defenders of Stalingrad." Hitler composes alibis. Goebbels's diary entry for 10 May reads: "[Hitler's] opinion of all the generals is devastating....*All generals lie,* he says; *all generals are disloyal; all generals are opposed to National Socialism [Nazism]; all generals are reactionaries."* By July, American armies enter Sicily. To overwhelm any criticism, Hitler says he sacrificed an army in Tunis to save Germany:

> *Naturally I have tried to reckon whether the undertaking in Tunis ...was justified....[It] succeeded in postponing the invasion of Europe by six months. More important still, Italy is as a result still a member of the Axis....The Allies would [otherwise]...push forward to the [German border] and as a result of the Russian breakthrough at Stalingrad, Germany would not have had a single man available to put in there. That would inevitably have led rapidly to the loss of the war.*

ITALY: the Axis in Ruins.

Losing Sicily and facing invasion of the Italian peninsula, Mussolini resigns July 25. Hitler blames the Italian royal house: *"Nothing! I always told him [Mussolini] that; he's got nothing! It's true he's got nothing. Those people took good care to ensure he had nothing to act with."* Hitler holds Rome, but admits to his staff that the situation is hopeless:

> *We must of course play the game from now on as if we thought that it was going to succeed.*

Hitler now calls up boys for army service. He claims an advantage in this: *"These young men are fighting like fanatics be-*

cause they come from the Hitler Youth. They're young German kids, mostly sixteen-year-olds. These Hitler Youth chaps generally fight more fanatically than the older people."

RUSSIA: the Sun Sets in the East.

While losing Africa and Italy to Eisenhower, Hitler fights in Russia against Manstein, who recalls: "I asked him to ensure the uniformity of [military] leadership by appointing *one* Chief-of-Staff....But Hitler...kept resorting to the personal aspects of the case, complaining of the disappointments he had suffered [and] quite bluntly [refusing to] put anyone...above Göring." On this point, Manstein sounds one of his rare doubts:

> Whether Hitler was really reluctant to offend Göring or merely used this as a pretext, I cannot say.

The struggle in Italy forces consideration of a truce in Russia. Air Field Marshal Erhard Milch tells his Führer: "Stalingrad has been the gravest crisis....You simply must act decisively to bring Germany out of this war." Ribbentrop agrees with Milch. But Hitler will not discuss terms. His schoolgirl excuse is monstrous and bizarre: *"If I settled with Russia today I would only come to grips with her again tomorrow--I just can't help it."* Hitler keeps the Army stretched thin. To mount an attack after Stalingrad means borrowing somewhere, but nothing tempts the Leader. Manstein recalls one effort:

> [As] on similar occasions, he avoided any real discussion of what I had to say....Nor did he dispute that the situation would develop in the way I [saw]. He [simply] treated every statement not bearing directly on the most pressing needs of the moment as sheer hypothesis.

Manstein remarks: "Hitler also argued that [1.] *if one fought bitterly for every foot of ground and made the enemy pay dearly for every step he advanced, even the Soviet armies' offensive power must one day be exhausted....*[But] our own divisions...

were themselves not far from exhaustion....[2.] *the present im-*
possibility, as he saw it, *of giving up the Donetz area....*[3.]
Hitler [droned] his quite astonishing knowledge of production
figures and weapon potentials....[Hitler insisted] that [4.] *[with*
rain] the broad valley of the Don might well be an impassable
[protection]....When I...refused to stake the fate of my Army
Group on the hope of a quite unseasonable change of weather,
Hitler finally agreed to the withdrawal of the Army Group's
eastern front....We had been in conference for four whole
hours."

A week later the Russians hammer at another gate: "[Hitler]
again passed a strict order to...*hold Kharkov at all costs....*The
SS Panzer Corps...evacuated the city on 15th February [1943]--
incidentally against the orders of General Lanz.....All the same
[Lanz] was replaced a few days later." Hitler adds new evasions when Manstein has a new plan: "[1.] Hitler at first refused to discuss [what] I was proposing. [2.] He would not admit
that there really were powerful [Russian] forces....[3.] Another
interminable discussion ensued [about] the Donetz area....[4.]
He could not take the forces for a large offensive from any of
the other theaters, nor could he find them from newly drafted
units....[5.] Hitler [resumed] the subject of weapons and weapons production, and [6.] it proved impossible to pin him down
on his intentions regarding the coming summer campaign."

Rancor here seeps into Manstein's recollection: "We lived, it
seemed, in two entirely different worlds." At last, an offensive
takes shape: "Operation 'Citadel'--the last major offensive...in
the east....was timed to start in the first half of May....Hitler
decided--against the advice of the two army group commanders
--to postpone 'Citadel' till June....The Army Group was not ultimately able to move off on 'Citadel' until the beginning of July
....And so [it] ended in a fiasco."

In a meeting at the end of August 1943: "[Hitler tried] to
ramble off into all sorts of technical details, [but] agreed that the

Army Group must be afforded vigorous support....The very next day....[Hitler] fumed with rage...[and] declared that *no forces could be spared.*" In the retreat: "Central Army Group ....had called on OKH to fortify the Dnieper [River] line....Hitler had turned down the request....[Hitler] had expressly ordered the retention of the bridgehead of Zaporozhye." When the Russians use Hitler's intact bridge to get across the river, he promptly fires Colonel-General Hermann Hoth as a scapegoat.

Manstein notes the continuing interference: "Hitler refused... forces to use on the operationally far more important northern wing....[where] First Panzer Army [faced] ultimate encirclement....It needed a desperate crisis on this northern wing before Hitler would face up--and even then most reluctantly--to these operational necessities." Even the ambitious lackey Martin Bormann complains to Joseph Goebbels on November 30: "It is so hard to get the Führer to make any decision."

A Look Backstage.

By December 27, 1943, the Russian front is collapsing. The evening is preserved in stenographic notes found among the few not burned at the end of the war. In the notes, Hitler merely drones on for hours to his captive audience: Keitel, Jodl and their assistants:

> *The enemy wants to ensure that we have no time to recuperate and so goes on fighting. That's all....Somewhere he comes to the end of his resources....You mustn't think he's like one of the old giants [of German mythology] who simply becomes stronger when he's laid out....He must get out of breath one day....*
>
> *The decisive thing is that in fact the morale of the troops isn't good....I'm a man who has personally built up and led perhaps the greatest organization on earth....People go on saying: we'll fight on to victory--all that fighting on to victory means to me today is to stabilize the thing somehow....*
>
> *We've withdrawn to a shorter line and found we couldn't hold that either. Alternatively we would certainly have been able to*

*hold it if we had been more mobile and units had had more spirit
of self-sacrifice. Then we'd have been able to save a lot. We've
had a classic instance. The whole Nevel catastrophe was caused
by the small-minded selfishness of the two Army Group commanders who acted like little egoists and wouldn't help each
other....*

[Pointing to the Crimean Peninsula] *We've simply got to
defend this second Stalingrad if at all possible. We can't just
cold-bloodedly turn our backs on it [just] because it's got nothing
to do with Field Marshal von Manstein's Army. We can't do
that; we must remember there will be men lost here....It may
happen that Turkey enters the war....If we withdraw here, the
Crimea is lost....I think the loss of the Crimea is the worst thing
that could happen. It would have the worst possible effect on
Turkey.*

In case of a defeat, Hitler fires the general in the field. Hermann Hoth is the latest victim of this policy. Hitler rubs it in:
*"[Manstein] was very much influenced by the jinx of Hoth at
Kiev. We're only just beginning to realize what a disastrous
effect that man had. He was the worst type of defeatist. There
are incredible stories which only come to light gradually. People are only just plucking up the courage to report them....*

*"[Manstein] refers to counter-maneuver. He shouldn't talk of
counter-maneuver but call a spade a spade--running away....
That's a typical example; we should have been able to hold this
[points to map]....It would have all been all right....[Pointing:
This is an] obstacle which is the last available and which must
be held under all circumstances. If we go back from there, that
will be a catastrophe."*

Hitler finally takes up the proposal from Manstein. In a nice
twist Hitler accuses the Field Marshal of reckless optimism:
*"The idea that he could quickly bring up these formations here
or bring down those here is a pipe dream. Everything in this
telegram is a pipe dream. It is just a dream world; there can be
no planned operations here any more. I'm happy if we can sta-*

bilize the situation; I don't expect more apart from that."

Collected below, but in actuality interspersed throughout the conference, is a series of asides--a sideshow. The man who hides in the woods storms about a problem he prefers, namely, the location of Manstein's headquarters: *"It's quite clear he's worried about Vinnitsa. His headquarters is here....They're too close up here. They'll lose their nerve. It would be better if he put his headquarters further back here....The first point is: I am sure he must move his headquarters from here--if people are under pressure like that they'll never make sensible decisions.... His Headquarters is badly placed in this situation; he's sitting here right on top of the focal point of the battle. His Head-quarters will be better somewhere else....He must move his headquarters straight away....One thing I think is essential: that he should get out of Vinnitsa straight away so that he doesn't lose his nerve. He'll lose his nerve and there's no sense in that....He must get out of Vinnitsa; there's no sense in that. There must be a special detachment at Vinnitsa to burn the whole headquarters down and blow it up. It is most important there should be no furniture left, otherwise the Russians will send it to Moscow and put it on display. Burn the lot."* Obviously planning to lose ground, Hitler mulls the furniture problem past midnight. With an astonishingly blithe attitude, Hitler simply filibusters when pressed to act on Manstein's proposal:

Hitler: [Retreat] is becoming a mania, a real disease. After all, this isn't a trifle....There's a break-through and we give up a colossal front of two hundred twenty miles. Two hundred twenty miles was the entire right wing of the army in 1914.

Jodl: But; my Führer, we don't want the sort of crisis where one day we have to say: "here's another army cut off."

Zeitzler: That's my view. I've reached the same conclusion as Manstein, but for other reasons....

Hitler: You've come to the conclusion, Zeitzler, that we must withdraw the whole front here?

Zeitzler: [Yes,] then we make some formations available.

Hitler: We won't get them up there in time....

Zeitzler: My Führer, the question is....

Hitler: The troops...just don't understand it when they have to abandon a position where they've spent all their energies digging themselves in....Each month we've produced more than two hundred thousand rifles...They've been lost here in the East as a result of these "successful withdrawals" during which the men chuck their rifles away....You may say: Stalingrad was something different; that happened over there. But here [points on map] *it's ridiculous. There are good communications here in all directions.*

Zeitzler: The communications are very bad here.

Hitler: They are bad, but nothing on the Stalingrad model.... If you bring [a division] back you get the whole of the front into a mess....We've seen what the results of these withdrawals are ....If we withdraw he may attack again straight away here [points].

Zeitzler: He can still attack this way, even if we don't go back.

Hitler: That's not right either; he's been attacking all the time. [Besides] I've got another report today about the other fellow's supply situation. This is the most miserable and precarious supply system there's ever been....[Besides] this may indicate a few tanks; one can't really tell.

Zeitzler: It didn't look that way today....

Hitler: Well, try and get the news....

Long and desultory conferences have become Hitler's nightly ritual. This one differs only in having a transcript that survived the war. The conference ends at 1:09 A.M. with no decision to either withdraw or relieve Manstein's beleaguered troops. They are thus left to their fate.

A Personal Problem.

Surrender is always on Hitler's mind. It comes up often in the course of his midnight conference. His shouting about the evils of retreat avoids talk about losing: *"That was the cry then: back! [The Crimea in February 1943] was a typical retreat, everybody lost their nerve. [Field Marshal von] Kleist included--everybody back!...We could have had that here. We mustn't try and make out that we couldn't have held that. It was just that the word went round: everybody back! Sometimes it becomes a real mania. If only we could now have some success somewhere! I have seen [only] two retreats during which I said: we can risk it....I read all the reports about these retreats. I could kick myself today that I gave permission for them. It wouldn't have been any worse up forward--on the contrary. But it's just as I said; it's all happened under pressure; the formations got back in the hell of a mess. The retreat was worse than any defensive battle."*

Zeitzler patiently tries to discuss military facts. Hitler takes the opportunity to elaborate further: *"We've come back this far on our own accord! That's demoralized the troops. They fought all right, Zeitzler. I spoke to innumerable people....This is the way it is: the men fight bravely, they repulse the enemy, they are brave and courageous, they fortify all their positions but then the word goes round: back!"*

Summary.

In all this rambling and preening before the captive audience of his generals, Hitler seems to ignore the war. No longer interested in how his generals perform their functions or what they think of him, he evidently is at peace with events and accepts the grinding down of his army. After seven more months, the generals try to kill him. After executing thousands of the supposed conspirators, Hitler will himself end his rule.

Epilogue.

So ends 1943. German forces retreat in Italy and Russia. Bombs fall on Germany around the clock after the destruction of Hamburg in August. Warlimont recalls the preparations against invasion from the West at year's end. They seem to be rather preparations for immobility and confusion: "There was no unity of command....No fewer than seven independent headquarters [existed], Commander-in-Chief West being merely number five....[All] were ordered to report on their plans and disposition to Hitler himself--not to OKW....In Germany there had been no [trained, professional] Supreme Commander since 1938 [when Hitler fired Blomberg]." Hitler simply notes:

If they attack in the West that attack will decide the war.

Chapter Seven

LEADING WITH THE CHIN

[1944]

Prologue.

Outgunned and losing ground in Russia and Italy, the German generals hope to drag out the war by clever maneuvers until the Allies will settle. But Hitler cares nothing for strategy or surrender. Does he care about survival?

RUSSIA: the Millwheel Grinding.

Manstein recalls: "On 4th January [1944]...I began by describing the new danger....the entire southern wing of the Eastern Front would be in mortal peril." Hitler offers only evasions, says Manstein: "Hitler even now categorically refused to evacuate the Dnieper bend or to give up Nikopol....As for giving us forces from the west, said Hitler, he *could not do this until an enemy landing had first been beaten off or the British did as he expected and tied themselves down in Portugal* [sic].... *There were so many disagreements on the enemy side,* Hitler added, *that the coalition was bound to fall apart one day.*" Manstein explodes: "One thing we must be clear about, *mein Führer,* is that the extremely critical situation we are now in cannot be put down to the enemy's superiority alone, great though it is. It is also due to the way in which we are led.

"Hitler's expression hardened. He stared at me....Not even in private would [Hitler] admit to having made mistakes or to being in need of a military adviser," says Manstein, who nonetheless maintained: "[forcibly removing Hitler] would lead to the collapse of our armies in the field." The Field Marshal notes, however, that Hitler turned his back on military reality: "[Hitler now demanded] National-Socialist [Nazi] education inside the army. The more difficult the military situation became, the greater importance he attached to *'faith'* as a guarantee of victory."

On January 27 Hitler contemptuously hints of impending doom: *"If the end should come one day, it should really be the field-marshals and generals who stand by the flags to the last."* This prompts Manstein to shout: "And so they will, *mein Führer!*" Hitler then strips him of an entire army, Manstein's only reserve force. The war of personalities takes precedence over the war of blood and bullets and torn flesh. Manstein notes the result: "Now the enemy was to force him to surrender the areas in question....The [German] armored divisions had only five serviceable tanks left!" In a small revolt, the desperate Manstein personally rescues two army corps at Cherkassy, as he recalls: "Hitler had called for the pocket to be held, but....[I] issued the order for the actual break-out without previously notifying Hitler in order to avoid any possibility of a countermand."

However, Hitler continues to weed out anyone who prefers survival to suicidal obedience, says Manstein: "[When] the town of Rovno was lost...Hitler...demanded the head of the general responsible....Sentence of death was passed not upon the officer originally accused, but on the divisional commander responsible for the Rovno area."

As a professional officer, Manstein cannot conceive that Hitler pursued unusual goals. Manstein tries to find excuses for his Leader: "Hitler, however, obviously went on counting on exhaustion and the weather to put an end to the enemy's offensive operations." But Manstein also criticizes: "[Hitler promised] he would have new divisions at his disposal....Had [Hitler] only put the personnel and equipment they required into our own bat-

tle-tested divisions, things might have turned out very differently." Furthermore: "Hitler thought he had found a new [defense]....*'strongholds'* [isolated garrisons]....[We] contrived to get them abandoned before they were hopelessly surrounded.... [After my removal] this method of Hitler's led to considerable losses....I could not overlook the faults of Hitler's leadership."
   In personality clashes, Hitler always wins. He traps the First Panzer Army March 19th. Manstein wants to save them: "Hitler, however, declined....On 23rd March....The Führer...still insisted that [First Panzer] *should mainly continue to hold the present front*....It was exactly the same as at Stalingrad in December 1942....On the morning of 25th March, I reached the Berghof [Hitler's remote mountain home]....[His evasions were, first] he tried to hold me responsible....[Then] Hitler asserted that all we (i.e. the Army Group) were ever interested in doing was 'playing at grand tactics [*immer nur operieren*]'....
   "Next Hitler declared that *according to the Luftwaffe there were very few enemy tanks to be seen, but that whole German units were running away from them*....[Later] Hitler's mood had completely changed....*'[I] agree with your plan....I have also decided--with great reluctance--to provide an SS Panzer [Tank] Corps.'"* Manstein returned to the Russian front. Five days later he was brought back to Bavaria and fired,, along with General von Kleist: *"All that counted now*, [Hitler] said, *was to cling stubbornly to what we held."*

The Struggle to Stay Loyal.
   Manstein still invents excuses for Hitler: "[He] [1.] believed in the power of his will not only to nail down his armies wherever they might be but even to hold the enemy at bay....[2.] fought shy of risks because of their inherent threat to his prestige and...[3.] for all his talent, lacked the groundwork of real military ability." But Guderian's sharper tongue finds Hit

ler jealous or touchy: "What a pity it was that Hitler could not tolerate the presence of so capable and soldierly a person as Manstein....Manstein [had] a sensible, cool understanding [and] was our finest operational brain....He formed his own opinions and spoke them aloud....Hitler [said] *'Manstein is perhaps the best brain...but he can only operate with fresh, good divisions'"* Guderian then drops the pretense of civility and deference: "The truth is that [Hitler] did not wish to [use Manstein] and was trying to justify his refusal by such circuitous excuses."

Captain Sir Basil Liddell-Hart gives the British military verdict: "[Manstein's] counterstroke which recaptured Kharkov [was] one of the most masterly in the whole course of military history....[But] Hitler's unwillingness to sanction any withdrawal forfeited each chance of stabilizing the front....The course of events continued to confirm Manstein's warnings. So in March 1944 Hitler...ended the active career of the Allies' most formidable opponent." Was it a personality clash, envy, or something else?

ITALY: Hitler Milks Defeat.

While Manstein wrestles him for Russia, Hitler keeps his other forces spread thinly in Italy, despite claims that an invasion of France may come soon. On January 28, 1944, Hitler declares his personal objectives for the "Battle of Rome": *"The battle must be hard and merciless, not only against the enemy but against all officers and units who fail in this decisive hour."* Warlimont finds the order: "berserk....Nothing was in fact achieved, except to ensure that in its hour of danger, the West [France] had available three to four divisions fewer than before. The West was bled a second time for the occupation of Hungary [although] quiet had reigned there for months." Warlimont believes the West is stripped because: "such was Hitler's rage and thirst for revenge against the Hungarian Regent, Admiral Horthy.

"On the night of 24 March [Hitler] began raiding the resources of the West in earnest....The West was now left without a single battle-worthy fully operational armored [tank] division at a moment when the invasion might come any day," notes Warlimont. Manstein gets the last tank divisions, but is fired before they arrive. They do rescue the First Panzer Army. However, says Warlimont: "[It was] Hitler's decision to retain these two divisions [in Russia]....It was not until 12 June, almost a week after the beginning of the [Normandy] invasion, that Hitler was persuaded, most unwillingly, to...order the corps to be moved back to the West."

NORMANDY: Hitler's Wait Ends.
Five thousand ships cross the English Channel undetected June 5 because the Luftwaffe has neither planes nor fuel to keep watch. Warlimont puzzles over Hitler's reaction: "He chuckled in a carefree manner and behaved as if this was the opportunity he had been awaiting so long....In unusually broad Austrian [dialect] he merely said: *'So, we're off.'*

"Rommel and the OKW Operations staff [agree] that every risk must be taken and all available forces concentrated for a rapid counter-attack." Nonetheless, Hitler refuses. Warlimont offers details: "I had brought a number of documents...Hitler dismissed them with a flood of objections and misgivings and, when I refused to budge, signalled to his aide to take away the maps and tables without looking at them....

"[Next] Hitler declared that *'it was obvious (that it would be) seven months'* before the Apennines [Italian defensive] position was ready. Kesselring's order to withdraw...was cancelled.... [and he] was in disfavor for several weeks....Jodl was careful to note[:]....'insistence [by Führer] on *the necessity of fighting for every square mile of ground and every week of time'*....Hitler insisted on quoting for the hundredth time the figures of men and material used in construction of the Siegfried Line[!]" Jodl drily records: "There were 4,000 concrete mixers."   Warlimont summarizes glumly: "The end result...our forces [in Italy], which were...completely exhausted [were] overrun....It was only then, [August] when it was much too late, that the first forces were released from Italy to reinforce the West."

The Allies land a million men in Normandy. Hitler again advises suicide for Germans: *"The fortress of Cherbourg is to be held at all cost."* While leaving for his mountain home, Hitler sneers at those who disagree: *"Rommel has lost his nerve; he's become a pessimist. In these times only optimists can achieve anything."* In a rare moment of prudence, Hitler privately acknowledges: *"If the invasion succeeds, then I must try to bring the war to an end by political means."* But Warlimont seldom hears prudence: "[June 17] Hitler merely re-emphasized his demands that *the largest possible forces should be thrown into the 'fortress' of Cherbourg....*The Americans captured Cherbourg, ten days later, [with the] several thousand additional prisoners ....[But] OKW was instructed by Hitler to *make a detailed inquiry to see whether his order had been carried out down to the last available man."*

Hitler then ordered four SS armored divisions brought together to prepare a strong counter-attack. The shrewdness was fleeting, laments Warlimont: "[Shortly] Hitler gave orders that those formations...should not wait to concentrate....This [piecemeal dribbling] put an end to the last hope of regaining the initiative....[Hitler] began to toy with the idea of using the newly-arrived armored formations to relieve Cherbourg....in face of the full weight of [Allied] air power...[How] obstinately Hitler clung to this new idea--even when on 26 June Cherbourg had fallen....

"[Hitler used] ruler and compass to work out the small number of square miles occupied by the enemy in Normandy and [to] compare them to the great area of France still in German hands....[Hitler] still refused to release...Fifteenth and Nineteenth Armies....Our repeated demands that the armored divisions should be pulled out of the front to reconstitute a reserve [were ignored]." As the crisis deepened, the generals writhed, but Hitler held fast. Warlimont notes: "General Freiherr Geyr von Schweppenburg, Commander of 'Armored Group West' [and] Rundstedt...stated that only by adopting 'elastic tactics' could we 'at least temporarily seize the initiative'....Field Marshal Rommel [agreed]....Geyr was relieved of his command [as was] Field Marshal von Rundstedt."

The Bomb Plot.

On July 20, a titled nobleman, Colonel Claus Graf Schenk von Stauffenberg, explodes a bomb in Hitler's staff conference; "just retribution," Warlimont calls it. Searching out conspirators, the Gestapo arrests seven thousand Germans and kills most of them. Warlimont turns bitter: "[Hitler's] actual injuries on 20 July had been minor but it seemed as if the shock had brought into the open all the evil of his nature....On the slightest occasion [Hitler] would demand shrilly that 'the guilty' be hunted down....As the fronts began to collapse in all directions [Hitler] would say over and over again...*'Anyone who speaks to me of peace without victory will lose his head.'*" Hitler keeps the blood flowing.

Guderian states: "What had been hardness became cruelty, while a tendency to bluff became plain dishonesty. [Hitler] often lied without hesitation, and assumed that others lied to him ....He frequently lost all self-control and his language grew increasingly violent." But Guderian's main concern was practical: "While our [mobile] panzer units still existed, our leaders had chosen to fight a static battle in Normandy. [The tanks] had been squandered and destroyed." Hitler placates his generals with pipe dreams August 1: *"I can hardly believe that the Russians would hand over the Balkans to the English. It may well be that something will happen as a result of tension be-*

*tween the Russian Bolshevists and the Allies....They will
certainly not act in concert.* "

Meanwhile, Hitler ruins victories, says Warlimont: "On the
afternoon of 7 August...[after] initial success at Mortain, Hitler
had issued a further order [to begin] *rolling up the entire Allied
position in Normandy!*...[He began] issuing a bewildering series
of orders...[until] the encirclement of the [German] army in
Normandy in the Falaise pocket on 19 August brought another
disastrous defeat...." Any listeners hear: "Radio Berlin's
frantic proclamations that week calling the Falaise battle a noble
achievement of German arms in buying time for the 'German
miracle' being organized." Warlimont concludes tartly:

> By clinging rigidly to impracticable plans [Hitler] had once more
> sent a great army to death or imprisonment without having any
> major strategic object to justify the sacrifice.

The scapegoat for Falaise, Field Marshal von Kluge, is sacked
after six weeks in charge. He commits suicide. Hitler denoun-
ces even the injured and hospitalized "Desert Fox" as a quitter:
*"Field Marshal Rommel is a great and spirited commander but
when the slightest difficulties occur he turns into a complete
pessimist."* (In October, he forces Rommel also to commit suicide.) Hitler hints Falaise was a failure of nerve and patriotism.
To divert attention, he gloats about surviving the July 20 assas-
sination attempt: *"It's like a western thriller."* Warlimont recalls: "On 19 August, the day of Falaise, Hitler's attitude was
similar to that following Stalingrad.... *'Prepare to take the offensive in November.'*" Whatever was in his heart, Hitler convinced others that he believed in his strategy. Guderian,
brought back as Chief of Staff, recalls: "Many, many times
Hitler was to say to me, dully: *'I can't understand why everything has gone wrong for the past two years.'*"

Hitler refuses to defend Germany. Warlimont notes: "On
August 22...our object now was to obtain Hitler's agreement to

proposals for co-operation with the [Serbian] nationalist leaders....[but] Hitler went off into a long historical survey of the *'danger of a greater Serbia'*....although the Russians were [at hand]." On August 31, retreating on three fronts, Hitler says he is not only blameless but on the verge of winning:

> *I've proved that I've done everything to come to terms with England. In 1940 after the French campaign I offered an olive branch and was ready to give things up. I wanted nothing from them....I proposed an alliance in which Germany would guarantee the British Empire....They wanted war and today they can't go back on it. They are reeling to their ruin [sic]. The moment will arrive when disagreements between the Allies will be so great that the break will come. Coalitions have always failed right throughout history.*

Claiming: *"no greater crisis than the one we've had this year in the East could be imagined,"* Hitler blames Manstein for Normandy: *"If I'd had 9th and 10th SS Armored Divisions in the West the whole thing would probably never have happened. No one told me about it."* Hitler himself had sent the 9th and 10th to rescue the First Panzer Army in Russia. He had kept them there. Since he takes no orders and little advice, he can claim, narrowly speaking: *"no one told me."* Whining petulance that is startling in the leader of a nation at war, he prescribes his rigidity to others. In a remarkably bald display of self-indulgent attitudes and misrepresentations, he dresses up strict obedience as *"iron determination"*:

> *I think it's pretty obvious that this war is no fun for me. I've been cut off from the world for five years. I've not been to a theater, a concert or a film. I have only one job in life, to carry on this fight because I know that if there's not an iron will behind it, the battle cannot be won. I accuse the General Staff of failing to give the impression of iron determination, and so of affecting the morale....German officers exist who make overtures [to the Allies]...and generals [exist] who surrender.*

In September Guderian, like Manstein before, struggles to save an entire Army Group cut off by the Russians: "I now became involved in a long and bitter argument with Hitler concerning the withdrawal of those valuable troops which were essential for the defense of Germany." Meanwhile, says Warlimont, Hitler keeps his generals hog-tied: "The commanders...were bound by Hitler's security instructions forbidding direct communication with neighboring theaters; the only information they received on the overall situation was that given them in broad terms by OKW once a week in the so-called *News sheets.*"

In the west, the big German offensive in December catches the Allies in the Ardennes by surprise, just as in May 1940. The line bulges westward; the Americans call their response the Battle of the Bulge. Guderian says: "[The OKW] proposed that the attack be made with a limited objective....but Hitler turned down this proposal and insisted on his more grandiose plan." Hitler prepares the German officers for death:

> War is of course a test of endurance....This test of endurance must under all circumstances continue as long as there is the slightest hope of victory.

Hitler admits Germany cannot maintain the static defense he has ordered; however, he does not admit he ordered it: *"From the outset of the war therefore I have striven to act offensively whenever possible, to conduct a war of movement and not to allow myself to be maneuvered into a position comparable to that of the First World War. If this has nevertheless occurred, it has resulted primarily from the defection of our allies."*

Hitler keeps Germany bleeding, meanwhile sustaining her loyalty to him with fantasies of miracles: *"The enemy...can never reckon upon us surrendering. Never, never....On the other side history is being made merely by mortal men--this coalition may dissolve, always on the assumption that under no circumstances does this battle lead to a moment of weakness* [i.e., surrender] *in Germany."* The *Wehrmacht* suffers 1,200,000 casualties in the three months after D-day.   Hitler blames others, then changes the subject: *"It was a major source of weakness for us that we had no strong states as allies, only weak states.... [But] for a time at any rate these states fulfilled their purpose. We were enabled for years to make war far from the borders of the Reich."*   Saying nothing of victory or survival, Hitler implies war is an end in itself.

At year's end, Hitler, insisting *"the battle must be fought with brutality,"* destroys the overmatched Second Panzer Division by demanding they continue attacking Bastogne.   He explains: *"We have had unexpected setbacks because my plan was not followed to the letter....[But] nothing will make the slightest change in my decision to fight on till at last the scales tip to our side."*   This assures many more dead.   A dejected Warlimont recalls Hitler's style:

> His flow of speech was incessant.   He refused all sensible measures; he demanded the impossible.   He clung undeterred to his principle of static defense and could not be persuaded voluntarily to give up anything or even to consider any long-term plans, however obviously necessary they might be.

Summary.

It was clear by the end of the year that Hitler intended to fight to the last German.   The Battle of the Bulge represented the final miracle of German arms--it was miraculous that Hitler could still gather sufficient men and equipment to make such an attack, it was miraculous that he managed to gather the forces so stealthily, and it was miraculous that the Allies had again failed to guard the Ardennes.

What had become ordinary and no longer miraculous was that Hitler once again at the Bulge ruined an offensive by overreaching and by rigid refusal to allow strategic maneuvers. Given this strategy for wrenching defeat from victories, even the near-miss of the German panzers running out of gas a mile from an enormous Allied fuel dump seems trivial. Hitler would certainly have squandered the advantage, had he won it.

The Battle of the Bulge cost Germany 120,000 casualties, the Russians were at the gates of Warsaw and the Americans filled France, but Hitler would not hear of peace under any circumstances. He promised sensational results from the world's first jet planes and ballistic missiles. And blood flowed on.

Chapter Eight

AN END IS MADE

[1945]

Prologue.

The Battle of the Bulge ends unsuccessfully for Germany because she has no more men and no more fuel. The synthetic gasoline factories built by Speer are bombed out or overrun. Hitler's military assistant, Field Marshal Wilhelm Keitel, the nominal Chief of the OKW, recalls: "Germany's defeat was absolutely clear. It was only the sense of military duty...which compelled me and all of us to fight on." Sustained by daily injections of amphetamines, Hitler in no way alters his program. Warlimont is beside himself, remembering Hitler's astonishing rigidity, and his ability to draw Germany on: "The determination of one man possessed of the devil governed everything; the machinery of command churned out orders in normal form though there might be no one to receive them. Yet the German soldier and...the German civilian followed this lead with self-sacrifice and energy."

To their deaths; the fervor of one single man keeps a nation at war when no one but him can see any further point. On the desolate twelfth anniversary of his rise to power, January 30, 1945, Hitler alone predicts victory. Germany does not dare doubt him; she has bled too much in her fantasy of a master race. Hitler drones on: *"However grave the crisis may be at the moment, it will, despite everything, finally be mastered by our unalterable will, by our readiness for sacrifice and by our abilities."* His will, their sacrifices.

Three days before, the Red Army passing the town the Poles call Oświecim find five thousand starving people living behind barbed wire alongside 368,820 men's suits, 836,255 women's coats and seven tons of human hair. Auschwitz becomes a household word, one to be discussed in the next chapter.

End Game.

The year begins in the same vein as before. Guderian glumly recalls trying to hold the Eastern Front: "The Russians' superiority to us was 11:1 in infantry, 7:1 in tanks, 20:1 in guns." Guderian exerts himself to find civil language for his Leader: "Hitler saw these matters from another point of view. He declared...an enemy bluff... *'It's the greatest imposture since Ghengis Khan,'* he shouted."   Even years later, Guderian speaks politely of the Leader's personality: "[Hitler's] mentality [was] becoming ever more extraordinary." Guderian is more pointed on Hitler's stream of bewildering decisions:

> On December 25th [1944]...Hitler ordered the transfer of...two SS divisions...the reserve [from Poland] to Budapest....This irresponsible weakening of an already greatly over-extended front was a matter of despair....The immediate transfer of our main defensive effort to the East still offered us a slender chance.... Rundstedt...gave me the numbers of three divisions...which were immediately available....Even this wretched pittance was to go, by Hitler's orders, to Hungary.
>
> [In January] Hitler had finally decided that the Western Front must go over to the defensive so that forces could be made available for transfer to the East....[but] to Hungary. On hearing this I lost my self-control....After I had disposed of the military reasons that he advanced he produced economic ones....[Furthermore] the troops we were to receive from the West were to be split up....Hitler refused to allow [either] the transfer of troops from the Western Front to northern Germany or the evacuation of [the army cut off there].

Guderian recalls the commandant of the Warsaw fortress reporting: "that the city...would have to be evacuated....[Hitler] at once lost his temper and ordered that *Warsaw be held at all costs.*" Budapest also falls, despite the troops wasted there, but Hitler diverts attention; he proposes to interrogate all officers connected with the loss of Warsaw. He also tries to rekindle an antique squabble: *"It's not you I'm after, but the General Staff. It is intolerable to me....That system I intend to smash."*

Hitler secretly arrests three colonels, pulling them out of their commands. Guderian is himself interrogated for several days. Hitler throws in the reserves: General Himmler. Here the professionals draw the line, as Warlimont notes: "Guderian had proposed that a new Army headquarters, 'Army Group Vistula,' should be formed to...stop the [Russian] breakthrough....Hitler now nominated Himmler as Commander-in-Chief of this Army Group! It was a vital and difficult job....Even Hitler was forced to recognize that Himmler was totally incapable...of command." Guderian himself recalls: "I had requested Hitler that a new army group be formed....He ordered that Himmler be given command....This preposterous suggestion appalled me.... Hitler [also] ordered that Himmler assemble his own [equally inexperienced] staff."

Hitler resists efforts to defend Germany. All German men between 15 and 50 are enlisted in the military, yet, says Warlimont: "Hitler vetoed the evacuation even of the most northerly part of [Norway]. No operations had taken place in the area for years, but troops were maintained there right up until the end of hostilities." A division of White Russians is organized to fight against the Soviets, but Hitler complains, on aesthetic grounds: *"I was always against putting the Cossacks into German uniform. They ought to have been given Cossack uniform and Cossack badges of rank to show that they were fighting for us. Much more romantic* [sic]."

Hitler buttressed his sensitivity with argument: *"It never occurs to the Englishmen to dress up an Indian as an Englishman. We're the only people who've got no shame because we've got no character."*

On January 27 Soviet troops arrive one hundred miles from Berlin. Guderian recalls: "I now proposed to him that all available forces be assembled in two groups east of Berlin.... But Hitler clung to his original plan, which was not to use these forces to defend Germany and, in particular, the German capital, but to employ them in an offensive in Hungary." Hitler solicits Göring to tell fairy tales about England making peace and helping Germany fight off Russia. Hitler asks: *"Do you think the English are enthusiastic about all the Russian developments?"* Göring's fawning response is: "They certainly didn't plan that we hold them off while the Russians conquer all of Germany....If this goes on we will get a telegram in a few days."

Speer presents his famous memorandum beginning: "The war is lost...." Hitler refuses to see him, telling Guderian: *"All he wants is to tell me again that the war is lost and that I should bring it to an end...Now you can understand why it is that I refuse to see anyone alone any more. Any man who asks to talk to me alone always does so because he has something unpleasant to say to me. I can't bear that."*

Ribbentrop and Himmler separately begin secret negotiations aimed at surrender agreements. As defeat presses in, Guderian snarls: "Tried and trusted officers at the front were, in the heat of the moment and without any proper inquiry being made, demoted by one or more ranks....Hitler's addiction to lengthy monologues did not decrease as the military situation became more acute. On the contrary, by means of interminable talk, he attempted to explain the reasons for the failure of the German Command, both to himself and to others, ascribing the guilt, of course, to innumerable circumstances and individuals though never, even remotely, to himself."

Guderian asks to shorten the Eastern Front, and explains: "[It is] to defend the capital. I assure you I am acting solely in Germany's interests." Whereupon Hitler jumps to his feet shouting his old slogan:

> *How dare you speak to me like that? Don't you think I'm fighting for Germany? My whole life has been one long struggle for Germany.*

But Guderian again criticizes his Leader: "This caused a new outburst of rage on Hitler's part. He stood in front of me shaking his fists....[An aide] had to pull me backwards lest I be the victim of a physical assault." Shortly thereafter, on February 13, a surprise attack is planned, but Hitler will not approve. Guderian insists: "We can't wait." Changing the subject, crafty Hitler shouts: *"I don't permit you to accuse me of wanting to wait."*

Guderian's plan calls for an experienced general to command the troops nominally under Himmler. Hitler again changes the subject: *"I don't permit you to tell me that the National Leader [Himmler] is incapable of performing his duties."* They argued without letup for two hours, says Guderian: "[Hitler's] fists raised, his cheeks flushed with rage, his whole body trembling, he stood there in front of me beside himself with fury and having lost all self-control. After each outburst of rage Hitler would stride up and down the carpet edge, then suddenly stop immediately before me and hurl his next accusation in my face. He was almost screaming, his eyes seemed about to pop out of his head and the veins stood out on his temples." Guderian stands his ground. But Hitler does not see military issues, only personal ones. When he finally gives in, he says: *"The General Staff has won a battle this day."*

February brings the Allies to the banks of the Rhine, at a cost of 57,000 German casualties. However, another 293,000 German soldiers accept or embrace captivity. Hitler still finds the prospects exciting, as illustrated by the photo on page 27. On March 8th the Allies take the bridge over the Rhine at Remagen intact. Guderian says: "Hitler raved and...five officers were summarily executed....[Later] a heavy battle was raging outside Stettin. Hitler now sent for Colonel-General Rauss, the commander....[Afterwards] Hitler turned to [us] and shouted: *'What a miserable speech! The man talked of nothing but details. Judging by the way he speaks he must be a Berliner or an East Prussian. He must be relieved of his appointment at once!'*"

Hitler reaches a shrill pitch in his efforts to keep Germany fighting to the last man. Warlimont notes: "At the beginning of March 1945 from the gloomy shelters of the Reich Chancellery thundered the empty threat to the soldiers of the Wehrmacht that their relatives at home would have to answer for it if they were taken prisoner unwounded....On March 19 there followed the order that before a further yard of German territory was relinquished to the enemy all industrial establishments and supply depots were to be destroyed--without regard even for the bare necessities of life of the population." Hitler now tells Speer:

> *If the war is lost, the people will be lost also. It is not necessary to worry about what the German people will need for elemental survival. On the contrary, it is best for us to destroy even these things. For the nation has proved to be the weaker, and the future belongs to the stronger Eastern nation. In any case only those who are inferior will remain after this struggle, for the good have already been killed.*

Germany proves to be the weaker, but the fight is fixed. Nominating a scapegoat, Hitler continues: *"The commanders have handled this wretchedly. From the top down they've drummed into the troops that it's better to fight in open country [i.e., with tanks] than in here."* With a month left in his life, Hitler still quibbles when Goebbels asks to turn a big east-west avenue in Berlin into a runway for planes: *"All right for [removing] the street lamps; but to level twenty to thirty yards of the Tiergarten either side...There's no need for more than fifty yards' width."*

Berlin burns while, on April 12, Hitler delights in the death of President Franklin Roosevelt. Yet again Hitler urges Germany on: *"Now that fate has removed from the earth the greatest war criminal of all time, the turning point of this war will be decided."* Nothing changes, and Hitler returns to accusations: *"The army has betrayed me, my generals are good for nothing. My orders were not carried out. It is all finished....Germany is lost. It actually was not quite ready or quite strong enough for the mission I set for the nation."*

Even Göring now joins the peacemakers; he confides to an aide: *"I'll stop the war at once [if I gain power]."* But reports claim Russian and American commanders are arguing about jurisdiction over Germany, and Hitler finds fresh cause to extend the war. His wording taunts broken Germany: *"Here again is striking evidence of the disunity of our enemies. The German people and history would surely brand me as a criminal if I made peace today while there is still the possibility that tomorrow our enemies might have a falling out!"*

On April 29, Hitler marries for the first time and writes his Final Testament, blaming "the Jews" for Germany's destruction. In the afternoon, he hears that partisans executed Mussolini. Hitler commits suicide April 30, 1945, along with his bride of thirty-six hours, the former Eva Braun. Usually kept apart from Hitler, she had come to Berlin two weeks earlier to join him for his final scene.

Epilogue.

Reasonable people have reasonable ideas. A conventional American view of Hitler's leadership, the *West Point Military*

History Series, pardonably emphasizes the American role in defeating Hitler:

> In the final analysis, the Second World War in Europe is the story of an unusually successful Allied coalition bringing crushing force to bear on an astonishingly resilient Germany, which was led to ruin by a short-sighted dictator....Hitler and his partners failed...[at] keeping the United States out of the war....Hitler's mistaken belief that he could fight a war whose duration could be measured in months was fatal. This belief... largely dictated the German failure to build an industrial base ....Relying excessively upon intuition and trusting too much in amateurs, Hitler also made strategic errors....Finally, perhaps the most telling German error was becoming ensnared in a two-front war.

"Short-sighted...mistaken belief...relying excessively upon intuition and trusting too much...becoming ensnared," these faults led to Hitler's downfall, say the Americans. However, Hitler's early triumphs are hard to explain using West Point concepts of foolish intuition and trust.

Just before killing himself, Hitler orders Goebbels to flee Berlin and the man blurts out another view of the defeat: "The Führer has made so many decisions too late! Why this one, the last one, too early?" Goebbels and his wife murder their six children, then commit suicide in the bunker. In another view, while on trial for his life, Keitel complains: "If he did not deceive us by deliberate lies, then he did it by deliberately keeping us in the dark and letting us fight under a false impression!" Keitel is hung at Nuremberg.

An alternative view of Hitler's career is that, beyond his own awareness, he successfully built himself a hideous suicide that took Germany and much of Europe down with him. In this view, when he screamed: *"Deutschland! Deutschland! Deutschland!"* he was cursing and mocking. In the depths of his mind, he may have planned a two-front war from the start;

he did warn of it. He may have planned to leave Germany in flames; he hinted at this possibility as well. Germany had cheated him of a military death--a hero's death--by ending the First World War early. Part Two will explore this need of Hitler's.

On November 5, 1937, Hitler had announced to his service chiefs his *"irrevocable decision to solve the German problem of living space no later than 1943-45, possibly even as early as 1938 and by force."* He kept his promise. Of every ten Germans, one no longer needed living space, and two more needed much less, due to injuries. Now consider the role the Holocaust played in Hitler's war against Germany.

Chapter Nine

THE HOLOCAUST AS STRATEGY

(*die Lebenslüge*)

Prologue.

He got them to kill off the Jews. That created dread and loathing for Hitler, and for Germany. Many men have started wars; only Hitler created murder factories, and only Germany has ever staffed them. No precedent existed for gathering, shipping and killing, year after year, according to published specifications. We shudder with revulsion and, even worse, with anticipatory guilt because, now that humans have done this, who can say for sure that he or she would not? We deny having such temptations, but we test ourselves by examining mechanical, remorseless murder in dramatic and literary works. We are no longer sure humans have a conscience.

The Holocaust-Shoah begs for outrage. But the *aktions* have already been described. The blank spot is Hitler's motive. Hundreds of speeches and millions of murders show his intensity. Yet seventy years of investigation have turned up no obvious grudge or injury; the historian Alan Bullock concludes: "[Hitler had] no personal experience [to explain] hatred of the Jews." Hitler himself never claimed any personal offense, only abstract, patriotic ones. He said an international conspiracy of Jews held vast power over Germany and the world; however, he showed no timidity about publicly attacking them. Something besides fear forced his hand. The murders were of no military value. Neither did they convey political or economic advantage.

The Holocaust had to have a personal meaning for Hitler. He never admitted it. Indeed, few people can give a good account of their inner workings. From the outside, we can infer the personal meanings. We can read between the lines of his speeches, assess his background, and examine the breadth of the results of the Holocaust.

The mountain of deaths has overwhelmed thought--the victims' screams remain deafening. But death meant little to Hitler, because neither did life. His disgust is the missing piece of the Hitler puzzle; it is critical to understanding him.

Even as a political newcomer in 1923, Hitler was boldly shouting: *"What does it matter if a couple of dozen of our Rhineland cities go up in flames. A hundred thousand dead would mean nothing."* For him, the ashes and corpses of the Holocaust weighed little. Hitler never saw a camp; in the abstract, death was simply a by-product of policy. Other goals moved him to action.

It helped no one directly. Since ovens do not fit into ordinary politics, many histories simply avoid discussing the Holocaust. They present Hitler as just Napoleon with a moustache. In contrast, the chapters that follow take up Hitler's defining act as central to his effort to settle with his family and to die for them and with them. First examine the paradoxical self-mutilation of Germany.

The Meaning in the Madness: Germany Today.

Large among the secondary effects of the Holocaust is the shame Germany bears. To be sure, racist slaughter did not begin or end with Germany: in the last century, Armenia, Nigeria, Cambodia, Bosnia, Guatemala, Vietnam, Rwanda and Native America have waded in their own blood. But only Germany has built death factories and laid railroad track for the purpose. An explicit national policy of methodical, deliberate murder punctures our myths about human nature. Besides her immediate, physical destruction in the prostrating defeat Hitler engineered and prolonged, he brought his Motherland enduring moral agony. Replacing the rubble of war, bold new architecture glitters in the western cities of Germany. She has yet to recover from the other, invisible wound. Germany lost again to the impossible odds of a War-against-the-World, but this time she also took poison, one that still contorts her politics. The corporal got revenge for his lost youth and for the 1918 surrender that he blamed for his dashed hopes.

His best generals saw through him and spoke up; he fired them. The preceding chapters discussed Hitler's military acts and failures to act, and their direct, immediate effects. Disguised by loud demands for German triumph, another agenda ruled Hitler's mind--beyond his own awareness. Over and over, Hitler worked against Germany. With the Holocaust, he struck again.

Hitler's suicide left the German Christians to take the blame; they may never be trusted again. Military adventures could distract, but not insulate Germany from the insidious campaign in the shadows. The slaughter created what might be called a public secret, one widely known, but always whispered. Death is never silent: within a month of the first mass shootings in the woods of Belarus, New York newspapers printed the story. Trying to overlook the murders heightened the tensions surrounding the project. Guilt for the deeds, shame for their bald exposure and the anxiety that builds up during enforced silence: all of these infected Germany when Hitler drew her into his *"destruction of Jewry."* The fateful companion to his fatal invasion of Russia, Hitler's crime against humanity created a new stigma and exposed a moral illness. Afterwards, he claimed success. The dimensions of this success have become clear: the Holocaust is measured not only by ashes and corpses, by numbered arms and eight hundred thousand women's coats in a single pile, but also by endless guilt.

Best-selling German author and television producer Guido Knopp says: "The Holocaust is the central experience of the war, and with the passing of time it has assumed a greater and greater importance." But Germans seldom discuss it. For this silence, the prominent poet Hans Magnus Enzensberger has created the term "*die Lebenslüge*," signifying a lie about life, a lie required in order to go on with life. Besides citing these men, Timothy Ryback quotes the major German newsweekly, *Stern*: "[The Holocaust is] a trauma that lies buried beneath hardened lava crusts of the German soul, a collective primal experience, never 'mastered,' never 'overcome,' that has instead been banished to the deepest recesses of the unconscious, from where it nevertheless continues to rumble from below."

Margarete Mitscherlich, a Frankfurt psychoanalyst, told Ryback the German spiritual problem is: "How can we express remorse for crimes we did not commit?" No one takes the blame for the Holocaust. Those who ran it followed orders; the rest were careful to know nothing. Mitscherlich's book, *The Inability to Mourn,* proved an explosive and controversial bestseller, stating: "[Germans] struggle with contradictory feelings of secret guilt and resentment--resentment, that is, of their burden of guilt--which make acceptance and healing impossible." Even a sensitive observer like Mitscherlich needs to believe: "They came in as innocents, and through their innocence they became guilty."

But the Germans were never truly innocent: the human race began with roving hunters who, if kind to their children, were quick to rip and tear; our species, including the Germans, has changed little, say the newspapers. *Hitler's Willing Executioners*--as Daniel Jonah Goldhagen calls them--let the mask slip entirely. Our mask, civilized urban life, consists of those strategies which are most productive over the long term. Courtesy, democracy and human rights are not divine inspirations promoted for their abstract symmetry; they work. They foster cooperative effort by millions of people and create a unified nation out of what would otherwise be a chaotic rabble. Lacking these elements, as Clive James recently put it: "Germany ceased to be civilized from the moment Hitler came to power." In a stealthy seduction, Hitler switched Germany to short-term strategies--an orgy of sadism. She now suffers a long-term loss of credibility, most of all, among the Germans themselves.

"It is impossible to exaggerate the pervasiveness of the shadow of Auschwitz [here]," says a recent *New York Times* bureau chief for Germany. Wrestling with their unsought legacy, some young Germans try to justify Hitler's pogrom by extending it. Germany reunited in 1990; as the occupying armies left, Nazi street gangs resumed racist violence. After forty-five years of enforced calm, again neighbors stood and watched, and some applauded. The victims are not Jews, now so scarce, but the scenes bring to mind Hitler's dying curse: *"Centuries will go by, but from the ruins of our towns and monuments the hatred...will always grow anew."* Any powerless minority will do as a target.

> [Given the desolate tone of this augury, a more pointed translation might be: Racism will be the death of Germany. As discussed in later chapters, the inner Hitler, deeply disheartened, saw in 1945 that the intoxicating appeal of racism for Germany had survived the total destruction he had arranged. Part of him marveled that, driven truly mad, she had not blanched at suicide; even that had not been too high a price for preserving her delusions.]

Officially, Germany now condemns the Holocaust as: "a crime whose immensity overwhelms the capacity of human comprehension." So proclaims Hitler's successor as Chancellor, Helmut Kohl. He must continually insist Germany has changed; he pleads to be forgiven his title: "This is a sensible government that makes sensible decisions." No other nation has to insist on her sobriety.

Throughout the foreign occupation, Germany hid any trace of Hitler. The site of his Berlin bunker was used as an anonymous junkyard. Now officially sanitized by the passage of time, the bunker is restored as a museum. The Wannsee resort hotel used to plan the Holocaust has also become a museum; at its opening, the Mayor of Berlin proclaims: "That a highly modern state, working with such brutal success, killed all the members of a race that it could capture, including mothers, children and old people--that is unique and without any historical parallel." For some Germans, discussion of the Holocaust includes a defiant strain of pride. Out of the context of a sombre museum opening, the declaration by the Mayor might seem ambiguous. In some ears its racism could sound like a boast.

Hitler identified himself with racism. In forcing the thoroughly racist pre-war world to oppose him, he forced it to oppose racism. The Holocaust shamed Europe and America into becoming officially race-neutral. Some countries offered compensation or "affirmative action" for past inequities. Germany took part in this repentance. However, racism resumes everywhere. With the international lull caused by the defeat of the Soviet Union, lesser matters come to the fore. New waves of immigration stimulate the urge to band together against outsiders. In tens of thousands of years of Neanderthal life, clinging closely brought advantages amongst competing hunting bands. A trading economy makes isolation stupid. But this is a new way of life, perhaps five hundred years old.

Our genes have yet to shift. As discussed in the Introduction, many Germans boast again of having a race all to themselves. This represents a combination of romantic myth, political nostalgia and stubborn, misguided patriotism. Facing the new outbreaks, Germany has only slowly come to denounce the resumption of Nazi street violence. Candlelight protest marches and a few well-publicized arrests slowed, but did not stop the murder and arson. The caution of the politicians reflects the division of the people. Arsonists who killed five "resident foreigners" in Moelln got 10-15 year sentences. Germany's Ombudsman for Foreigners quotes a 1992 poll showing that in Hamburg, thirty-five percent found racist street gangs "understandable." Germany needs such an Ombudsman because she rarely awards citizenship to immigrants. In a continuing insanity, Germany calls a full ten percent of her adult population "foreigners"--she still and again rules out millions of people. Many of these non-persons have lived and worked in Germany thirty years and more.

Berlin plans a prominent memorial to the Holocaust. But a memorial states a position, for or against what happened. No public figure can recommend a memorial in favor, yet a memorial against the Holocaust would be against Germany. This problem has mired down the project. One popular solution denies continuity. In this view, the current Germans are not descended from the aggressors of 1939, nor from the one-third of the electorate who voted for Hitler in 1932, but from the 1945 survivors of aggression, within the nation that was the first to be overwhelmed by the Nazi gangster clique: Germany. President Richard von Weizsäcker recently called the Allied victory "the liberation of Germany." After quoting him, Jane Kramer summarizes: "Germans want their past to have happened to them. They want to have suffered from themselves, the way everybody else suffered from them."

Germans have become identified with evil, at least in popular dramatic works in the U.S. Dependably, the villains of modern melodramas have thick German accents and personal characteristics like Hitler's: coldness, explosive rage, off-hand murderousness, conspicuously neat clothing--generally all black or all white--excessive formality, close-cut hair, and harsh and exacting attitudes towards others, including their own accomplices. Dramatic plots often identify villains as Nazi sympathizers seeking a return to power from long-secret hideouts. The forty-five-year cold war against Russia did little to supplant this dramatic cliché. One immigrant actor, Arnold Schwarznegger, has achieved enormous popularity caricaturing vicious, unfeeling, indestructible Germanic monster-men. Christopher Walken contributes his brilliant lunatic twist as well to hollow-eyed versions of mechanical men, without joy and without scruples.

No one can now deny that humans have a dark side. However, many prefer to believe that mostly Germans have it, or that they alone have the insolence or ignorance to show it. Germans who travel abroad face wariness and unspoken accusations--their grandparents created the pall of self-doubt that now hangs over us all. We watch closely for any hint of aggressive behavior, even someone breaking into line. Ryback heard Guido Knopp make the routine denial of guilt: "The average German had little idea of what was happening to the Jews at the time." However, Knopp went on: "Germans knew that something was going on, but…'they knew enough to know that they didn't want to know more than they knew.'" Knopp protests that the bombing of German cities and the battle deaths dazed everyone. Meanwhile Hitler killed the Jews, stripped the cities of air defense and kept the battles going. To justify his scorn and his withdrawal from life, a sardonic Hitler forced into the open the casual, animal viciousness humans share with every other predator on earth.

The Romance of Racism.

Murder always has appeal as a simple and final solution to conflict. Wanton butchery is not hard to grasp; examples are common in a well-armed country like the U.S. Harder to comprehend is the endurance of the mass hysteria and romantic abandon of a Germany who saw her problems coming from her remaining Jews, by 1939 a quarter-million citizens, not quite one-third of one percent of all Germans. (For an American comparison, this percentage in the total U.S. population is the same as that of Korean-Americans or, to focus on religion, of Seventh-Day Adventists. The Jewish presence in the United States is far larger.) How easy life would be if only the source of its difficulties was so clear and so concentrated. Obviously, one advantage of picking on a very small minority will be its weakness. Yet the German idiocy was sincere: her bureaucrats labored mightily without, however, resolving the fundamental issue: what is a race?

The gentlemen should not be blamed for their failure; the only secure division of the human race is the one between the living and the dead. Any other attempted distinction produces a gray area containing individuals not clearly included or excluded. The Nazi bureaucrats met at Wannsee in celebration of *"the final solution to the Jewish problem."* The Foreign Office accurately predicted that gathering Jews for slaughter would meet no resistance except in Norway and Denmark. When invited, Holland, France, Ukraine, Romania, Yugoslavia and the Baltic states leapt at the chance to murder their citizens.

But the Wannsee party degenerated into a shouting match. Half the meeting and two additional meetings were consumed in trying to find a way to extricate intermarried Jews and their children from German society. Wannsee was chaired on January 20, 1942, by an SS General: Reinhard Heydrich. The issue was bucked down to his deputy, Lt. Col. Adolf Eichmann, and other lesser lights; they met six weeks later. Czech partisans then killed Heydrich in May, but twenty middle-rank executives doggedly met again on October 27, only to fail as the others had. Strong advocacy of forced sterilization by some and of forced deportation by others showed that the racists were fervent. But disobedient Christians and Jews had interbred for centuries, yielding 125,000 Germans of mixed parentage and 28,000 Jews married into Christian families, alongside the remaining 250,000 *"full Jews."* Outwitted by human nature and by G_d, Germany killed only the 250,000 and left the others to wander. Hitler called them *"mischlinge,"* or mixed-breeds--as if there were any other kind of human.

It was all so viciously romantic, the pipe dream that a pure race would bring an orderly, harmonious, womb-like society--no more conflict, no more deceit, no more competition--supported on the backs of the lesser races, of course. Hitler talked racism while Margaret Mitchell wrote *Gone with the Wind*, with its kidnapped Africans feeling honored to serve Europeans. Mitchell admitted her work was fiction.

Hopelessly quixotic, Germany listened. The slow work of a thousand generations has expanded human loyalty to take in city and nation, and to give up violence in return for the security, comforts and abundance of civilized life. In bad times, the lessons have to be repeated.

The Attitude of the Young.

In Germany and Austria computer games based on the Holocaust are illegal but popular. In the most optimistic interpretation, they may represent the attempt of the new generation to acknowledge the oppressive legacy they cannot evade. The Simon Weisenthal Center in Los Angeles offers a $25,000 reward: "for information leading to the arrest and conviction of those responsible for the production and manufacture of Neo-Nazi hate games in Germany." But the Center's Holocaust survivors are as impotent as the Germans who survive; their common history will not change.

On their merits, evil ideas need no repetition, but the history of Germany cannot otherwise be told. The game *KZ Manager* invites the player to simulate running a concentration camp [*KonZentrationslager*]. To win, the player gains credit for killing and torturing prisoners and for selling gold teeth and lamp shades made of human skin. However, the game begins with Heinrich Himmler's morose 1943 address to his SS officers: "I want to tell you about a very grave matter in all frankness. We can talk about it quite openly here, but we must never talk about it publicly....I mean the evacuation of the Jews, the extermination of the Jewish people....Most of you will know what it means to see 100 corpses piled up. Or 500 or 1,000. To have gone through this and--except for instances of human weakness--to have remained decent, that has made us tough. This is an unwritten, never to be written, glorious page of our history."

Apart from the single word, "glorious," the speech is sombre and mournful, freighted with shame and guilt. Himmler, speaking for Hitler, insists they are "decent [and] tough," not bloodthirsty, spineless sadists preying on unarmed civilians. The computer games serve as history lessons. The games present sensational aspects of Nazi policy that older Germans will not discuss. The Weisenthal Center reports neo-Nazis as the source for these computer games, and fears that they will incite racial hatred. Unfortunately, history is full of racial hatred, with or without games.

In fact, the games ridicule racism. The Himmler speech warns about it. Hitler, by carrying racism to an extreme, shamed it. Few teenagers will be drawn to trading in gold fillings. The games mock the Nazis, not the Jews; *Aryan Test* begins with a sneer: "To the protector of German Youth, the only decent youth which must be protected from the decay in morals which is caused by the Jews." The derision continues: "The entire German population is to undergo the following Aryan test by order of Dr. Joseph Goebbels." These words carry little seduction. The games reflect the struggle Austrian and German children face when they learn their national history of being vicious losers. While mocking the generation that took Nazi propaganda seriously, games shrug off the horror, to make being German more bearable. Lacking the great spellbinder who invented and propelled the Nazi lies, the games depend for popularity on being forbidden essays on forbidden subjects. The remedy for today's violence is to confer citizenship on the throngs of "foreigners" raising families in Germany--ten percent of the population. Young rowdies with nothing to lose will always seek weak, isolated victims. It is the same game whether the thugs call themselves Cossacks, Nazis or rapists.

Hitler's Work.

At the end, Hitler claimed he had taken vengeance: *"I have made it quite clear that this time the real culprit must expiate his guilt."* In 1945 he called the Jews his target, but in 1924 Hitler had warned Germany: *"The great crime the German people committed [surrender in 1918]...can be expiated only by prodigious efforts, perhaps by very great and cruel sufferings."* He killed an equal number of German Christians as they murdered Jews, an eye for an eye, a million eyes for a million. Into the bargain, Hitler branded Germany a criminal nation. He killed no one; Germany stands convicted.

Hitler expected outrage. He claimed the war was worth starting: *"even if the world does hate us now."* Still haughty six years later, he declared: *"I know that by tomorrow millions of people will curse me."* Erik Erikson concludes that, overall, Hitler had been: *"a gang leader who kept the boys together by demanding their admiration, by creating terror, and by shrewdly involving them in crimes from which there was no way back."* Hitler himself asserted the evil of his death factories: *"I have to do it, because after me no one else will!"* He separately warned: *"We've burned all our bridges behind us. There is, gentlemen, no going back any longer."* Hitler mocked Germany's moral qualms--and his own: *"To find internal peace...rid the race of the consciousness of its own guilt....The feeling of being guilty...paralyzes every sincere and firm decision.* " He insisted: *"Freeing men from...the dirty and degrading [ideas of] conscience and morality [is my work].* " After the orgy, the ideas returned as his vengeance. He could be certain that the shame and secrecy he orchestrated would provoke moral questions, even where the murders did not. The commandant of Auschwitz received only verbal orders to construct the gas chambers and ovens. So impressed was he with the shame of the project, he did not tell his boss or his wife. She would need to overlook ten thousand people a day arriving at their camp, with none leaving.

Germans dutifully registered, collected, shipped and murdered. Unlike Ukrainian pogroms, four years of methodical harvesting cannot be laid to a drunken rampage. Orderly mendacities about work and resettlement soothed the victims. Despite holding the grand title *SS Obersturmbannführer*, the appointed gatherer of Jews, Adolf Eichmann, when he was captured, tried and hung, frightened the world precisely by being so banal, a cog in a machine: no horns, no tail.

After the war, the German generals denied hearing even rumors of genocide or of millions being shuffled across Europe. Even at the highest level--the twenty-three defendants in the dock at Nuremberg--all except Göring were aghast at the thousands of corpses filmed when the death factories were seized. Keitel said: "I didn't know--I'll never be able to look people in the face again." Jodl: "It is shocking." Admiral Erich Raeder modestly insisted he had only known of three concentration camps. Hans Frank wept; "Horrible!" he exclaimed, then added: "Don't let anybody tell you that they had no idea! Everybody sensed that there was something horribly wrong with this system, even if we didn't know all the details. They didn't *want* to know!" Fritz Sauckel, the slave-labor chief, trembling all over, insisted: "It is a shame! It is a disgrace for us and for our children--and for our children's children!" Even Göring admitted nervously: "I can see that the German people will be forever condemned by these brutalities."

The Total Isolation of German Generals.

It is a mark of Germany's loathing for her past--that is, for herself--that her military heroes claim they were consistently ignorant and isolated, throughout the six years of war. They contend not even rumors reached them of a major national and international policy and program using German troops to make public, mass, daylight roundups all over Europe that consumed scarce railway equipment and fuel, and a whole bureaucracy.

The foremost military hero on the German side, Field Marshal von Manstein, proclaims near-total ignorance despite hundreds of hours of attendance at Hitler's conferences, and informal daily contacts with colleagues as he ranged over the entire Russian front, from Leningrad to Sevastopol. Ridiculous in another context, his plea for amnesty runs: "It was not granted to me...to perceive Hitler's true nature....Rumors of the kind that circulated at home hardly penetrated to the front....The anxieties and problems which the fighting brought us left little time for reflection on matters of wider interest." Manstein thus claims (1.) dealing with Hitler taught him nothing, (2.) he heard little news and (3.) he ignored what he heard.

By contrast, the sacked Field Marshal is harsh concerning Hitler's generalship: "In the military sphere, however, I could not overlook the faults of Hitler's leadership." But he did overlook them, claiming: "to remove him by violent means in wartime [would crush Army morale]....[But] I often used to wish that I could leave." Hitler granted the latter.

The commandant at Auschwitz, Rudolf Höss, (no relation to Hess) testified: "We were required to carry out these exterminations in secrecy, but of course the foul and nauseating stench from the continuous burning of bodies permeated the entire area and all of the people living in the surrounding communities knew that exterminations were going on at Auschwitz." Nonetheless, Guderian, resurrected as Chief of Staff for the final months of the war, heard nothing of any murder camps: "Hitler and Himmler succeeded in keeping this part of their program strictly secret." General Warlimont, although a section chief at Supreme Headquarters throughout the war, was merely more elaborate in his denials. Dismissing his writing of the "Commissar Order" that initiated mass executions, he says: "None of those officers who took part in the discussions or in the drafting of these orders had the smallest inkling that...the SD [*Sicherheitsdienst* Security Police] would proceed, immediately the [Russian] campaign had begun, to the systematic mass murder of Jews." Wanting it both ways, Warlimont also claims to have quietly weakened the policies of which he was nonetheless ignorant: "[Hitler] was open to no counterargument; his intentions could only be countered with any prospect of success by working under cover."

Warlimont boasts he deleted any mention of Jews or commissars from the final written orders of March 1941. He was clearly trying to conceal authorization of the Holocaust, but he pretends humanitarian interests forced him to write on the draft orders: "remains to be seen whether a <u>written</u> instruction of this sort is <u>necessary</u>." He lobbied the point, and ultimately Hitler gave only verbal explanations for the reference, "special tasks [of] the Reichsführer SS." In his diary on 3 March 1941 General Alfred Jodl, Warlimont's immediate superior, quotes the Führer: *"The Bolshevist-Jewish intelligentsia must be eliminated."* Yet Warlimont insists: "The Commander-in-Chief [of the Army, von Brauchitsch] had no idea what were the real tasks of these 'Special Employment' organizations [the SD and the police]." Warlimont says no more about Jews.

The army did nothing to interfere with Hitler's decisions. Unlike the generals who claimed shocked virginity after the war, Halder had his diary; on September 19, 1939, it acknow-ledged the plan to exterminate the Polish Jews, along with the "intelligentsia, clergy, nobility." And Warlimont notes the reaction to Hitler's 1941 "Commissar Order": "The cream of the German officer corps [they] sat before him in stubborn silence, a silence broken only twice--when the assembly rose first as he entered...and later when he departed....Otherwise not a hand moved and not a word was spoken but by him."

Volumes have been written claiming that only in Germany could this have happened and that the blind obedience beaten into German youth creates a nation of sheep who carry out or-ders without question. Any straw is grasped in the effort to help the world get back to sleep, to forget the inhumanity of which humans are capable. Nonetheless, an American psycho-logist, Stanley Milgram, showed that ordinary college students would torture people. When, for his own reasons, Hitler want-ed violence, he milked it from his hosts. Perhaps he moved slowly not to awaken anyone too soon.

Genocide As Strategy: the West.
Hitler launched the Holocaust-Shoah to change the attitudes of the western democracies. His campaign of purely economic persecution had succeeded in persuading half the Jewish Ger-mans to leave their country when President Roosevelt organized a fateful meeting of the western powers for July 1938. At Evian, France, to assure an air-tight united front, countries of every size met to ward off the Jews Hitler had been forcing out.

Various parties proposed to force all Europe's Jews to move to Africa. Poland had begun calling for such a resettlement of her three million Jewish citizens the previous year. The main obstacle was how to smooth their reception. "British opposi-tion" to Jews entering Palestine kept that possibility off the agenda at Evian. The historians Richard Breitman and Alan Kraut have insisted on President Roosevelt's good intentions, but note that his State Department offered "implacable resist- ance" to Jewish immigration. They also note anti-Semitism among Roosevelt's friends and relatives. In the U.S., as well as in Germany and elsewhere, huge radio audiences listened to anti-Semitic hate-mongers during the economic depression of the 1930's.

The net result of Evian was to stop Hitler's forced-emigration program. *Newsweek* called Evian "slamming the[ir] doors against Jewish refugees." Hitler boiled. His Foreign Ministry insisted: "The ultimate aim of Germany's Jewish policy is the emigration of all Jews....[There] will be an international solution of the Jewish question." Responding more eloquently, Hitler extorted Czechoslovakia in September at Munich, then abruptly expelled all Polish-born Jews one day in October, then created the barbaric rampage known as *Kristallnacht* in Novem- ber. His persecution of German Jews accelerated dramatically. On January 24, 1939, Hitler opened a Central Office for Jewish Emigration. On January 30, he formally offered his alternative plan--war and Holocaust.

Hitler shouted: *"If the international Jewish financiers in and outside Europe should succeed in plunging the nations once more into a world war, then the result will not be the Bolshe- vization of the earth, and thus the victory of Jewry, but the annihilation of the Jewish race in Europe!"* He mocked his au- dience by inventing *"Bolshevik financiers."* He also mocked Evian: *"It is a shameful example to observe today how the entire democratic world dissolves in tears of pity but then, in spite of its obvious duty to help, closes its heart to the poor, tortured Jewish people."*

Murder was still just an idea. But the U.S. State Department continued to fight off immigrants. In December 1940, when Hitler put French Jews in camps, ready to ship, Undersecretary Sumner Welles branded it an effort to "force our hand on the refugee problem." Most caught in the camps went to the gas chambers finally, having no exit. Prof. Raul Hilberg points out: "The expulsion and exclusion policy...remained the goal of all [Nazi] anti-Jewish activity until 1941....the bureaucracy was still thinking in terms of emigration only." Prof. David Wyman agrees. Hitler did not even mark German Jews with the notorious yellow stars until late in 1941, after Shoah began.

Hitler finally started mass killings of Jews--to prove they needed help. In his first five years as Chancellor, he had killed less than two hundred, despite the venomous froth he lavished upon them in every speech. He had killed more Nazis, those considered political opponents.

Hitler's program of social and economic exclusion had ancient roots. Even the organized terrorism of *Kristallnacht*, November 9, 1938, merely put into deeds the raging invective of Martin Luther, who had suggested four hundred years earlier that the Jews should be forced to depart: "[leaving] all their cash and jewels and silver and gold [or] that their synagogues or schools be set on fire, that their houses be broken up and destroyed...and they be put under a roof or stable...in misery and captivity." For years Hitler had urged the creation of a Jewish homeland on the French-controlled island of Madagascar, far away in southern Africa. Evian said, *non*.

Killing his newest hostages, in June 1941 Hitler began mass shootings of Jews in conquered Soviet territory. Improvisation of the initial gas chamber at Auschwitz from a wooden house came a year later. After its successful bid for the SS contract, the Topf Co. then began construction of crematoria. Each of the five had an attached gas chamber with a capacity of two thousand and a towering smokestack, but these did not begin murdering until February 1943. After an inspection complaint by Richard Glück, Commandant Rudolf Höss put up a line of trees to screen the gas chambers.

Albert Speer recalls the pall cast by the murdering: "Thereafter, Hitler spoke with somber and ambiguous undertones....

'We can only go forward. We've burned all our bridges behind us.'" To emphasize the vileness of the enterprise, Hitler never signed any piece of paper concerning the Holocaust-Shoah, and when the Soviets approached the death camps, he exhumed and burned the early, pre-crematorium corpses. The bones were pounded into dust to be thrown into rivers, as if to remove all evidence; the guards then shot the Jews who had done the work. The cover-up activity served to publicize and intensify the shame of the slaughter. When overrun, the camps were deeply moving to the Russians, the British and the Americans. Hitler's Holocaust strategy suggests a conclusion which few will grant.

Genocide As Strategy: the Jews.
Israel exists as a direct result of the Holocaust. The Jewish survivors of Hitler fought off the Arabs. Jews from around the world resettled their homeland after two thousand years of wandering.

No one could possibly imagine that Hitler intended these results. He expressed the harshest enmity towards Jewish people. However, he did proclaim the need for a Jewish homeland. He did compliment Jews for keeping their faith, despite being scattered among hostile peoples. Nazi policy for the first eight years of Hitler's reign did urge the citizens of Germany to leave, if they claimed Judaic ancestry. Many went to Palestine.

At a resort hotel in Wannsee, outside Berlin, in 1942, an anti-Semitic conference responded to the one at Evian in 1938. The Holocaust was as much a result of one conference as the other. The Holocaust forced the West to protect the Jews. Before, President Franklin Roosevelt refused to let the ship *St. Louis* put even her thousand such people on American soil. After the Holocaust, President Harry Truman formally recognized the State of Israel within her first hour and guaranteed her survival. Can Hitler have intended this? The following chapters take up Hitler's Jewish question.

Epilogue.

Fifty years after his death Germany remains awash in Hitlerism. He was a tremendous salesman of ideas, an extraordinary orator who could pivot with the mood of an audience and mold it. Germany remains preoccupied with the questions he asked about race. The U.S. also has concerns about race, concerns shifted and stirred up by Hitler and never resolved since.

Why did he lose and why the Jews? A man with such a grasp on the human soul, unfettered by any moral bond or barrier, strident, reckless, fulminating hatreds, was he simply undisciplined? Did he charge off wildly, beyond the limits of prudence? Held by his combination of terrorism and cajolery, people would follow him anywhere, to the moon, or into a desert without stopping for water. There was no natural restraint on him, no one to publicly object. Did he not see that Russia was big? He certainly kept off England. Of course, England had her planes swarmed against him. England proves he had some discretion. But in the end he fell, he jumped or he was pushed.

Alternatively, perhaps the war was a success and ended just as it began, on Hitler's schedule, at his whim and by his design. His Walther pistol ended the war as surely as his invasion of Poland started it. Should there ever have been any doubt about how it would come out? The psychoanalyst Walter Langer foresaw the ending. The next chapters clarify whether Hitler was a mad dog finally cornered by the forces of reason and justice, or a wily and twisted sorcerer who got the whole world dancing to his ghastly tune.

Having reviewed how Hitler disarmed, disfigured and disemboweled Germany, Part One of this work is complete. Hitler conquered Germany. He got her to commit suicide alongside him. He spread out her armies to be picked apart. He dipped her hand in blood and left her for the dogs of war. He exposed beyond denial the evil potential of her people--leaving the human race heartbroken. Part Two will take up his inner reasons for this ferocity, reasons of which he himself never became aware, so they drove him steadily along *"with the precision and security of a sleepwalker."*

PART TWO

―――――――

THE MAKING OF

A MONSTER

Prologue to Part Two

As Tolstoy put it: "All happy families are like one another; each unhappy family is unhappy in its own way." Part Two searches Hitler's background for forces that might lead to a war on people who were German or Jewish or both. To be sure, he never admitted he had seduced and punished Germany; he made his threats against the Jews. In each case, the results did not entirely match the advertising. But undercurrents in the mind can push us along without our being aware. Profound trends from childhood operate unseen on our judgement. The horrors Hitler brought to the world reenacted the tensions and events of his early life.

Some will object that such a search is too complex; others, that it is only too simple. Too complex because the data on human motivation are always and unavoidably incomplete--there is no x-ray of the mind. Also, Hitler can no longer help. But Hitler alive in Spandau Prison could not tell us much more than he already has with his words and deeds. He was not a judicious historian of his own life, if ever anyone is.

Some call the matter simple and dismiss Hitler as unlucky or crazy, or both. This cuts off discussion by ignoring the internal workings that lead people to risk their lives on luck, or to do things that, to others, seem crazy.

Some prefer not to inquire too deeply into the chemistry of horror. When a man becomes a monster, shoot him and look away. Any eruption from the dark underside of human life threatens the social convention that people are and should be orderly, predictable and well-regulated. The rest, the mad and the bad, we simply exclude.

Hitler has puzzled generations of investigators. Sly even in death, he had a right to be complicated. Hitler grew up in a silken trap: he had a coddling but controlling mother and a distinguished but brutal father. Adolf became dedicated to evading control by anyone. However, he could not evade his memories. To this day many Germans think of Hitler as the most fanatical German nationalist in history. Yet Part One has shown that Hitler marched always towards disaster. His Holocaust sealed simultaneously the fates of Germany and the Jews, reversing their traditional postures: the one ineradicably shamed, the other seared into tenacious militancy. Both agree: Never again!

Hitler claimed righteous indignation and vengeance as the basis for most of his policies. He invented that solution in order to survive despite the complex web of constraints that his childhood created. As the pioneer family psychiatrist Carl Whitaker put it: "There are no individuals, only pieces of families." An inventory of the stresses on the Hitler family shows how Adolf was their captive.

Chapter Ten

FATHER:

THE JEWISH PROBLEM

Prologue.

Secrecy shrouded the conception of Adolf's father, Alois. The birth of Alois was recorded as illegitimate, with his paternity left unstated, and his mother died ten years later without publicly naming her mate. Alois took his mother's name. She left him to be raised on a farm, where illegitimacy would ordinarily have been no more than an excuse for rustic drollery or a bit of bawdy gossip. But once grown, Alois, smart and ambitious, managed to enter the civil service. He then found the uncertainty of his origins a stumbling block. For his even more ambitious fourth son, Adolf, the uncertainty proved overwhelming, devastating and unforgivable.

Born Under a Cloud: Father.

In 1837 Maria Anna Schicklgruber gave birth to her only child, Alois. She was forty-two, but had never married. She returned home pregnant after venturing from her native Waldviertel region, in northern Austria, to the city of Graz, where she had been employed as a maid in the home of the Frankenbergers. Of them, three things are said: they had a grown son at home, they paid years of child support for Alois, and they were Jewish.

Testimony by Hans Frank at the 1946 Nuremberg war crimes trial provided the information above. Frank had sufficient credentials as a supporter of Hitler to be among the twelve whom the tribunal sentenced to hang, so his testimony has to be given some weight. Conceivably, a bitter Frank might have drawn on his own anti-Semitism to call his defeated Leader a Jew. During the war, Frank served Hitler as the Governor General of central Poland; Frank did uproot and ship out a million of its people, for being Jews. However, if the grandfather story was fabricated as a cynical maneuver, the reaction of the Court was hard to predict--the ancestry of the late tyrant was not of legal interest. Favoring the truthfulness of Frank's account is the well-documented religious conversion he experienced following Hitler's suicide. Frank determined to clear his conscience, and preserved the diary he had kept for years, even though it contained more than enough evidence to hang him. On the day Frank's diary was read in court, he was overheard in conversation. Göring advised stonewalling in the name of "the German sovereign." Frank exploded: "He got us into this, and all that there is left is to tell the truth!"

Before the war, Frank, an early Nazi, had been Hitler's personal attorney. In 1930, the press had questioned the origins of the racist politician. At that time, Hitler did not have the power to silence them. According to Frank, Hitler sent him to check on what might be found out about the secret grandfather. William Hitler corroborates Frank's claim. William, Adolf's English nephew (the son of Alois, Jr.), says British papers published an interview with William concerning the family's ambiguous origins.

Either Adolf did not know his lineage, or he wanted to find out how much his political enemies were likely to discover. Adolf also brought William Hitler and his mother, Brigid, to Germany for a meeting. William reports Adolf raging: *"How carefully I always kept my personal affairs out of the press!*

These people must not know who I am. They must not know where I come from and from what family....Even in my book I did not say a word about such things, not a word, and now accidentally my nephew is discovered. Investigations are made, and spies are sent to dig up our past." (Evidently a reference to Frank's mission.)

Adolf Hitler also corroborated Frank's report; his actions show that he believed it. He declared persons like himself, with only one Jewish grandparent, to be non-Jewish. He gave his own group a different name, *"half-breeds* [Mischlinge].*"* Hitler decided he needed to exclude himself after the violent outbursts against Jews in 1938 known as *Kristallnacht.* Adolf had already ruled in 1935, *"for the Protection of German Blood and Honor."* Mentioning no other occupations, that otherwise brief and vague edict concerning sexual contact specially prohibited Jews from employing Christian women under age 45 as housemaids.

Apparently Hitler understood that his own housemaid grandmother had, at 42, given him a Jewish grandfather. The new law would have prevented not only the clouded birth of Alois, but also that of Adolf. Both of their Germanic, Christian mothers had first become pregnant while working for Jews as maids. Another unspoken fantasy target of the law might have been Adolf's fatal liaison with his own housekeeper, his niece, Geli--to be discussed later.

For Adolf's family, questions of race had always been fraught with tension. So said Adolf with artful delicacy in his autobiography, *Mein Kampf*: *"I do not remember hearing the word [Jew] so much as mentioned at home during my father's lifetime. I think the old gentleman would have considered it uncultivated to emphasize the designation at all."*

Warned by the forced silence at home, the boy Adolf passed off his father's ancestry as German at a time and place when race was critical. Power struggles between ethnic groups roiled the politics of Hapsburg Austria-Hungary a century ago. The groups had been thrown together as one nation only a short time, and the Germanic minority dominated. Meanwhile, the small Jewish population of Vienna doubled due to immigration from newly annexed territory in the east. The immigrants from the closed ghettoes of rural towns brought distinctive clothing and rituals that made an easy target for politicians. One mayor of Vienna even led a mob to destroy the offices of a Jewish newspaper.

Adding insult to injury for Adolf, the name, "Hitler," had been newly invented by Alois in 1876, when he was thirty-nine. Before that, being both illegitimate and unclaimed, Alois had used his mother's family name, Schicklgruber. The new name resembled that of the man his mother took in marriage when Alois was five. However, her husband, Johann Georg Hiedler, had not claimed Alois as his son following the marriage, as a Catholic father would do. Nor did Hiedler consent to raise the boy. When Alois's mother died, Hiedler gave Alois to a brother to raise. Alois ran away to Vienna at thirteen, found his way into the Customs Service and did well. He married the spinster daughter of a bigwig. He then got a priest to change the baptismal record to indicate a father for the infant Alois. Alois proposed Johann Georg Hiedler, already long dead. His mother, Maria, being also dead, Alois brought for witnesses three illiterate peasants. The X's they signed served as the only proof of Alois's claim. The priest would not sign the change.

Born Under a Cloud.

The circumstances that preceded his birth assured Adolf he would never have a moment of peace. Not helping matters, his restless and irascible father dragged the family through a dozen houses. Little Dolfi attended seven different schools; he was always the stranger among the provincial Germanic Catholic boys who became, however briefly, his neighbors. Further-

more, his unusual name he knew to be fake. A clouded ancestry, and a father who forbad talk of race, made for shame and
anxious secrecy. Whether the secret died with Grandma Maria
or was whispered within the family--or was cat-called in the
streets--Adolf knew at least that his grandfather was a secret.
He became a moody loner. On any given day, he might be discovered to be a Frankenberger, not a Hitler or a Hiedler.
Later, the Gestapo would look repeatedly for further information. In his youth, as well, Adolf found the whole subject of
ancestry painful. In four years of close and exclusive adolescent
companionship, August Kubizek heard little about Adolf's kin-
folk: "Adolf spoke but rarely of his family....[He] preferred to
describe the [Waldviertel] landscape."

Hitler wanted nothing to do with his family's past. When he
annexed Austria to Germany in 1938, he had his father's home
village, Döllersheim, obliterated--including the grave of his
wayward grandmother, Maria. He gave the area to the tank divisions as a training site. When he heard that his mother's
ancestral home in Spital had been marked with a plaque, he
flew into a rage and ordered it removed. His father died when
Adolf was 13; his mother, when he was 18. Except for his
half-sister, Angela, and her daughter, Geli, with whom he briefly resided, Adolf had little contact with relatives after his
mother died.

Jew-Baiting as a Family Matter.

Adolf had to face his father's eminence, shame-ridden ancestry, brutal discipline and early death. Little else in his life
might explain Hitler's anti-Semitism. Living in small towns,
the boy Adolf apparently had few contacts with known Jews.
Later, in Linz, Edmund Bloch, a Jewish doctor, treated Adolf's
mother for several months. She nonetheless died of breast
cancer. Some authors have suggested that made Adolf hate all
Jews. However, Hitler showed nothing but gratitude towards

Dr. Bloch, sending him a postcard of thanks in 1908 and giving him passage to America when the Holocaust started. Various Jewish art dealers in Vienna marketed Adolf's watercolors, but the next Jewish person identified in Hitler's life was the Lieutenant who got Adolf decorated for bravery with the Iron Cross, First Class, during World War One. Hitler never claimed any personal grievance against anyone Jewish. He complained bitterly about various schoolteachers and generals, but they were all Christians.

Hitler characteristically blamed others for his every misfortune, but the fervor of his volcanic, lifelong assault against Jews could not have come entirely from exposure to cultural influences. Living on the streets and in the homeless shelters of Vienna between 1908 and 1913 may have freshened a pre-existing animosity. Often hungry himself, Adolf knew some Jewish people were well off. Using the language of the anti-Semitic newspapers, he came to call them *"guests."* They had resided in Germany and Austria-Hungary just a few centuries. He called the Holocaust his *"final solution* [Endlösung]" to the Jewish problem.

Based on his ancestry and his early experiences with his father, Adolf "Hitler" had strong reasons for finding both Jews and anti-Semitism to be problems. He protested too much about their evil; he had to be drowning out other feelings. This would be consistent with the attitudes towards a parent. He often gave the Jews compliments in passing, for sticking to their principles, for sticking together, and for surviving centuries of persecution. The Jews were what he could not dare to be, and what he was sworn not to be, and what he could never be sure he was not. And what he feared he would be found to be.

Another man of illegitimate birth was suspected of concealing Jewish ancestry, and became a ferocious anti-Semite. He also called for their extermination [*Untergang*]. This was the composer and amateur philosopher, Richard Wagner. Hitler admired him enormously, once declaring: *"Whoever wants to understand National Socialist Germany must know Wagner....At every stage of my life I come back to him."*

His Father's Son.

Besides sharing their clouded ancestry, young Adolf had daily contact with his father. When Adolf was six, Alois retired from the Austro-Hungarian civil service. For the next seven years until he died, Alois was a formidable presence in their successive homes. His eldest son, Alois, Jr., simply ran away. The youngest, Edmund, died. That left Adolf as the only son. Adolf's younger sister, Paula, recalls that thereafter:

> It was especially my brother Adolf who challenged my father to extreme harshness and who got his sound thrashings every day. He was a scrubby little rogue, and all attempts of his father to thrash him for his rudeness and to cause him to love the profession of an official in the state were in vain.

Adolf tells it: *"Then barely eleven years old, I was forced into opposition [to father] for the first time....I did not want to become a civil servant, no, and again no. All attempts on my father's part to inspire me with love or pleasure in this profession [father's] by stories from his own life accomplished the exact opposite. I...grew sick to my stomach at the thought of sitting in an office, deprived of my liberty; ceasing to be master of my own time and being compelled to force the content of my whole life into paper forms....One day it became clear to me that I would become a painter, an artist....My father was struck speechless. 'Painter? Artist?' He doubted my sanity, or perhaps he thought he had heard wrong or misunderstood me. But when he was clear on the subject, and particularly after he felt the seriousness of my intention, he opposed it with all the determination of his nature.... 'Artist! No! Never as long as I live!' ...My father would never depart from his 'Never!' And I intensified my 'Nevertheless.'"*

Adolf's older half-brother, Alois, Jr., left, but remembers hearing: "When Adolf was about eleven years old he refused to put up with the maltreatment of his father any longer and resolved to run away from home with two other boys....[Father] was furious and beat Adolf so violently that when he returned home he was afraid that he had killed him." Their father, Alois, Sr., was considered by a colleague: "very strict, exacting and pedantic, a most unapproachable person." This hardness probably reflected his own youth. Alois, Sr., started life as his mother's only companion, but in dying or before, she abandoned him to foster parents. He ran away at thirteen to make his own way. Adolf wrote that his father was a man of: *"iron energy and industry....a lifetime's struggle for existence had made him domineering."* In admiration, Adolf himself learned endurance: *"I resolved not to make a sound the next time my father whipped me. And when the time came--I still can remember my frightened mother standing outside the door--I silently counted the blows. My mother thought I had gone crazy when I beamed proudly and said, 'Father hit me thirty-two times!'"*

In this account, Hitler's mother, Klara, participates as a voyeur of the sadism of the father. The outwardly meek and servile woman had her eldest surviving child, Adolf, fight her battles with her husband, while she watched from the wings.

"Hard and determined as my father might be...his son had inherited...a stubbornness like his own." So claimed Adolf. Kubizek heard widow Klara argue with Adolf: "Our poor father cannot rest in his grave because you *will* flout his wishes." Kubizek recalls: "Whenever [Adolf] heard the word 'civil servant,' even without any connection with his own career, he fell into a rage." Alois had died when Adolf was only thirteen-- Alois must still have seemed a towering and imposing figure. Kubizek notes the conflicted reverence later: "Hearing him speak of his father, one would never have imagined how violently he disliked the idea of being a civil servant....Adolf spoke

of his father with great respect. I never heard him say anything against him, in spite of their differences of opinion about his career." Adolf had converted his angry feelings about his father--who had been too important and too frightening to oppose--into furor over civil service. Adolf also reviled the Austro-Hungarian Empire, his father's employer: *"The Hapsburg house [of Austria] was fated to bring misery on the German nation...[I have] warm love for my German Austrian homeland, profound hatred for the Austrian state."* Adolf's mother being of unimpeachably German stock, his words carry the personal meaning that Adolf remained loyal to her and still took her part against his father. Adolf always insisted he was a German nationalist, to the end.

Consequences.

While passing for German, Adolf could never feel himself securely a member of any group, not the Germans and not the Jews. On any day, Adolf Hitler's ancestry might be discovered, his name properly not Hitler or Hiedler, but Frankenberger. Warding off any possible suspicion, he trumpeted both virulent contempt for Jews and fervent German nationalism.

Hitler's struggle to pass for German opened the door for the Holocaust. Subsequent chapters will take up the nihilism and rage which permitted and fueled radical action; his inner burning originated in his personal history. From adolescence, Hitler was always in a rage, making broad, abstract attacks on society at large. As an isolated person with few pleasures, unattached to life, Hitler felt little restraint in turning his murky and conflicted philosophy into harsh reality. And no one interfered: at Evian the West showed it cared not; in the war that followed, American bombers purposely bypassed Auschwitz.

In fantasy, killing off all Jewish people solved Hitler's own Jewish problem: if the Jews had never come to Europe, his grandmother and his mother would have mated within their

German tribe. In this fantasy, Adolf's youth would then have been untroubled. If the Holocaust also replied to, opposed and exceeded the viciousness of the half-Jewish father, so much the better. Emotionally misshapen and alienated, Hitler pursued his own thoughts without restraint. He did not ask approval from anyone. He resisted advice when it was offered. His way was to announce conclusions. Hitler spent much of the war at his headquarters in the East Prussian forest. To dignify hiding out, he called it Wolf's Lair and had himself called "Wolf." Seen from there, Jews were not a huge range of complex creatures, each with unique feelings and ideas, but a single, abstract entity to be erased. For that matter, so was the German Army.

However, Hitler described himself as a wanderer, much as he described his fellow Jews. By his direct experience in his youth, when he had changed houses and schools so often, with his made-up name, Adolf knew what it was to be an unwelcome and uneasy outsider. Informed by his own early sufferings, he praised the endurance of the Jews. For them to live with persecution and exclusion was more painful than death, in Hitler's eyes. Forced emigration proved a half-measure, halted by Evian.

In his caring for his tribe, Hitler then gave the Jews a quick and quiet way out. Hitler was emphatic in his preference for death over a life of obloquy and shame. He alone could find the monstrous Shoah a rescue. It did force the world to confront the logical conclusion of racism, so long and so smoothly concealed within the whispers and innuendoes of polite and democratic societies, the whispers or catcalls the boy Adolf had himself feared or even endured.

Then the world thought better of its thousand years of mindless scapegoating of Jews, and Israel was restored. In this one sense, Hitler used strategy like that of Gandhi and Martin Luther King, confronting the world's rulers with the unacceptable violence implied by their racism--violence otherwise carried on piecemeal and quietly. Quite unlike Gandhi and King, Hitler created the violence by his own orders, as the Leader of the Germans. Hitler called himself an artist. Indeed, no physical contact occurred between him and the other elected heads of state. The heaped corpses served as props. What has been so far the ultimate violence in human history can also be considered as a ghastly kind of artistic production--performance art at its largest--impressing upon an otherwise inattentive public certain feelings and ideas, the feelings of an artist who, whatever his lies, remained at heart an Austrian of mixed race.

[Footnote: the special role of England reflected the loyal aspect of Hitler's feelings about his father. Adolf told Ciano Britain was essential to the world and told his generals nothing would be gained by beating her. He had told Göring England would never be a target. Dunkirk can be seen as a suicidal plea for peace with England; Hess's flight, as a delusional one. Even late in the war, Hitler asked America and England to join him to crush Bolshevik Russia. Adolf gave England the organizing and sheltering role his father had once held. For the less savory aspects of Alois, the Jews were to serve: when British bombers demolished Hamburg one night in 1943, Hitler insisted that the air commanders, at least, must have been Jews or part Jewish.]

Summary.

His father gave Adolf a Jewish problem, and the viciousness to stage an orgy of revenge and rescue, to solve it. The profligate Alois was the perfect model for the *"seductive, race-destroying"* Jew Adolf bragged about in *Mein Kampf* and elsewhere. On the other hand, Adolf had a Germanic mother. She gave him his passionate allegiance to Germany--an allegiance poisoned with outrage, as discussed in the next chapter.

Chapter Eleven

MOTHER AND THE GERMANS

Prologue: Racism as a Lure.
As a boy, Adolf Hitler, like all children, loved his mother, and she clearly loved him. But other emotions complicated their life together. Even after her death, this clash of emotions continued to torment Adolf--all his life, in fact. They prevented him from starting a family or even having close companions, male or female.

His mother happened to be of Germanic stock. Hitler often referred to Germany by the unusual term, *"Motherland,"* instead of the much more common "Fatherland." This blending of images in Hitler's mind, mother and Motherland, set him on a course of deceptions, self-deceptions, seductions and revenge. Hitler's guileful suicide led Europe to catastrophe. To be sure, no mathematical proof will ever link the misgivings of an infant to affairs of state half a century later. Nonetheless, for a decade, Germany was Hitler, as he often announced. And Hitler, more than most, kept the character he had as a boy.

The hopelessly intertwined knot of strong feelings that grew up between Adolf Hitler and his mother inspired the vainglory of his racist siren song. Viewed from its results, Hitler's delirious racism, so romantically pro-German on its surface, cunningly taunted and mocked Germany to her ruin: *racism as a lure.* At the end, in March 1945, he ordered Germany leveled, but from early on, his speeches gave hints of a destructive rage against his *Mutterland*.

Adolf's rage came from actions taken by Klara Hitler in all innocence. After her first three children died, she bore Adolf and held him close. But held too close too long Adolf, smothering, became lethally bitter. If he never criticized his mother openly, few do. Trained and constrained to be his mother's savior, he dreamt of escape and revenge and *Lebensraum*--that is, the freedom to become himself. This quest he made a national program. Torn by his inner conflicts, Adolf as a teenager had lost hope that life could ever be worth living. How to conquer the world without leaving home? His later solution to his quandary was earth-shattering.

Hitler's inner turmoil had roots in the courtship of his parents. His father's clouded ancestry gave his mother's clearly Germanic derivation great importance. Her struggles with her half-Jewish husband redoubled Adolf's own concerns. In Adolf's mind, racism became a kind of shorthand for family life.

Born Under a Cloud: Mother.

At the age of sixteen, a farmgirl of purely German stock named Klara Pölzl had the opportunity of living in the distinguished home of an Inspector of Customs of the Austro-Hungarian Empire, to earn her keep as a housemaid. She called the Inspector, "Uncle," because he had spent several years of his boyhood under the care of her grandfather. In this way Klara moved in with Alois Schicklgruber and his first wife, just when he invented for himself the name Hitler and claimed her grandfather as his relative. If Klara's arrival prompted his name-change, the slick opportunism of Alois would be similar to that later shown by his son. Klara calling Alois Uncle would have reminded him of the possibility of claiming it in public.

At thirty-nine, Alois was more than twice the age of his new housemaid. His wife, Anna, was older still, fifty-three. The details of life in the Schicklgruber-Hitler home have not been preserved, but when Alois took up in earnest with a cook at the local inn, both Anna and Klara left. Anna soon died, and Alois married the cook, Franziska, who was by then pregnant for the second time. Franziska Matzelsberger got sick in turn, left for the countryside and died. Klara Pölzl returned to care for Franziska's two children by Alois. Alois got Klara pregnant too, and at twenty-five she became his third wife. He was not much for sentiment. Klara remembered the afternoon of the ceremony as routine, with Alois going to his office: "My husband was already on duty again."

Klara bore three children. Then an epidemic of diphtheria took them all. In 1889 she had a fourth, Adolf. Five years passed without another birth. She was able to devote herself to Adolf, her one and only survivor. Klara later told Adolf's friend, August Kubizek: "that Adolf was a very weak child and that she always lived in fear of losing him, too." Another son and a daughter, Edmund and Paula, came later. Adolf remembered his mother as: *"devoted to us children with unchanging loving care."* But this seeming praise can be read as a complaint: that his mother rigidly insisted on treating him like a baby.

Adolf himself believed he needed extra care. He saw himself as weak but brave, claiming: *"association with extremely robust boys which sometimes gravely worried my mother,"* and insisting he was: *"a boy who was certainly anything but 'good.'"* Later, he concluded defiantly: *"Young lads belong with other young lads, and away from their mothers. A mother's love is too great to keep her from constantly making every effort to help the boy, to pamper him, look after him, and even do his thinking for him....[A boy at home] is like a hothouse plant....[Better] to fight for his rights...[than] run to his mother to cry his heart out....practicing for a life of cringing servility....Those who grow up at home are more likely to feel a different longing [not gratitude, but]: away from this place!...The boy who hangs around the house....is much more likely to see what is bad, ignoble, negative, and ugly."*

An over-close and confining, worried mother hovered always near. Enticed by her coddling, yet undermined by her concern, Adolf fought off protection. Other boys seemed *"extremely robust,"* but he forced himself to join them. Then and later, Hitler strained against a temptation to return to *"cringing servility."* Childhood games of cowboys-and-Indians-on-the-Danube absorbed Adolf. They drew from his ominous reading: in the pulp westerns Adolf read as a boy (and all his life) the cowboy is a lonely hero, and the Indians all get killed.

Born Under a Cloud: Adolf as Savior and Prisoner.

On his mother's side, as well as his father's, the circumstances that preceded Hitler's birth insured that he would never have a moment of peace. Besides having three children dead, Klara had an unfortunate marriage. Whatever Adolf's nature, and whatever happened to him once he was born, his bed was already made.

The balance of power was far from equal between Adolf's parents. After Klara, with the special permission of the Catholic Church, married her Uncle Alois, she continued to care for him and his two children by Franziska: Alois, Jr., and Angela. There was no honeymoon. Besides the ignominy of being third among his wives, Klara had married while pregnant. After the death of Alois, the local newspaper described the arrogance of this profligate customs officer, calling him: "universally well-informed, [and] able to pronounce authoritatively on any subject." The paper might have added that he was well known at the tavern. In short, Klara's marriage brought her little companionship. She còmplained to Kubizek: "What I hoped and dreamed of as a young girl ha[d] not been fulfilled in my marriage. " This identifies her as a dreamer who, like her son, blamed others for the difficulties of life. Yet, having nursed the previous wives on their deathbeds and replaced them sexually, she knew Alois's character and habits. In a fateful twist of mangled purpose, Klara had returned to and married someone who guaranteed her not joy or warmth, but grounds for righteous anger. This attraction to disaster she passed on to her son.

Klara was further isolated from neighbors and from her family by having to follow Alois to his successive posts. Furthermore, due to his mania for moving, twelve different addresses were recorded in one town. Accordingly, she could be pardoned if she looked to her children for human warmth and closeness. Between his push and her pull, Adolf got chosen to be her savior--every boy's dream, but a nightmare if it happens. He spent his life trying to embody the role.

A savior is also a prisoner, constrained by his mission to put aside the ordinary pleasures of life. Adolf was born into ceaseless, unrewarded toil. The work was emotional responsiveness and attentiveness instead of physical labor, but his assignment proved exhausting nevertheless. Robbed of his childhood, Adolf became a grim and severe person. It took a gifted listener, August Kubizek, to become Adolf's friend. Gustl was his only friend when they were teenagers in Linz. The two boys then shared an apartment in Vienna for a bleak and painful year. Kubizek recalls this young Adolf, still a teenager:

Hitler [was] a deeply serious man....One thing he could not do was to pass over something with a smile....He never came to the end of his problems....Many other qualities which are characteristic of youth were lacking in him....I never heard him use an ambiguous [or foul] expression or tell a doubtful [or immoral] story....I never saw him take anything lightly....For him the world was hostile and empty....There was no end to the things, even trivial ones, that could upset him.

A difficult closeness--really a mutual capture--had enveloped mother and son. Kubizek found he was nearly their only caller. On her deathbed, Klara still worried about her Adolf, by then eighteen years old. She begged Kubizek: "Go on being a friend to my son when I'm no longer here. He has no one else." Of this harsh view, Kubizek says: "I realized then how much his nature resembled his mother's....There was a peculiar spiritual harmony between mother and son which I have never since come across....He loved his mother above everything; she was the only person on earth to whom he felt really close, and she reciprocated his feeling to the same extent."

"His nature resembled his mother's," especially a possessiveness that blurred and overwhelmed identities. Forinstance, Adolf once told Gustl Kubizek: *"I can't bear it that you should mix with other young people and talk to them....[Besides] we should both dress in exactly the same way, so that people would take us for brothers."* Kubizek recalls further evidence of how identities melted together in Adolf's mind: "He [once] shouted at me rudely asking *whether I was his real friend or not; if I was, I should share his interests."* In his fantasies, Adolf showed the same attitude. As an adolescent, he loved a young woman from afar. He claimed the distance did not matter: *"What is in me is in Stefanie too."* Kubizek recalls: "He used to insist...*everything would become clear [between them] without as much as a word being exchanged....*Adolf would not believe that Stefanie had not asked after him, for he took it for granted that she was longing for him just as much as he was for her....[Had he ever approached her,] Adolf would have sought in vain for those grandiose thoughts and ideas with which he had surrounded her to such an extent as to make her the female image of himself." Adolf had better luck as Chancellor. Crowds roared when he would say: *"I am Germany, and Germany is I."*

Despite believing his identity fused with others, Hitler could also show a flinty quality. He abandoned Kubizek in Vienna without a word. When they next met, thirty years later, Adolf had become the Führer of Greater Germany. His character had not changed; he seductively purred: *"I am still tied up by the war. But, I hope it won't last much longer and then I'll be able to build again and to carry out what remains to be done. When that moment comes I shall call you, Kubizek, and then you must stay with me always."*

With his mother as with Kubizek, Adolf felt free to leave, but he could not stand to be left! After first deserting his mother for Vienna, on his return he strained every nerve and fiber to hold her back from escaping to her grave. Klara's doctor called the struggle a sign of affection and mourning: "[Adolf's] attachment to his mother was deep and loving. He would watch her every movement so that he might anticipate her slightest need. His eyes, which usually gaze[d] mournfully into the distance, would light up whenever she was relieved of her pain.... In all my forty years of practice I had never seen a young man so broken by grief and bowed down by suffering as young Adolf Hitler was that day [his mother was buried]."

Lessons Learned.

One lesson Adolf gleaned from his mother's attitudes was racism. Given his bond with her, Adolf's fulminant racism must have echoed something in her; he would not have strayed far from her viewpoint. Evidently, Alois's "mystery" father was not shrugged off, but instead provided Klara an opportunity to avenge her husband's arrogance.

Another lesson was sensitivity: conscripted to meet his mother's demands for attentiveness and responsiveness, Adolf developed extraordinary talents. Kubizek swears: "By God, nobody on earth, not even my mother who loved me so much and knew me so well, was as capable of bringing my secret desires into the open and making them come true as my friend [Adolf]....[He] was full of deep understanding and sympathy.... Without my telling him, he knew exactly how I felt. How often this helped me in difficult times! He always knew what I needed and what I wanted."

This Adolf became: "the loud-speaker which magnifies the inaudible whispers of the German soul until they can be heard by the German's conscious ear....the first man to tell every German what he has been thinking and feeling all along," as Hitler's favorite psychologist, C.G. Jung, wrote. Jung and Germany failed to notice that Adolf magnified only the destructive, racist "whispers of the German soul," exploiting them for an apocalyptic seduction. His mother's racism incited the boy Adolf against his own father, causing Adolf to feel like a parricide and an outcast. In return, Adolf incited his motherland to the racist folly that branded her an outcast.

The Price of Genius.

The narrow life that induced Adolf's unusual skills also created vengefulness towards mother, expressed indirectly, so as not to break contact. In their battle, only words of love were spoken out loud. Kubizek says: "How often did she unburden to me the worries which Adolf caused her....Gradually I learned to understand the suffering this woman endured. She never complained, but....the preoccupation with the well-being of her only surviving son depressed her increasingly."

Someone who never complains and yet communicates great suffering has unusual powers. Such a person can exert subtle, yet pervasive influence. This person's pleas cannot be denied, because they are never openly stated. Adolf complained that a mother can corrupt her son, even: *"doing his thinking for him."* By contrast, his father's abuse had been clear and physical. Adolf defended himself against being influenced by holding onto his first opinion; this was called "inflexibility" by the docile Kubizek: "There was in his nature something firm, inflexible, immovable, obstinately rigid....Adolf simply could not change his mind....It was just this inflexibility that was responsible for Adolf Hitler's causing such innumerable sorrows to his mother."

As Führer, Adolf would insist: *"Any change in my attitude would certainly be misunderstood as giving in...and would bring a landslide."* He took pride in his obstinacy. Warlimont recalls Hitler boasting: *"It was always my habit, even as a boy --perhaps it was naughtiness then, but on the whole it must have been a virtue after all--to have the last word."*

For Adolf to do battle with his mother, the one person upon whom he depended, proved an agony. Kubizek tells of seeing a teenager in "deep depression":

[Adolf] was at odds with the world. Wherever he looked, he saw injustice, hate and enmity. Nothing was free from his criticism....He wallowed deeper and deeper in self-criticism. Yet it only needed the slightest touch...for his self-accusation to become an accusation against the times, against the whole world; choking with his catalogue of hates, he would pour his fury over everything, against mankind in general who did not understand him, who did not appreciate him and by whom he was persecuted.

Albert Speer, Hitler's close associate during the war, recalls: "While looking [at architectural models] he spoke with unusual vivacity. These were the rare times when he relinquished his usual stiffness." Kubizek agrees: "Freshness and liveliness-- this was missing completely in Adolf's work...His intention was not to express any of his own emotions." As General Franz Halder heard Hitler say: *"You should know first of all that you will never be able to discover my thoughts and intentions until I give them out as orders....You will never learn what is going on in my head. As for those who boast of being privy to my thoughts--to them I lie all the more."*

With all his wariness and anguish, Adolf barely mentioned his mother in *Mein Kampf*, or anywhere else. He often boasted of his father--both the achievements and the beatings. However quiet he was about his mother, Hitler did talk about: *"the great German Mother country."*

The Great German Mother Country.

From boyhood on, Hitler saw Germany in violent opposition to Austria-Hungary. At thirty-six, he published his views: *"The safety of Germanity first required the destruction of Austria....The Hapsburg house [ruling Austria] was fated to bring misery on the German nation....[I have] warm love for my German Austrian homeland, profound hatred for the Austrian state....By resisting the Jew I am fighting for the Lord's work."* The last statement connects with the others through Alois, the half-Jewish customs officer for the Hapsburgs. These taunts describe in metaphor Adolf's daily defiance of his father.

As with his mother, Adolf's connection to Germany was at times a rapturous mingling of identities. One speech went: *"I am Germany and Germany is I. That is the miracle of our times that you have found me. And that I have found you, is Germany's joy and fortune....Whatever you are, you are through me, and whatever I am, I am only through you alone."* With his mother's picture hanging over his bed at each of his residences, the solitary Leader excused his bachelorhood by claiming: *"My only bride is my Motherland."* When his death coincided with Germany's, it made a *Liebestod*--the joint suicide of lovers that Richard Wagner favored in his operas.

The Rienzi *Solution: Suicide as Heroism.*

Suicide fascinated Hitler from adolescence onward, but he wanted company. Even in death he had to merge. He sometimes acknowledged his temptation in denying it; Warlimont recalls hearing: *"[I have] known nothing but struggle and with it only one principle: strike, strike and strike again! In me they...are facing an opponent who does not even think of the word capitulate.* " Hitler wanted to combine his own death with some larger event. In adolescence, he wrote poems about a young woman. He dared not talk with her; he would instead die with her. Kubizek shudders to recall:

> [Adolf] exclaimed. *"I will make an end of it!"*...Adolf contemplated suicide seriously. He would jump into the river from the Danube bridge...but Stefanie would have to die with him--he insisted on that....Every single phase of the horrifying tragedy was minutely described.

Kubizek recounts the stresses on Hitler then: "He had spent two years living with his mother....[in an] aimless, day-to-day mode of life...[with] dangerous fits of depression....He was anxious to escape the atmosphere that prevailed at home." At eighteen, Hitler decided to study art in Vienna, a hundred miles away. Anxious to keep him home, his mother exploded: "He's as pigheaded as his father. Why this crazy journey to Vienna?" Unable to discuss his mother or his confusion about her, Adolf claimed instead: *"There is only one thing to be done. I must go away--far away from Stefanie."* He stayed away until the end of that year, 1907. His mother was by then on her deathbed. Adolf's show of grief impressed her doctor.

The prospect of death with a chaste love had preoccupied Adolf Hitler long before Eva Braun was summoned to the bunker. This romantic and extravagant personal solution riveted Hitler's attention when he first saw Wagner's opera *Rienzi.* Kubizek solemnly recalls:

> It was the most impressive hour I ever lived through with my friend....We were in the theater...living breathlessly through Rienzi's rise to be the Tribune of the people of Rome and his subsequent downfall....[Afterwards] as if propelled by an invisible force, Adolf climbed up to the top of the Freinberg [mountain]....Adolf stood in front of me; and now he gripped

both my hands and held them tight. He had never made such a
gesture before....His eyes were feverish with excitement. His
words...erupted, hoarse and raucous....Never before and never
again have I heard Adolf Hitler speak as he did in that hour....

He transferred the character of Rienzi...to the plane of his own
ambitions....He conjured up in grandiose, inspiring pictures his
own future and that of his people....He was talking of a *mandate*
which, one day, he would receive from the people, to lead them
out of servitude to the heights of freedom.

But the heights of which Adolf spoke represent only the middle
part of the opera. Adolf did not openly acknowledge the
ending, when the people, unworthy and ungrateful, turn on the
hero and set fire to his castle. The hero remains at prayer
within, despite having been excommunicated. Damned from
above and below, he refuses to flee. His faithful sister, seeing
the fire, enters the castle to die at his side. Richard Wagner
combined struggle for the heights with fiery death for the doomed couple, bound by their sexless, selfless union. Losing
everything except his honor, Rienzi dies on principle and on
purpose.

Hitler revised the staging. In his version, after leading the
German people out of servitude to the heights of power over
Europe, he lost his war and then declared that the people were
to blame:

*If the German people were to be defeated in the struggle, it must
have been too weak: it had failed to prove its mettle before
history and was destined only to destruction.*

By April 1945 the weak, unworthy and ungrateful people let the
Russian army shell Berlin and let the British and Americans
cross the Rhine. Only then did Hitler-Rienzi invite Eva Braun
to join him. His "Political Testament" offered a libretto for the
ghoulish finale:

I have therefore decided to remain in Berlin and there to choose death voluntarily....I die with a joyful heart in my knowledge of the immeasurable deeds and achievements of our peasants and workers....I myself, as the founder and creator of this movement, prefer death to cowardly resignation or even to capitulation....Commanders must set a shining example of faithful devotion to duty unto death.

[Eva Braun] came to this city, already almost besieged, of her own free will in order to share my fate. She will go to her death with me at her own wish as my wife. This will compensate us both [sic] for what we lost through my work in the service of my people....My wife and I choose to die in order to escape the shame of overthrow or capitulation. It is our wish that our bodies be burned immediately in the place where I have performed the greater part of my daily work during the twelve years of service to my people.

No leader of a great nation can openly advocate poetic extravagances. Hitler never asked to be trapped in a burning castle. Nonetheless, he was the first to find a parallel between his course and that of *Rienzi.* In 1939, just before beginning the war, Hitler invited his rediscovered friend Kubizek to a festival of Wagner operas. Kubizek heard Hitler tell Wagner's widow about wandering in the mountains on first seeing *Rienzi.* Hitler concluded solemnly: *"In that hour it began."*

Six years later, forced to acknowledge the imminent defeat of Germany, Hitler did not again mention *Rienzi.* However, he offered:

We may be destroyed, but if we are, we shall drag a world with us--a world in flames.

Chapter Twelve

THE MESSIAH OF DEATH

(Holocaust as Symbol)

This work and especially this chapter attempt to answer two questions: why did Hitler lose, and why did he focus on Jews? Hitler revived grave doubts about human nature when he showed the beast in eighty million people. Nothing could excuse their Leader; however, we need to know what plagued him, so we can head off the next life-hater. Temporarily suspend the conventional views and weigh his enormous morality play of good vs. evil, World War II. What did it say?

Hitler's defining crime was the Holocaust, but did he jump into it, accidentally fall, or was he--by his lights, in his view-- pushed? He created economic and social barriers against Germans who still worshipped in the old way. Half left. The western democracies meeting at Evian in 1938 stopped this outflow. Only then did Hitler threaten to murder the Jews, and he did not begin in earnest until 1941. He kept the genocide remote from himself and, therefore, abstract. What did it mean to Adolf, whose attitude towards death had always been unusual. The would-be hero had often praised suicide, and his military adventures reflected that view: the German General Staff opposed every one of his invasions as reckless. Some call him a gambler; however, he played on and the Germans lost. Moreover, during the actual fighting he fired many of Germany's most able generals: Guderian, Manstein, Rommel, Halder and others. Hitler's strange tactics largely bypassed Britain, Moscow and

St. Petersburg-Leningrad (despite staging a gruesome seige), yet he ordered the destruction of Germany herself. He took an opera he saw at the age of fifteen as a model for his career; he claimed: *"In that hour it began."* However heroic his fantasies, World War One had ended with Hitler under psychiatric care for claiming blindness. Thereafter, he loudly blamed Germany for surrendering; he insisted the war had ended too soon for him. How does all this add up?

Conclusion.

Offering himself as the savior of Germany and believing that, Hitler nonetheless lived in agony over his secret Jewish grandfather and his ancient conflicts with his parents. In a *"final solution"* beyond his own understanding, he exposed, extended, taunted and crushingly punished German racism. His brutality towards Jews shamed the anti-Semites of the West into allowing the revival of Israel. Rash and ruthless, Hitler invented quick, radical solutions to what he saw as social problems, then he lied, seduced, shamed and terrorized until he got his way. The war and the Holocaust settled his unconscious debts to his parents and helped him feel bold. Hitler consistently strove for a hero's death, from his youth, on through the vicious cleverness of his early years as Chancellor and the rigid posturing later. At the deepest level, a good death was the most he hoped for. Along the way, he became a monster who devoured German and non-German alike. Having astonished the world, he declared his campaign a success: he had made himself unforgettable.

This concept of Hitler's career comes from emphasizing its results, and his formative years, not his propaganda. His true motives remained for him--and for Germany--largely unseen and unsuspected. Some say his motives are irrelevant: if Hitler did hate the Germans and love the Jews, that would not change the results. Holding this issue at bay, first examine how Adolf

Hitler might have grown so misshapen. After outlining his early life, we can consider its consequences.

A Brief Chronology. Shame infected the Hitler household. The parents kept outward appearances ordinary, what with father's government job and mother's domestic skills. But Adolf was born into a cauldron of secret torments. Grandfather could not be mentioned. Adolf's parents met in a courtship of master and servant. After ten years, Klara became pregnant. Alois had invented a new name, Hitler, on Klara's arrival. Half his age, she had begun as the housemaid of Alois's first wife, only to become, eventually, his third; Klara remained deferential. Then a catastrophe befell them: an epidemic killed all three of their shared children. The two motherless children from father's prior marriage lived in the home; they escaped the epidemic. Alois, Jr., was by Adolf's birth seven, and Angela was six.

Adolf Hitler was born the year after the epidemic, on April 20, 1889, in what is now Austria. Before Klara had another child, she devoted five years to Adolf. Then came Edmund and, two years later, Paula, her last. Alois, Jr., ran away from home because of father's beatings. But Adolf did very well in school until Edmund died and left Adolf, at eleven, the only son in the home; he had long been the main focus of his parents' attentions and a party to their struggles.

Father died when Adolf was thirteen. Then Adolf made friends with August Kubizek, and began lecturing to him. When Adolf was eighteen, his mother died and he moved to Vienna with Kubizek. Turned down twice by the art school ("too few heads" in his test drawing), Adolf educated himself. Living on a small pension, he sketched buildings and visited the library, the opera, and the legislature. He railed against society and avoided women. Kubizek studied music. After a year, Adolf abruptly deserted Kubizek to live in a homeless shelter.

He became known as a crank who argued politics. By day he sold his small watercolors of buildings (thus he painted houses, yet was never a housepainter). In 1913, at twenty-four, he emigrated to Munich. When the multi-ethnic Austro-Hungarian Army attempted to draft him, he got a doctor to say he had bad lungs. Then World War One started, and Hitler immediately volunteered--but for the German Army. He won the Iron Cross, First Class, for valor, but ended the war in a military hospital under treatment for hysteria.

Following his recovery, the German Army sent outspoken Corporal Hitler to infiltrate and influence new political parties. By 1920 a practiced orator, he helped form the National Socialist German Workers Party [*Nationalsozialistischen*, the Nazis]. In 1923, Hitler led them in an armed uprising in Munich which was crushed in a day (the so-called Beerhall Putsch), but his speeches at his trial won him fame. He published *Mein Kampf* in 1925. A world-wide economic depression brought the Nazis enough followers to make them the chief political party in Germany, and Hitler was named Chancellor January 30, 1933. The Reichstag legislative building then burned down. Hitler blamed his political rivals, the Communists, claimed an emergency and took total control of Germany. The major events of his twelve years as Chancellor have been discussed in Part One. But what meaning did this life have for Hitler?

From Boy to Man: the Making of a Monster.
Even monsters start out as helpless babies. Misused, the baby strains to turn the tables. Each life is invented to wring out survival, both physical and emotional. Born as innocent as any, seeking only nurture, protection and respect, the infant Adolf maneuvered to extract what was not freely provided. His failure enraged him, estranged him and pointed him towards suicide. Children are people, and people have feelings. Children

remember everything. What is too early to remember in words is etched in our bones.

After losing three children, when her fourth, Adolf, arrived, Klara held him as close as the fingers on her hand. Her clinging and interference strangled Adolf. She demanded loyal service equal to the care she forced on him. If her hovering proved a strait-jacket, her demand for loyalty unto death became a ghastly burden. Adolf had no life apart from her, but neither could he stand being her prisoner, weapon and shield; he worshipped and envied from afar the apparent power and freedom of his father. However, Klara recruited her little boy to do battle with her husband. Father being stern, aloof and generally absent, Adolf depended on his mother, and so was compelled to do her bidding. He still needed to balance between the giants who ruled his world--one by day, one by night--the world into which he had been thrust by no choice of his own.

Neither parent focused on Adolf's feelings, so Adolf never grew independent--yet he hated being dependent. Rage though he might at his condition of servitude, he was afraid to let go. Children batten on respect and attention to develop a sense of safety, comfort and permanence. This permits them to form their own opinions and plans. Convinced of their importance and feeling solid and substantial, they learn to care about themselves and then, by imitation, about others. Adolf never got that far. However, having no legs of his own, so to speak, he could not stand back and criticize. His rebellion took its strange shape from being forced entirely underground.

His father, Alois,. had no identity beyond his work. Alois relied on his uniform, his frequent changes of address and his gruff manner to shield him from close scrutiny. But there was no way to evade his own doubts. More insidious and more corrosive than his brutality, the doubts infected his family as well; insecurity of self became part of the family's internal politics and a lifelong, blinding agony for Adolf.

Father also asked for loyalty. Schooling would prepare Adolf to follow Alois into the Austro-Hungarian civil service. Unlike the covert, vague but pervasive demands of his mother, his father's was open, verbal and specific; accordingly, it could be openly opposed. Adolf wrote: *"Hard and determined as my father might be...his son had inherited...a stubbornness like his own....My father held to his 'never' and I redoubled my 'nevertheless.'"* Adolf exerted himself so that: *"the so-called wisdom of age does not choke the genius of youth."*

Mama's Boy and Father's Son.
The whipsaw of competing loyalties bore down on Adolf all his life. As a compromise, he pledged to take his mother's part, yet followed his father's example. He stood up to his father daily, and was thrashed soundly. But he also adopted his father's dignity, and refused to cry. This regimen of dancing back and forth was both too intense and too confusing. Distracted from developing his own point of view, Adolf was unable to say anything about personal matters. Kubizek recalls: "Adolf spoke but rarely of his family." Unable to criticize and forbidden to leave his family, Adolf instead would arrange the symbolic death of all concerned; this *"final solution"* to his dilemma blended leaving and not leaving. In a chilling self-description, Hitler once said:

[Some find] in nihilism their final confession of faith. [They are] incapable of any true cooperation, with a desire to oppose all order, filled with hatred against every authority. [Their] unrest and disquietude can find satisfaction only in some conspiratorial activity of the mind perpetually plotting the disintegration of whatever at any moment exists.

In the battle with his parents for emotional survival, he had lost. The result was the macabre Hitler of the photograph on page 27, exulting over his plans to rebuild his hometown of Linz--after *"the disintegration of whatever...exists."* This photograph of joy was taken in February 1945, with the Red Army a scant hundred miles away. Hitler's reaction suggests *"nihilism"* and *"hatred against every authority,"* even his own. The cunning dictator in his last months still bore the scars of his youth: harried by demands for service from his parents, he never achieved the benevolence that comes with self-respect. However, his agitated ambivalence helped him as an orator; it left him free to adopt the mood of any audience. A close associate of Hitler's early years in politics, Ernst Hanfstaengl, describes the shapelessness at the root of Hitler's mesmerizing oratorical power:

> His brain was a sort of primeval jelly or ectoplasm which quivered in response to every impulse from its surroundings....His characteristics were those of a medium, who absorbed and gave expression, by induction and osmosis to the fears, ambitions and emotions of the whole German nation. [He could harmonize because] no single aspect of his temperament was so firmly developed....You could never pin him down, say that he was this thing or that thing, it was all floating, without roots, intangible and mediumistic.

Hitler gained oratorical and political power by his extreme fluidity; only his personal life suffered. Having been too often drawn in by his mother's appeals, he came to deny any love or attachment whatever. In his experience, they had simply increased his vulnerability. Hanfstaengl reports: "He even kept his senior partners [Göring et al.] at arm's length. There was no warmth in his opinions of them." Kubizek recalls: "Adolf hated sentimentality of any kind. The more anything touched him, the cooler he became." Hitler took a small dog with him in the trenches during World War One, and was heartbroken when it was stolen. But he came to mock the memory: *"It's crazy how fond I was of the beast."*

Having been so entwined with his mother, Hitler was never confident of being unlike her, that is, masculine. Like a textbook of machismo, he reassured himself with repeated demonstrations of *"hardness."* At the same time, having depended so much on his mother, he was never sure he would get away with his daring rebellions. When Hitler began his epochal murders, he apologized as if speaking to his mother:

> *When I think about it, I am extraordinarily humane.* [Pause.]
> *[But] I see no other solution but the extermination [of the Jews].*
> [On a different day:] *I would prefer not to see anyone suffer, not to do harm to anyone. But then I realize that the species is in danger and...sentiment gives way to the coldest reason.*

In these passages Hitler spells out his identity problem. Each day, Hitler first claims to be kind like his mother, then immediately corrects himself to say he is distinctly unlike her and is instead harsh, like his father. Adolf made very similar excuses, chatting over two different lunches. Kubizek, in their adolescence, also heard many repetitions from Adolf: "There was in his nature something firm, inflexible, immovable, obstinately rigid....Adolf simply could not change his mind." Saddled with an "ectoplasm which quivered in response to every impulse from its surroundings" (per Hanfstaengl)--an automatic urge to please--Hitler relied on rigidity to ward off anyone who might seek to influence him or to *"do his thinking for him"* (his complaint about mothers).

"I would prefer not to see anyone suffer": true to his word, Hitler refused to visit any of the murder factories, and he rarely approached the battle fronts. Reality might shake decisions based on abstract thinking. *"The species is in danger"*: this strange claim--one of his few recorded rationales for the Holocaust--had coded meanings for Hitler. First, *"species"* meant Adolf and his Germanic mother, both of whom he avenged, or even protected retroactively from Alois, by removing all Jews. Second, he also must refer to Germany and the world being in danger from himself, Adolf Frankenberger-Hitler, the part-Jew. (He had just strewn almost all of Germany's able-bodied men

across Russia.) Third and most piquantly, he could also say he was saving Germany from continuing to be German by the public exposure of her worst tendencies: racism, militarism and suicidal vainglory, in a context that assured terrible retribution.

Always, Adolf was back and forth. Like his father, Adolf took pride in wearing a uniform. Father and son were each glad to belong to a group, at last. But Adolf also endorsed the scrubbing of his house-proud mother. Kubizek saw: "Even more than from hunger, [Adolf] suffered from the [slightest] lack of cleanliness, as he was almost pathologically sensitive about anything concerning the body. At all costs, he would keep his linen and clothing clean." For this fastidious, insecure, chaste vegetarian, each additional notch of disenchantment had cut further into his attachment to life.

Hitler's final solution was to be a mama's boy and at the same time, his father's son. By his unconscious calculations, he had to hurt one to help the other. Screaming for vengeance, in his unseen text he would dishonor them both, to honor them both, simultaneously. He marched the German Army into Russia without a defined target or a winter coat, and began to murder all the Jews he could find. In this manner, he closed the books with his father's people and his mother's as well.

A Boyhood without End.

Adolf's image of his father was frozen at the time of father's death. The authority figure of Adolf's world still had the gigantic, ominous and omnipotent quality that a severe father has for a young boy. Adolf's mother also undermined Adolf's emergence from childhood with her over-protection and her fearful insistence that he was too weak and sickly to mingle with *"extremely robust boys."* Crippled by each of his parents, even after their deaths, Adolf endlessly worked at proving manliness --to convince himself. Another Viennese, Sigmund Freud, had the goal of helping patients recognize that their dramatic complaints were based on ordinary misery. Hitler did the opposite. The troubles of mishandled children may seem far removed from those of a shrewd and vicious Leader of eighty million people. However, the final solution Hitler designed for his problems translated the ordinary misery of a single family into a global catastrophe.

The problem itself is common enough. The psychiatrist Margaret Mahler found many children whose actions, on their small scale, resembled Hitler's strutting. There is a turning point, a time of strain and confusion when children start to leave mother's side for brief expeditions on their own--if mother approves. If she does not approve, as Klara Hitler did not approve (a late example was her scorn for Adolf's "crazy trip to Vienna"), a lifelong conflict is set in motion. Adolf's own demands for *"blind loyalty and obedience"* signal what the atmosphere of his home had been--in parenting, you get out what you put in.

In such captivity, any hint of independence risks bringing down wrath and rejection. A desperate show of rage and power, such as a child's tantrum (or a despot's military invasion), gives the child (or adult despot) temporary reassurance, but does not resolve the conflict. Mahler describes the situation:

> On the one hand is the toddler's feeling of helplessness [without mother]...and on the other hand is his valiant defense of...the emerging autonomy of his body. In this struggle...[with] anger about his helplessness, the toddler tries...to approximate the forever lost illusion of omnipotence....[Accordingly] he may get caught up in an uncertainty...[which is] the effect of insufficient separation [from mother]....As a result, fusion, or reengulfment, remains a threat [and lure] against which the child must continue to defend himself.

Hitler kept his mother's picture hanging over his bed, and slept alone; he took no other wife. (Eva remained merely an occasional houseguest.) Adopting at times the other side of the same game, Adolf would refer to Germany as if he himself was an over-involved and possessive mother: *"I am Germany and Germany is I....Whatever you are, you are through me, and whatever I am, I am only through you alone."* Despite such boasts, he also feared getting too involved. He was "caught up in an uncertainty" like the children in whom Mahler saw "emerging autonomy....[despite] insufficient separation." Recall from the previous chapter that Hitler warned: *"Young lads belong with other young lads and away from their mothers."* Without acknowledging his sarcasm, Hitler raged on: *"A mother's love is too great to keep her from constantly making every effort to help the boy, to pamper him."*

No one wants to be eaten alive or to go naked, but through Adolf's first years, Klara forced her only surviving child to choose between the extremes of being engulfed and overwhelmed, or being abandoned for being independent. So began Hitler's impossible struggle. Leaving home brought the death of his mother, but Adolf's tensions continued. He insists he was *"anything but good,"* but his warning against coddled boys who run to mother gives a different picture of his youth. He praised his father's *"iron determination"* and called himself *"ice-cold"* with the *"coldest reason."* To fight engulfment, he imitated this over-simplified, monolithic view of his punishing father. He struggled to seem evil.

The German psychiatrist of families, Helm Stierlin, contributed a profound essay on Hitler reviewed in the next chapter. There and elsewhere he reports work with adolescents who resemble Mahler's toddlers. He finds the emotional "binding" of children both common and devastating:

[In] mystifying the child about what he feels, needs, and wants ....separation [from mother becomes] the number one crime.... The resulting conflicts can be unbearably intense and guilt-laden as Hamlet (among others) has shown....The child suffers an archaic, terrifying ambivalence. Caged into a closeness from which there is no escape, he loses all [or fails to achieve a] sense of autonomy....This triggers murderous wishes--i.e., wishes to bite, mutilate, and destroy the mother--...and [triggers] self-destruction...[despite a] sense of uniqueness and strength.

The dealings of mothers and children have in most hands been cautiously and respectfully reviewed--indeed, nearly exempt from evaluation. It has taken the art of a Shakespeare to broach the subject. But there is no fundamental reason to believe any human emotion would be necessarily excluded. It all depends on how the love affair plays out as the junior partner gradually gains strength and experience. Some romances end in respectful compromise, some in death. Even compromise includes a degree of frustration and annoyance that the parties choose to accept, but not necessarily forget.

Which emotions carry through from childhood? It seems they all do. In Stierlin's view, the caged and murderous son, Adolf, "becoming newly bound-up (or symbiotically fused) with Germany," could turn his rage on her. The evidence of Part One is that Hitler did "mutilate and destroy the mother[land]," before proceeding to self-destruction. It is a tall order to imagine that a charismatic leader would, even in a trance, set out to ruin his own country; however, in Hitler's case, the only question is, why? No one doubts that he did ruin Germany, step by step.

Respect and Identity.
He could be only a slave or a conqueror. Limited to either appeasing or opposing the will of others, Adolf Frankenberger-Schicklgruber-Hitler had no clear identity of his own. Forced by his parents to an extreme of anguish and obligation, one way or the other, he could find no resting point. Death was the only way out, a conclusion he reached as a boy. In revenge for his years of service as a handmaiden, he claimed a dramatic setting for his departure, with a large and attentive audience, and the total destruction of those who had sentenced him to a wretched

life of Sisyphean agony. He called his life: *"mein Kampf [my struggle]."* He came to monstrous acts; he struggled without end.

In his conscious thinking, this struggle took the form of promoting nationalism and racism. A Germanic mother had pitted Adolf against a half-Jewish father. Railing at Jews coincided with family politics, as did trumpeting the virtues of Germans. Since Adolf's father had illegitimate children with Christian women, Adolf called Jews wily seducers who polluted *"German blood"*--and left each listener to define and defend his or hers.

His positions grew more radical from a sense of dishonor brought on by his mother's coddling and her claim that he was weak and sick. By way of compensation, he wanted to appear *more* honorable than others. He ordered what they did not dare suggest.

Forced to oppose the father he admired and copied, Adolf tired of life early, becoming grim, over-serious and depressed. His big brother ran away and his little brother died. With his father's death, Adolf at thirteen became the man of the house. Struggle had been honorable, but victory was bitter--it would always remain intolerable. Beneath awareness, he felt guilty for surviving; he slid out of school. Having been drafted into his mother's camp, he crept toward vengeance for that burden. Perceiving her opposition to his father as a kind of racism, he found racism to be the crucial problem facing society. Still serving two masters, Adolf declared Jews evil, but at the same time proved them the opposite: helpless and helpful. Not constrained by ties to anyone, Adolf was free to take up the most brutal and direct methods. Still smarting from Evian, on *Kristallnacht* Adolf burnt every synagogue and put every tenth German of Jewish heritage into Dachau or the like. Still the West made no response; all borders remained nearly closed. In his appalling way, Hitler worked to end racism. With the Holocaust, finally the world listened.

It was savagery, but Hitler meant to be shot and cremated with the other Jews. His suicide was the goal and cornerstone of his plan. For Hitler, disgusted by life and sensitive to shame, as one who knew what it was to crave respect and identity, to him the gassings were mercy, as well as revenge. With one stroke, he could serve both his masters. In any case, he saw only numbers on a page, the body counts. He never visited a slaughter house or a labor camp. He himself injured no one. The Germans did it.

Politics Echoes Boyhood.
The 1919 Treaty of Versailles that ended World War One punished Germany harshly. The treaty made a natural target for Hitler, given his family background. He blamed Jews-- English Jews supposedly demanded the Treaty and German ones (*"the November criminals"*) foisted it on Germany. As he protested, the spell-binding orator drew on his feelings of having been betrayed and captive. His boyhood never ended.

Still raging at his confinement as a child, Hitler the politician insisted on *Lebensraum*, the freedom to expand. Yet conquering Poland made him feel *"hated"* by the world, that is, isolated and abandoned. This shudder of fear came because he had symbolically broken his mother's restrictions. He retained a fear of losing his bond with her. And without access to an external viewpoint such as that described in Chapter Fourteen, he could not revise nor escape the emotions his personal history had given him.

Punishment was his way around this dilemma, and had always been the path to reunion. His mother authorized and supported his impudence; the small boy would not have been so brash without backing. Klara took voyeuristic pleasure in the beatings, counting the strokes; they also insured Adolf's allegiance to her. In his turn, Adolf became a voyeur of sadism, one never sadistic himself.

In the repeating cycle of his youth, Adolf would muster his nerve and oppose overwhelming authority, to show himself not a cowering mama's boy. This earned harsh punishment. The punishment would drive him to the solace of his mother's bosom once again--until the next day. As Chancellor, he never ceased searching for a punishment that would, paradoxically, end his pain by sending him back to his mother, at last as dead as she.

He advocated hatred and aggression with all of his enormous powers of persuasion--but he could not forgive hatred or aggression. Hitler punished Germany for betraying the supplicating, *"humane,"* feminine (mother-like) Hitler and for embracing the fierce, *"ice-cold,"* masculine (anti-mother) Hitler. The more vicious the impostor racist nationalist could persuade Germany to be, so much the worse should be her punishment. In particular, for murdering defenseless women and children in the Holocaust, Germany would pay endlessly. Hitler had ranted against the Jews since his days of wandering Vienna, but when it came time to punish those who actually killed this Jew or that Jew or all the Jews, the world-criminal would be his vaunted *"Deutschland! Deutschland! Deutschland!"*

Echoing his struggles with his father, Hitler's attitude towards constituted authority alternated between reverence and scorn. This alternation extended to any standing structure, whether political or architectural. The scale merely expands: personally owning an entire nation faced Hitler with the international order, then led by Britain. Out of respect for his mother, he could not let authority figures alone. Out of respect for his father, neither could he prevail.

No one should ever forgive Hitler. His early life tells how he came to be a monster and what kind, exactly, but he was personally responsible for the deaths of fifty million people. He was personally responsible for the systematic murder of peaceful civilians: six million Jews and millions of Roma gypsies and

Slavs, including Soviet prisoners of war. Hitler was personally responsible for plunging Europe into war in 1939, and for keeping her there long after Germany's defeat was obvious. He teaches that human nature has a dark side, one that any ruthless opportunist can draw upon. He teaches that fairy tales can have shattering endings.

Impact of This Concept.
Why dither over the quality of the murders done by this twisted recluse? At issue are peace of mind and confidence in the human race (the only well-defined race). If Hitler was just an ordinary guy who had a run of luck, he could happen again any time. If Hitler had complex, hidden motives and enormous political gifts, favored by events--a rare person perhaps never to be seen again, a phenomenon, not just a catastrophe--then we can sleep better. The popular belief is that Hitler hated Jews and loved the greedy gamble of aggressive war. But hate and greed are too common. Racism alone does not make a society pluck out its own eye, as Germany did, gassing her Jewish citizens. Greed alone is not enough to make a society commit suicide by waging a war of one-against-all. Hitler was anti-racist, and racists might pause before adopting his destructiveness. [Burning southern black churches can revive national concern for minority rights--Selma revisited.] Because Hitler mocked German nationalism, tin-drum patriots have to explain the suicidal edge when they seduce their countries into war.

In dramatic works, the mass media present cold-blooded violence as an ideal, a token of personal maturity and freedom, vicious but impressive, almost honorable. This ideal was adopted by Hitler. If he was a Mama's boy strutting, his pose may lose some of its lustre.

If Hitler proves to have been irreparably damaged as a child, the system of harassment that shaped him may come into question--both the hovering mothering and the ferocious fathering.

As discussed further in Chapter Fifteen, the eldest surviving child is usually a mother's mainstay. The limelight brings both preference and obligation for the child. Prudence dictates that neither should be carried to an extreme, but the weaker the marriage, the more reliance falls on the shoulders of the first-born, and preference corrupts.

The Romance of Racism.
How pleasant to believe we are better than they! The joy of such beliefs has dazzled great masses of people throughout history. The resulting murderous eruptions are common enough--nearly annual--but in daily life, racism has to be polite to work. Murder is hard to ignore. Racism is about preference, quiet, chilly and incremental. Rather than injure directly, it simply bestows a gift elsewhere: the "No Irish need apply" job advertisements of a century ago, or the more recent "White only" toilets. Murder interrupts; inflammatory and provocative, it cries for vengeance. Our American lynchings have traditionally been one at a time, at night, performed by parties unknown, a mob, preferably hooded. Isaac Babel created literary horror with his detailed accounts of Cossack pogroms that had always been anonymous and remote. Ukraine is unbowed by those private, piecemeal sins, but Germany now continually apologizes for her official, public orgy. Chancellor Helmut Kohl pleads: "This [now] is a sensible government that makes sensible decisions."

Hitler ruined racism. Each foreigner killed in Germany gets world-wide media attention as a victim of racism (Germans killed in Miami are merely statistics). Martin Luther King, Jr., could take a handful of murders and bombings and turn a whole nation around. A few murders, and the official, public, televised racism of Birmingham, the firehoses and head-busting of 1963, carried the United States Congress that would not raise a finger for the Jews of Europe twenty years before. President

Lyndon Johnson could declare in front of a joint session: "*We shall overcome!*" No one laughed at the "we." The world held its breath.

Each generation must first admit it is racist, to learn to leash its racism. Hitler's lesson may need repetition. Lacking a major external enemy, America may once again declare herself a racist nation of white Protestants, mostly illiterate. Hitler also poisoned nationalism, by equating it with racism: the German nation was one race, one *"Volk,"* as he called it. He built a cheap automobile to give conceit a shape, make the *Volk* idea seem real--and mock it as shabby. He proved that a nation that flatters itself into reckless aggression will reap the whirlwind. This was the same lesson the Corsican Napoleon had taught Corsica's French conquerors, one hundred thirty years before. The message bears repeating, and the Austrian Hitler forced Germany's *Wehrmacht*, in its summer clothes, to live off Russian snow.

As Napoleon had, Hitler kept pushing the button for more war until he made his lesson clear. Corporal Hitler openly despised the German military caste with its saber-cut cheeks and courtly airs. He remained the student who had been drawn to Vienna for its culture: the art school, the opera, the library. There, even a homeless shelter was good enough for him. For those who would be high and mighty, he taught about gullibility and racism.

In reality, we are all nearly identical. That is why we can intermarry and swap blood, kidneys, hearts and livers. The biochemistry of mitochondrial DNA mutation suggests that we are all descended from one individual, one hearty mother Eve whose progeny now cover the earth; anthropology says that she lived in Olduvai Gorge in Kenya. In short, we are all Africans. Those who wandered out of the sunlight have faded to white or yellow over the millennia. Presumably, the ones forced to leave early were mostly the riff-raff.

Strenuous efforts have been made to link mental acuity to skin pigment. However, the existence of a stupid tribe would imply that somewhere on earth, the smart died off. In this fantasy land, foolish sons and daughters were more likely to survive. This bizarre notion manifests the genes for gullibility and racism that were favored by the original conditions of human life. These genes predominated during our evolution. To survive hard times, the hunting-and-gathering bands needed gullible men to risk their individual lives to protect the women and children, game lairs and fruit trees from the hated and supposedly inferior men of the next little band.

We have to diet. Like the tastes for salt, sugar and fat--also developed in times of scarcity--the ancient warlike traits no longer serve us well in urban life, with its overfed managers, diverse populations and global economy. Less fat, sugar, salt, racism and gullibility. Of course, these things will always be appealing; we are made that way. But we know better, so we limit our binging. We wish we were recognized as superior beings by our race (that is, without having to work for it). We hope the next President or Chancellor is going to be completely fair, honest and wise. But we know better.

Counter-Arguments.

Many have read in Hitler's actions only ordinary motives of pride, greed and anti-Semitism. His stream of blunders they explain by claiming Hitler had two heads, one smart and the other dumb, sleeping by turns. But why would he hate Jews so much--more than anyone in recorded history? Even a half-Jewish father beating him does not explain such explosive rage. Father's beatings did not break Adolf's runaway half-brother, the bigamist saloon-keeper, Alois, Jr.

Neither can Hitler be explained as the product of aberrant genetics. His first thirty years brought not even a drowned cat as an augury of his future. Some claim evil exists to test our virtue and belief, but this evasion has lost meaning in a century renown for the global scale of its evil, a century that has nearly worn out the terms "death march" and "fire storm" and "genocide." Working in Connecticut courts, I have evaluated fathers (steadily employed, sober, white) who repeatedly and secretly broke the bones of their own infants. Humans have the capacity for limitless savagery--usually incited by what they themselves have suffered.

Even Hitler's greatest blunders have their defenders. Dunkirk might have been an effort to appease England and reach agreement on spheres of interest. Or it was a sop to Göring, to give him the glory of finishing off the Tommies. Stalingrad bought time; hanging on permitted the orderly retreat of the huge Caucasus salient by tying up the Red Army. However, Britain might well have made peace had Guderian been allowed to take her army. And the rash Caucasus strategy itself needs explaining.

There is much to explain. The arch-racist of modern history was a victim of racism. The most fanatic German nationalist led his country into the doomed repetition of World War One he had sworn to avoid. He then repeated Napoleon's disastrous invasion of Russia. As an ending, the champion of defiance and determination crawls into a rat-hole and shoots himself--after getting Germany to destroy herself and after getting his companion, Eva Braun, to do the same. No ordinary man could have done all this, and no simple explanation works for Hitler.

Hitler was searching for catastrophe, from first to last. However, during the earlier period, his opponents stumbled in astonishment. They changed, not Hitler. They learned to ask no quarter and to give none. Hitler thundered that only honor and duty should concern Germany; meanwhile he repeatedly took her too far and then interfered with her Army. In the time of diplomatic victories, he insisted he preferred military victory. But military victories only prompted him to announce new and larger aggressions. Once he was losing, he would allow no changes whatever in strategy. Instead, he promised magical weapons and magical events: Britain or America would quit or fight Russia. He never announced his personal goals; he did not know he had them. He did not know he meant to push Germany until she broke, then mock her. He praised Germany as a seduction into suicide: praise as hate. He cursed and murdered the Jews and restored their homeland: curses and murder as love. Calling himself the Leader [*der Führer*], he proved to be the Messiah of Death; that was the balm he offered one and all. It seemed sweet enough to him. All Hitler sought for himself was a glorious death.

The Prior Image of Hitler.
The seven major psychological studies of Hitler are reviewed in the next chapter. Each has contributed to the view taken here. All agree that Hitler saw in the world around him images of his family's internal struggles. Memories of childhood preoccupied him and shaped his major decisions. This inner tumult made Hitler unable to work, marry or start a family. Shut out from life himself, he took views which were not realistic or humane. He did claim both of those qualities; he hoped to be allowed to join the dance.

Besides specialists in the workings of the mind, others have tried to grasp Hitler. His major American biographer, John Toland, saw the stunning contradictions in Hitler's results: "When he died so did National Socialism and the Thousand-Year Third Reich. Because of him, his beloved Germany lay in ruins. The greatest irony of all was that the driving force of his life--his hatred and fear of Jews--was thwarted. He had intended the elimination of six million Jews to be his great gift to the world. It would lead, instead, to the formation of a Jewish state."

A renown British authority on Hitler, the Oxford don Alan Bullock, leaves unspoken his suspicion that Hitler actively courted disaster: "The baffling problem about this strange figure is [whether]...he was swept along by a genuine belief in his own inspiration [or]...deliberately exploited the irrational side of human nature, both in himself [sic] and others, with a shrewd calculation." Bullock instead carps: "[Hitler as egotist:] It was when he began to believe in his own magic, and accept the myth of himself as true, that his flair faltered....[As manipulator:] It is easy to forget the astute and cynical politician in him....[As amateur:][He showed a] mixture of calculation and fanaticism."

Bullock again suggests Hitler abused Germany: "As soon as the interests of Germany began to diverge from his own, his patriotism was seen at its true value--Germany, like everything else in the world, was only a means, a vehicle." In recent *New Yorker* interviews with Ron Rosenbaum, Bullock goes farther: "The man [Hitler] destroys himself...making the German Army stand in front of Moscow....[And] the man could have had half of Russia on his side against Stalin [by sparing Ukraine]." Bullock sees several faces at once: "Hitler wasn't a madman. He was an extremely astute and able politician....He was the great actor who believed in the part....I originally took him as solely interested in power; I now think the ideology is central....this belief he was the man sent by Providence." Ultimately, Bullock concedes: "The more I learn about Adolf Hitler, the harder I find it to explain."

Hugh Trevor-Roper, likewise an Oxford professor raised to the Peerage for his work on Hitler, agrees: "His character remains elusive. It remains a frightening mystery." Trevor-Roper remains impressed: "Even when he was dead they carried out his wishes....He certainly had an extraordinary power ....He was convinced of his own rectitude....[and] took himself deadly seriously....[and as] a rare phenomenon....He was not an adventurer....The fact is that he nearly won the war....There were three or four moments in the war when he really could have won it." Ominously, Trevor-Roper feels that Hitler was not like most historians: "Hitler was never confused about anything." If he did not win the war, presumably he chose not to.

Ernst "Putzi" Hanfstaengl, himself a published historian and a Harvard graduate, was Hitler's intimate from 1920 until 1934; then the Nazi foreign press officer fled for his life. He recalls Hitler in the Munich Beerhall Putsch of 1923: "To a great many staid and established members of the audience he represented little more than an adventurer. Nevertheless, they had been tempted by the voluptuous picture of power he had painted for them." Hitler then told Hanfstaengl his method:

> When I talk to people...I always talk as if the fate of the nation was bound up in their decision....Every individual, whether rich or poor, has in his inner being a feeling of unfulfilment....Slumbering somewhere is the readiness to risk some final sacrifice, some adventure, in order to give a new shape to their lives....It is my business to canalize that urge for political purposes....Millions of their countrymen died in the [First World] war, and when I appeal for an equal sense of sacrifice, the first spark is struck.

Affectionate to the end, Hanfstaengl paints a forlorn Hitler drunk with power: "Momentum had driven him into an extreme position from which there was no escape....His limited provincial mind had finally swallowed this twisted Nordic and Nazi myth...[that] provided him with the one [firm] mental buttress in a dream world of infinite proportions....[He was] like an airman in a fog, who loses all contact with the earth." Despite the tender apologies of sycophants, much remains to be explained.

War is popular. Whether won or lost, it defines and unifies each nation involved. But the Holocaust proved Hitler strange.

Robert Wistrich, the Neuberger Chair of Modern European History at the Hebrew University of Jerusalem, writes in *Antisemitism, the Longest Hatred*:

> This intensely ideological, mystical and deeply irrational character of Hitler's antisemitism...made the Holocaust possible. In his eschatalogical world-view...the "final solution of the Jewish question" was indeed the key to world history, to the future of Germany, of European civilization and of the white, Aryan race ....In its fanatical intransigence [Hitler's final] testament represented the...bimillenial disease that had been raging intermittently in the heart of Christendom.

Wistrich calls Hitler "mystical and deeply irrational." President Franklin D. Roosevelt sounded a similar religious note on D-day (June 6, 1944), calling Hitler and his Nazis "apostles of greed and racial arrogance." But Hitler practiced no religion; the extermination had its roots in his personal history. The tensions of his early life made him a suicidal hate-monger.

Only Lose, Only Valiantly: 1941.

Hitler wanted to be stopped and punished. His twin offensives of 1941 renewed his effort to get to an ending quickly. Confined in boyhood, Hitler could not stand to wait passively. He attacked all along the thousand-mile-wide western lip of Russia. The Germans would have made only a single wave, had they stood shoulder to shoulder. Their only hope was the punching speed of the tank divisions, but these Hitler hobbled. At the same time, tortured by his father's ghost, Hamlet-Adolf killed his father's people and waited to be beaten for it. Already forced onto the defensive, and with winter crushing his troops, Hitler declared war on the U.S. immediately following Pearl Harbor: he pressed to quicken his defeat.

Hitler did as much damage as he could. The invasion of Russia could have aimed for the oil fields at Baku. However, nothing in the advance planning suggested Baku as a principal target. Rather, Hitler later announced his *"economic"* interest in Baku as a cover story for avoiding Moscow--as a way not to win, and a way to prolong the carnage. Overmatched, another man might harbor his forces and fight a delaying game. The strategy of the professionals in OKH (the German Army's General Staff) from 1939 onwards was to play for a stalemate, but Hitler had a different end in mind. As in his boyhood, he needed to defy valiantly the overpowering odds and to lose, valiantly. He sounded this theme when first notifying the German people that they had opened war. Hitler thundered many righteous excuses, then ended with bleak and foreboding talk of surrender and death. Despite having begun an unprovoked war, Hitler did not offer to win:

> *[Unless] victory is secured...I will not survive....Should anything happen to me....[Never] surrender....We are facing a hard time....with a ridiculously small State....[The] November 1918 [surrender] will never be repeated....I myself am ready at any time to stake my life--anyone can take it...so I ask the same of all others....It is quite unimportant whether we ourselves live.... [There is] sacrifice that is demanded of us....[We are] resolved never to surrender...[instead] master every hardship and difficulty.*

The stakes, said Hitler, are my life, and yours: *"I am ready to stake my life; I ask the same of all others."* The viper Hitler-Iago smoothly hisses: *"It is quite unimportant whether we ourselves live."* Hitler held Germany fully accountable, to the last man. From age fifteen to fifty, he put them all into battle. He had truthfully promised:

> *The German people has learned its lesson, and a collapse such as Germany underwent thanks to her credulity [in 1918] will not be repeated....One should cut off all possible lines of retreat oneself....I would not think of some rotten compromise.*

Cutting off retreat kept blood flowing and bombs falling; it assured the complete destruction of German military capability and of Germany. The Holocaust-Shoah branded her forever. The Messiah led the Jews to freedom, and Germany, too. Each was free of the other and he was free of both. So ended his life's struggle.

Hitler and Suicide.

Hitler committed suicide. Eva Braun Hitler, his wife-for-a-day, committed suicide next to him. Remarkably, it was her third try since taking up with Adolf. A previous attempt occurred when he left a pistol with her, then abandoned her. A year earlier a similar oversight had cost the life of Geli Raubal. Another intimate acquaintance of Adolf, Renate Mueller, leaped out a window to her death soon after their brief liaison. Unity Mitford put a bullet into her brain as well. In all, six women committed suicide, of the seven reputed to have spent time alone with Adolf.

Hitler's hope of inciting the suicide of a woman dated back at least to age fifteen, when he told Kubizek in great detail of his plan to jump off a bridge with his loved-from-afar Stefanie. In the trenches of World War One, he was called "the woman-hater" because of his unusual abstinence. He had nothing to do with women until he was nearly forty; public scrutiny then forced him to deflect rumors he was homosexual. By then he had discovered methods to bring about his long-desired result, and his niece, Geli, shot herself after a spat. She had complained: "My uncle is a monster. You have no idea what he demands of me!" Adolf attended the autopsy on her corpse.

His liaisons had been very brief, but the rising politician reluctantly confined himself to Eva after her second suicide attempt: *"Obviously I must now look after the girl."* Adolf first asked the surgeon who sewed up her neck: *"Do you think Fräulein Braun shot herself simply with the object of becoming an interesting patient and of drawing my attention to herself?"* Reassured in the negative, Hitler announced: *"You hear, the girl did it for love of me."* Years later, he exulted again over Eva: *"the girl who, after many years of loyal friendship, came of her own free will to [Berlin], already almost besieged, in order to share my fate. At her own request she goes to her death with me."*

Adolf brought about a mixture of rage, despair and self-loathing in his women friends. His method has gone unrecorded, although several hinted that his sexual preferences were unusual. Renate complained that he lay on the floor groveling and begging her to kick him. In any case, he spent little time on women. He took Eva into his bunker-mortuary only for their final two weeks of life. When he enticed Germany to her doom, it was done openly, with public speeches full of harsh shouting and soaring hopes. The sorcerer worked his wiles with an audience of one or one million. Adolf-Iago had an astonishing ability and an insatiable appetite for getting others to ruin themselves.

The Jews were victims of his cajolery, too. Had they either resisted or dispersed, the Holocaust could not have happened. Again, promises: the Jews stood in orderly lines to wait for trains, having been promised that there would be work for all at the other end. Elie Wiesel, in his book, *Night*, wrote about his whole town ignoring the pleas and warnings of a man who had escaped after such a train ride. Few could believe that gas chambers waited to kill them. As a boy, Wiesel did not believe it even when he stood in front of the heaped corpses of children burning in a pit. No one had ever seen or heard of such a thing, so how could it be? Why waste skilled workers with a war going on--why would anyone bother?

'To defy and to avenge, no matter what the cost': these were Hitler's watchwords. If the world would not willingly accept Jews, he would make it wish it had.

Hitler and Moses.

The Holocaust made the surviving Jews eager to leave Europe, and shamed the British and Americans into making room for them. The Jews went back where they came from. After the treacherous and devastating collaboration with Hitler by France, Holland, Italy, Romania and Hungary, most Jews who survived wanted to leave Europe. The Poles actually killed those who tried to return. Symbolically, the Messiah led the Jews back to the Promised Land, across the bodies of the six million. To use the term, Messiah, may seem a sacrilege; the title began with Moses, who led the Jews out of bondage and into Israel the first time. But Moses did not do his work gently:

The Bible and the Torah tell us that Moses led his people wandering through the desert. In metaphor or in fact, they spent forty years in the "terrible wilderness, wherein were fiery serpents, and scorpions and drought." [Deut. 8:15] Those who had been enslaved in Egypt perished. The Bible explains this as the Lord finding fault and cursing them: "Surely there shall not one of these men of this evil generation see that good land, which I sware to give unto your fathers." [Deut. 1:35]

Moses himself was barred. In fact: "All the generation of the men of war were wasted out....for indeed the hand of the Lord was against them, to destroy them." [Deut. 2:14-15] Here the Haftorah comments: "The generation of murmurers did not perish entirely from natural causes. God hastened their annihilation, so as to enable their children to pass over the Jordan." [Ht p.745] The Bible makes clear that destruction in those times included "the men, and the women, and the little ones, of every city, [leaving] none to remain." [Deut. 2:34] The Haftorah comment calls this "extermination." [Ht p.747]

Hitler efficiently murdered six million Jews. He had first tried to persuade his coreligionists in Germany to leave. Hitler could say that his appointment as Chancellor proved Germany no place for Jews. Hitler insisted on staying behind to add his burnt corpse to the others. This too echoes scripture. Moses is quoted: "Furthermore the Lord was angry with me for your sakes....I must die in this land...but ye shall go over, and possess that good land....The Lord thy God is a consuming fire." [Deut. 4:21-24]

Tauromachia.
Another way to view Hitler's career is as a kind of bullfight. The Spanish bullfight is hardly a fight: the bull nearly always dies, because the man has the tools to kill the bull. The drama depends on how close the bull comes to winning, but the choice is up to the man. The bull is scorned if he does not try to kill when given the chance. The man is scorned if he does not bring the bull close.

Hitler led Germany through furious charges. His capework was magnificent, using first the Jews, and then small victories, and finally just the words, Honor, and Fatherland, to drive the bull to distraction and exhaustion. At last the Russians stormed the Chancellery, and the sword passed swiftly downward to pierce the heart.

The German bull had rare bravery. Hitler showed it well. Several times the bull seemed close to success. Hitler earned both ears and the tail as trophies for his capework and his deft sword: so impressive had he been the authorities destroyed everything he built, to prevent its use as a shrine. Such was his monument.

Chapter Thirteen

OTHER VIEWS

Prologue.
Journalists, diplomats and finally, historians and psychoanalysts have pondered Hitler ever since 1923, when his trial for an unsuccessful revolution brought him his first national exposure in Germany. The early investigations provided the facts on which my work is based, and many of their insights have been useful, either in stimulating my own, or in confirming my approach. The confusion of the historians was noted in the previous chapter. However, the psychologists and psychiatrists agree that certain events and tensions twisted young Adolf's development, producing a man with unusual strengths and weaknesses. Each view emphasizes a different piece of the puzzle. My effort has been to fit together these views as well as recent scientific studies of young children, to create a new understanding of Hitler as a man with strange motives which were hidden even from him.

A young person feels smothered and oppressed when subjected to constant concern, anxiety and interference. Ruinously extreme mutual devotion embittered Adolf Hitler and his mother. Fathers can also become over-involved, as noted in the discussions of Judge Daniel Paul Schreber by Sigmund Freud and, separately, by Morton Salzman. A routine of interruptions is harsh no matter how quietly delivered nor whether done in the name of love, protection, education, discipline, religion or any other excuse for sadistic harassment.

Hitler never stopped defending himself; despite this red flag indicating emotional abuse in early life, few mention the harm done Adolf by over-attention. As noted below, Helm Stierlin, Rudolf Binion and Norbert Bromberg briefly allude to this critical problem; others, not at all. However, psychiatrists such as Melanie Klein and Margaret Mahler have explored the overprotected child's profound confusion and anger. The previous chapter quoted Mahler regarding the continuing battle by children caught and encapsulated by an intrusive, over-attached parent. When Hitler made similar cries of rebellion and vengeance, Germany listened.

However, once Hitler had won Germany's loyalty, her demand for his leadership made Germany another oppressor, and another target for his rage. For public consumption, Hitler designated foreign enemies: the Versailles Treaty victors, the Jews of the world and the Bolsheviks. He never complained verbally of any personal memory of oppression except at the hands of his schoolteachers. Instead, the war was Hitler's two-edged protest, uniting him with Germany and then, in striking her down, cleaving her from him. His emotional life never emerged from the child's struggle between trying to separate and trying to belong, a struggle in which he involved all the world. Such is the conclusion of the present work. Now review the prior studies of Hitler's outlook. Noted below are all seven of the major psychological studies in English.

Emphases of the Early Work.

Dropping on Germany a million copies of Walter Langer's report would have ended the war early--by 1943 Langer had predicted for Hitler a dramatic suicide. But the Office of Strategic Services and the Central Intelligence Agency kept the report secret for twenty-five years. Langer also saw that Hitler's feelings about his mother had echoes in his statements about Germany. Acknowledging Langer, Helm Stierlin considered how Germany took on personal, maternal meanings for Hitler. But the first recognition of the intensity of Adolf's rage towards his *"Motherland"* came from Rudolf Binion. Alice Miller's discussion of brutality focused more on the physical abuse of the young Adolf by his part-Jewish father. Erik Erikson emphasized Hitler's power not merely to lie but to create myths. Erich Fromm analyzed Hitler's death-loving destructiveness. Norbert Bromberg noted Hitler's disordered personality and abrupt changes in outlook.

Others have offered valuable material on Hitler. Part One quoted the generals who worked with him closely--those impartial enough to have criticized his decisions and to have been dismissed by him. Other chapters have referred to August Kubizek's personal experiences with the adolescent Hitler, as well as the comments on Hitler's personality by the British historians, Alan Bullock and H. R. Trevor-Roper.

Langer, Stierlin, Miller, Bromberg, Fromm and Erikson are all psychoanalysts, investigators who do painstaking, detailed research into individuals and families. Binion is a historian at Brandeis who has written extensively on Hitler. Their views of Hitler's personality are presented in more detail below. The first to publish his views was Langer, although few besides President Roosevelt saw the original edition of his work.

Langer.

Others have failed to see even after the fact the significance of Hitler choosing suicide. Walter Langer predicted it beforehand, in a passage that deserves special emphasis:

> **Hitler might commit suicide....Not only has he frequently threatened to commit suicide, but...it is the most likely possibility....It would not be a simple suicide. He has much too much of the dramatic for that, and since immortality is one of his dominant mo-**

tives...he would stage the most dramatic and effective
death scene he could possibly think of. He knows how
to bind the people to him, and if he cannot have the
bond in life he will certainly do his utmost to achieve it
in death.

This sweeping summation in 1943 proved entirely accurate in
predicting the manner of Hitler's exit two years later. Langer
only did not recognize that the war itself was Hitler's "dramatic
and effective death scene." Caught up in the catastrophe, no
one could imagine that Hitler had set the world on fire to em-
bellish his suicide. The composer Richard Wagner had used
such an image, but only in operas. Hitler had more imagina-
tion. He had his death always on his mind. Langer noted that
on Hitler's brief tour of newly conquered Paris in June 1940,
his main interest was the tomb of Napoleon. To others, that
triumphal tour of the conquered capital might have seemed the
pinnacle of Hitler's career. Hitler instead felt challenged by the
sepulcher of carved white marble; he burst out: *"I know how
to keep my hold on people after I have passed on....My life
shall not end in the mere form of death. It will, on the
contrary, begin then."*
      Interviewing dozens of prisoners of war and refugees who had
spent time with Hitler, Langer understood him to be preoccupied with "[a] basic fear of death....that demands that he become immortal....The great danger [in 1943] is that if he feels
he cannot achieve immortality as the Great Redeemer he may
seek it as the Great Destroyer....**He will fight as long as he
can....The course he will follow will almost certainly be the
one that...wreaks the greatest vengeance on a world he despises.**" [emphasis added] Langer was the first to note Hitler's
oath:

*We may be destroyed, but if we are, we shall drag a world with
us--a world in flames.*

In Langer's view: "[Hitler] has not lost complete contact with the world....There is a definite moral component in his character no matter how deeply it may be buried or how seriously it has been distorted." But Langer also saw that no notion was too horrible for Hitler, who felt his every threat had to be carried out, to avoid appearing cowardly. Langer understood that Hitler was trying to appear bold and determined, and as: "[one who] struggled endlessly against overwhelming odds and obstacles....'never-say-die.'" The confusing result was ruthlessness mingled with guilt. Suicide might appear a way out of the struggle between belonging and separating, an identity crisis Langer called a "Jekyll-and-Hyde [alternation between] a very soft, sentimental, and indecisive individual....[and] a hard, cruel, and decisive person with considerable energy."

Violent crime or a split personality usually signals terrible abuse in childhood. Years before Kubizek published corroborating anecdotes, Langer recognized: "that [to Adolf the] whole world would appear as extremely dangerous, uncertain and unjust." Langer finds echoes of Adolf's struggle with his father: "Throughout his later life we find him searching for a strong masculine figure....[However,] in the end he turned upon them one after another." Raised under his mother's wing, Hitler wanted to avoid ever again needing a protector. Langer saw this reaction: "To grow strong became the dominant motive of his life....The whole 'Führer' personality is a grossly exaggerated and distorted conception of masculinity....[a] cover-up for deep-lying tendencies that he despises....[He] has managed to convince millions....[but] he must prove to himself, over and over again, that he is really the type of person he believes himself to be....Every brutality must be followed by a greater brutality."

Germany would suffer because Hitler denied feeling rage towards his mother. Langer concluded: "Hitler has written very little and said nothing about her publicly [but] every scrap of evidence indicates that there was an extremely strong attachment ....[Yet] she was overprotective....[Therefore] his distrust of both men and women is so deep that in all his history there is no record of a really intimate and lasting friendship....Unconsciously, all the emotions he had once felt for his mother became transferred to Germany....Hitler almost always refers to it as the *'Motherland.'*" As he had done with his mother, Hitler blurred any distinction between his emotions and Germany's, says Langer: "The madness of the Führer has become the madness of a nation....a reciprocal relationship exists between the Führer and the people."

In sum, Langer's views are very close to the conception presented in this work regarding Hitler and his mother. Remarkably, this is a case of parallel inspiration, separated by forty years. His work came to my attention after early drafts of my own had already been written and privately circulated. The discovery was most reassuring.

Erikson.
Condemning Hitler as a spellbinder and myth-maker, Erik Erikson angrily called him: "the most ruthless exploiter of any nation's fight for a safe identity...[an] expert of the cheap word....[whose] pathological attachment to his mother [made for] a two-faced image of maternity: the mother...[sometimes] treacherous, and in league with sinister forces." Without making an explicit connection to Hitler's struggle with his mother, Erikson also saw Hitler "openly despising the [German] masses."

Erikson agreed that Hitler had goals beyond victory, including a taste for catastrophe. The analyst sees World War Two as "superbly planned and superbly bungled" and says Germany was "trapped into" it by her evil "[Pied] Piper." Himself a refugee, Erikson struggled at length to explain how Germany went wrong. He spent little time examining Adolf's personality

or childhood experiences, and dispensed with Alois Hitler briefly: "[Adolf's] father was a drunkard and a tyrant." He quoted
unnamed psychiatrists saying, respectively: "[Adolf was] a psychopathic paranoid, [an] amoral sadistic infant, [an] overcom-
pensatory sissy [or] a neurotic laboring under the compulsion to
murder." Contenting himself with explaining how Hitler performed, rather than why, Erikson stated his own verdict. In
accord with Chapter Nine of the present work, Erikson's conclusion emphasized Hitler's effort to contaminate Germany forever:

> [Hitler] was first of all an adventurer....[who] knew how to ex-
> ploit his own hysteria....[and to] represent with hysterical aban-
> don what was alive in every German....[Hitler became] a gang
> leader who kept the boys together by demanding their admira-
> tion, by creating terror, and by shrewdly involving them in
> crimes from which there was no way back.

Miller.
    Although seeing that: "[humans] suffer from the tragic com-
pulsion of having to avenge, decades later, traumata experienced at an early age," Alice Miller nearly ignores Klara Hitler's subtle, but pervasive, oppression. Instead, Miller presents
Adolf Hitler as a survivor of his father's physical abuse. She
overlooks Alois, Jr., the older half-brother of Adolf, who survived the same hippopotamus whip. Junior led an undistin-
guished life after running away from home, dodging from Austria to Germany to England and back. Junior's mother, Franziska, died when he was two. However, Adolf's mother stuck
by him. Klara, so preoccupied with her "sickly" son, was
merely the stepmother of Junior. Therein lies the difference.
    Miller blames the father's brutality for Hitler's frequent
nightmares of being persecuted. But Alois was not a sadist like
the older Schreber who stayed home to make a religion out of
"disciplining" his sons. Alois was a promiscuous and opinion-
ated man who left home each day to work or, after retirement,

to drink. Persecution came to Adolf at the hands of a mother
dedicated to the protective confinement of her only surviving
child. Furthermore, her extreme cleanliness would have created a constant whirlwind of scolding. Despite her focus on the
physical, Miller does view Adolf's mother with concern:

> All the biographers agree that Klara Hitler loved her son very
> much and spoiled him....a contradiction in terms if we take love
> to mean that the mother is open and sensitive to her child's true
> needs....[Adolf's] relationships with women, his perversions,
> and his whole aloof and basically cold relationships with people
> in general reveal that he never received love from any quarter....
> His mother was not capable of love but only of meticulously ful-
> filling her duties.

Thus Klara gave Adolf good reason to hate her. Miller infers
that Adolf would also be angry at his mother for failing to protect him from his father. However, Hitler admired his father's
strengths. Paradoxically, Adolf wished for the father's courage,
in order to shrug off the father's abuse. In words that equally
protest his mother's coddling, Hitler demands that childhood
should be the opposite of his: *"I want the young to be violent,
domineering, undismayed, cruel....There must be nothing weak
or gentle about them."*

Mercilessness is memory with a reversal of fortune, says Miller: "It is possible for a child to forget about the extreme acts
of cruelty he or she has endured and to idealize their perpetra-
tor. But...the drama now unfolds in front of the spectators with
an amazing resemblance to the original situation....The child
who was once persecuted now becomes the persecutor....[How-
ever] beating is a never-ending task--behind it hovers fear of the
emergence of one's own repressed weakness, humiliation, and
helplessness." Miller neglects to note that the same pressures
made seduction a never-ending task for Hitler: he betrayed
Germany as his mother betrayed him. For the racism he hated
in her, he punished Germany.

Father's mixed race added to Adolf's pain and to his confusion. "There is probably no more reliable common tie among the peoples of Europe than their shared hatred of the Jews," offers Miller, who is Swiss. She believes secrecy about grandfather Frankenberger and the made-up name created a "state of constant jeopardy." By screaming anti-Semitism, Adolf tried to cleanse himself. His hands were free since, notes Miller: "There were no bonds of affection between Adolf and his father." In daily life, Adolf was nonetheless "the awestruck admiring child," she says, with the conflicted result: "In Hitler's view, the Jews were characterized by a specific mixture of Lucifer-like grandeur and superiority...on the one hand and ugliness and ludicrous weakness and infirmity on the other."

Hitler was a great impostor. Dr. Miller and many others still believe in: "the savage fanaticism of Hitler's later actions, which represent a gigantic struggle to purge his self [of] degradation." She only overlooks that he purged his degradation by transferring it to Germany. Like so many, she accepts his claim of good intentions towards his Mother(land): "In symbolic terms...the liberation of Germany and the destruction of the Jewish people...could have made him like a happy child growing up in a calm and peaceful situation with a beloved mother." Miller finds that the Holocaust was Hitler's retroactive cleansing of his pedigree.

He could struggle so long as he did not win. Success always created strains in Hitler. Acknowledging a completed victory would tap rage long forbidden to him--rage against his Germanic mother as the undeserving beneficiary of the victory. Without noticing these conditions, Miller did find Hitler emotionally stymied, and condemned to repeat:

> If the path to experiencing one's feelings is blocked by the prohibitions...or by the needs of the parents, then these feelings will have to be lived out....The persecution of the Jews permitted [Hitler] to persecute the weak child in his own self...[to avoid] grief over his past pain.

Fromm.

Erich Fromm offers a devil theory of Hitler, saying he was a self-invented "necrophilic beast" who loved death. Ignoring the strains of Hitler's youth, Fromm poses the question: "How can we explain that these two well-meaning, stable, very normal, and certainly not destructive people gave birth to the future 'monster,' Adolf Hitler?" This question will seem ironic or rhetorical to readers of the present work, but Fromm found no answer. Endorsing the conventional public behavior of the parents and disregarding their private hollowness and sadism, Fromm finds Hitler's defects to have arisen spontaneously, as a quirk of nature. Contradicting Erikson, Fromm applauds Hitler's father, Alois: "a real self-made man....by no means a drunkard....He was not a tyrant, but an authoritarian who believed in duty and responsibility....[He] never beat his son; he scolded him, argued with him...but he was not a frightening figure." This sweeping exoneration dismisses the unanimous testimony of all three of Alois's children who are on record, and much other information. Fromm says not a word about Adolf's grandfather problem.

Seeing "Hitler's hatred of life," Fromm agrees with the other analysts that intense conflicts roiled Hitler's "malignant incestuousness" with his mother: "Hitler's fixation to his mother was not a warm and affectionate one...he had never felt close to her." Getting it backwards, Fromm blames the "mother-bound" child for the coolness: "[Adolf could] live in a kind of 'paradise' where nothing is expected of [him] and everything is provided...even though [mother] is not loved or cared for in a personal way." Completing this astonishing whitewash of the older generation, Fromm calls Klara "a kind and concerned mother...[with much] loving behavior....[without evidence of] deeply hidden hostility or a lack of contact." Yet Fromm observes misery in the paradise of his fantasy:

[Hitler became] a withdrawn, drifting boy....[then] an extremely narcissistic man without any interest in anybody or anything... [but] with a burning wish to conquer, and filled with hate and resentment....His plans to rebuild cities were an excuse for first destroying them....Hitler was in a way a grotesque figure: a man driven by the passion to destroy, a man without compassion, a volcano of archaic passions--trying to appear a well-bred, considerate, even harmless gentleman.

Despite noting Hitler's suicidal taint and his "passion to destroy," Fromm gives the routine verdict that defeats shamed him: "Everything depended now on wiping out the [latest] humiliation by taking revenge on all his 'enemies' and devoting his life to the goal of proving that his [inflated] self-image had not been a fantasy but was reality."   This says Hitler lost because he lost; defeat drove him crazy.   However, Fromm remains perplexed by the military blunders, and blames them on "poor contact with reality....weak will [*sic*]....[and] defective judgement."

In his third effort, Fromm recognizes dark forces at work [emphasis added]:   "Hitler stoked the fire, closed more and more avenues of retreat, [and] brought the whole situation to a boiling point where he would *have* to act as he did.   With his self-deceptive technique he spared himself the difficulty of having to decide....**Unconsciously, and in spite of all apparent efforts to the contrary, his course was set toward catastrophe.**"

Giving several examples, Fromm also sees Hitler staving off guilty feelings: "[Hitler] stopped eating meat after the suicide of his half-niece Geli Raubal, who had been his mistress.... Hitler did not get involved in any of the [physical] fighting with political opponents....He was never present at a murder....It was impossible for his generals to persuade him to visit the front....[Hitler] has not shed blood as long as he avoided *seeing* the corpses."   Fromm's concept of not-seeing has led to the cur-

rent view that survivors of abuse have split-off multiple personalities which must discreetly ignore each other's actions.

As a refugee from Hitler, Fromm refuses to applaud the man.
Instead he warns: "Hitler was no genius, and his talents were
not unique....There are hundreds of Hitlers among us who
would come forth if their historical hour arrived." Fromm does
acknowledge Hitler's danger for Germany and his dark side:
"Hitler was a Jew-hater...it is equally correct to say that he was
a German-hater. He was a hater of mankind, a hater of life
itself."

Stierlin.

In contrast, Helm Stierlin does find Hitler unique, for the
combination of: "his high energy level, his passion for power,
his force of will, his sense of certainty, his belief that he was
chosen by destiny, his radicalism, his hatred of Jews, his crav-
ing for ever more *Lebensraum*, his--seeming or real--quest for
self-destruction, and his ability to recruit followers." Stierlin
considers many of these qualities, positive and negative, to be
based on the intense and prolonged relationship between Adolf
and his mother. Hitler transferred onto Germany his struggle
with his mother, says Stierlin. Stierlin says mother, for her
part, embraced fiercely her only surviving son, rendering him:
"bound and delegated....to absorb her [babying] regressive gra-
tification and, in so doing, [to] nurture her; to redeem her worth
as mother; to provide her with vicarious power and importance;
and, finally, to avenge her." Stierlin reports work with adolescents who resemble Mahler's toddlers. As noted in the previous chapter, he says the emotional binding of children is both
common and devastating:

> [In] mystifying the child about what he feels, needs, and wants
> ....separation [from mother is] the number one crime....Caged
> into a closeness from which there is no escape, he loses all sense
> of autonomy....This triggers murderous wishes--i.e., wishes to

bite, mutilate, and destroy the mother--...and [triggers] self-destruction.

The caged and murderous son, "becoming newly bound-up (or symbiotically fused) with Germany," as Stierlin puts it, would presumably also become viciously rageful against Germany. However, Stierlin, once a *Wehrmacht* rifleman, still believes in his former Leader's patriotism. So do the generals quoted earlier; faith in your superior is part of military discipline. Stierlin claims that Hitler's hatred of Germany came after "the tides of war turned." As a teen-age soldier, Stierlin could not have understood that Hitler himself turned those tides. Even as a mature doctor, Stierlin respectfully quotes Hitler's grandiloquent mythology: *"For the greater a man's works for the future, the less the present can comprehend them....The laurel wreath of the present touches only the brow of the dying hero."* Stierlin finds in these words only heroic qualities: "[Hitler's] defiant loneliness...unyielding self-confidence...[and] total absorption in his projects." However, the passage conceals vicious scorn. Folded into the classical images of heroes, death and laurel, Hitler's convoluted rhetoric offers two angry curses: (1.) orders that seem crazy prove that only the Leader sees the way, and (2.) death in war leads to glory. Hitler demands blind obedience even in the face of disaster.

Wavering in his faith, Stierlin quotes without comment some harsher views. He notes that Binion wrote: "[The war] was a sure recipe for military and national suicide." The biographer Joachim Fest described Hitler's "strategy of grandiose perdition [and] all-out will for catastrophe." Stierlin bends enough to find: "self-destruction in the creative process [*sic*]....[and in Hitler's] reckless risk-taking; his longing for, and preoccupation with, death; and his (covert) invitation to be punished and controlled....It was Hitler's and Germany's problem here that for a long time no really limit-setting and punishing authority was forthcoming."

This nostalgia for father-the-punisher mingled with anger, concludes Stierlin: "[Adolf showed] precariously ambivalent attitudes [of] idealization, obsequiousness, and, as time went by, increasing resentment, contempt, daring defiance and vindictive fury [towards his father]." Stierlin calls the harshness of the illegitimate father a menace to the household. However, a Jewish doctor treated Klara in her last months. Stierlin blames the doctor for Hitler's fulminant anti-Semitism. As noted in previous chapters, Hitler sent the doctor, Edmund Bloch, a grateful postcard and later rescued him from the ovens. Stierlin discards the testimony of Hitler's attorney that Alois was half-Jewish. Nonetheless, Stierlin concludes: "[Hitler] grappled with conflicts his family bequeathed him. As an artist, he turned Germany and the Western world into a gigantic participatory theater."

Bromberg.

Like Fromm, Norbert Bromberg finds Hitler universally rageful: "Hitler hated not only Jews but also Blacks, Poles, Russians and ultimately Germans, indeed all mankind including himself." Hitler's childhood left him snarling, says Bromberg: "The great frustration in Adolf was a result of his mother's overanxious treatment of him....[It gave] reasons to dread his mother and even hate her....His identification of his mother with Germany and therefore also of Germany with himself... made for the furious intensity of feeling...his passion to rescue Germany....[that proved] a most destructive aspect of his political policy."

Broadening the war assured defeat. However, Bromberg claims it was a show of "masculinity." He does not recognize the result as a goal, "ignominy and self-destruction." Bromberg instead concludes: "Power was his sole program; all the rest was window dressing....Hitler's vain efforts to disavow unacceptable [mother-like] tendencies by demonstrating 'masculinity' in ever more power and in greater conquests persisted and became more unrealistic until he overreached and brought about his own ignominy and self-destruction."

The Jewish question is more complex for Bromberg. He concludes that Hitler's paternal grandfather was probably Jewish. However, Bromberg sees Hitler's fear of being surrounded by Jewish power as an echo of life with Klara: "[Hitler's] excessively solicitous, pampering mother...[caused his] lasting tendency to see all others as well as himself as either all-good or all-bad....He also hated as well as loved her."

Bromberg announces a bizarre discovery that remains unrecognized in the literature: "[Hitler experienced] a displacement of his fear from women to Jews....around 1928 [*sic*]." Loading hatred of women onto Jews would have been for Hitler a way of shifting hatred from mother to father, as happens in many families. Why this would occur abruptly in 1928 is less clear; Hitler had preached anti-Semitism to Kubizek in 1908, and to the world after 1920.

However, Bromberg also finds anti-Semitism a result of shame: "In his great shame, [Hitler] saw himself as a nonperson, an image which he tried to neutralize by bursts of being a superperson, almost divine. The objectionable image, [along] with the dangerous and evil image, was also projected on the Jews."

Binion.

With little to say about Hitler's father or the Jews, Rudolf Binion concludes that Hitler drew murderous rage from being entangled with his mother, then: "He recreated his infantile situation, with Germany in his mother's place....*'Whatever you are, you are through me,'* he told his (German) followers, *'and whatever I am, I am only through you alone.'*" Held close by his mother, Hitler learned to sense the feelings of others. Binion quotes with approval the Swiss psychologist Carl Jung: "[Hitler] is the loud-speaker which magnifies the inaudible whispers of the German soul until they can be heard by the German's conscious ear. [Hitler] is the first man to tell every German what he has been thinking and feeling all along." This one-sided relationship created rage, as Binion sees:

> Hitler took to remarking that for Germany the wages of defeat was death and increasingly with the addendum that those wages were well earned. [Hitler said:] *"Get one thing straight...in this war there is only...victory or ruin. Should the German people fail...then it should go to ruin [and] perish"*....Here was the nether side...the hate hitherto buried beneath his consuming love for a mother who had unfitted him to outgrow that consuming love for her.

Such evidence pushes Binion to quote the historian Golo Mann: "There was no attempt that failed to the regret of the attempter; there was only an insane enterprise that was *bound*...was *intended* to fail."

Summary of the Personality Studies.

The psychoanalysts agree the intense relationship with mother dominated Hitler's boyhood. Fear of a repetition kept him an isolated and childless bachelor. Several state that mother's loveless protection and control made childhood a prison for Adolf.

It may seem far-fetched to suggest that a powerful politician might act out impulses stemming from his youth. But Hitler's leadership of Germany apparently served as a vehicle for his feelings about being bound by his mother as her delegate, avenger and savior. Langer and Stierlin describe this. Hitler sought vengeance for his captivity under his mother, but conflict between loyalty and rebellion left him suicidal. Binion saw that, not to die alone, Hitler, all unaware, made war on Germany.

Miller, emphasizing the brutality of Hitler's father and his potentially Jewish origin, sees father as the basis for Hitler's anti-Semitic fear and ferocity. Bromberg agrees on the Jewish ancestry, but concludes mother-hatred became Jew-hatred, a version of the familiar use of expendable, peripheral fathers as family scapegoats. Langer, although writing before Hitler's suicide, is the one who recognized that Hitler, having foresworn the pleasures of life, cared most about his place in history. As refugees, Fromm sees Hitler as a death-lover; Erikson sees him as a cunning gangster.

The insights of the seven analysts support the view that Hitler was an impostor who fooled Germany and the world. He masqueraded as a fanatic nationalist, but his aim was vengeance against Germany, the Jews and the world. He preached racism as a way of hiding from racist persecution himself. His wretched, terrified and terrifying life was invisibly guided by the stresses and conflicts of his childhood as he replayed on an enormous stage his family's drama. His intended role was to become a mythical hero, one who loses valiantly.

Conventional military histories assume leaders seek to win. Most studies of the Second World War find Hitler's direction unconventional. All see that the windy Austrian tramp crucified Germany. He started an unwinnable war and prolonged it to be sure of the most bitter possible end. Outside Stalingrad (Volgograd), exposed to the elements, lie miles of unburied German and Austrian bones where their owners once lay breathing. The bone donors had likewise lain exposed to the elements and their enemies on the level, open plain barren of landmarks or any tree or rock or gully to take cover by. The soldiers were frozen in place by the Führerorder not to retreat even a yard and frozen also by the winter of 1943. That crop of young men's bones yet winter in Russia, the crack specialized rapid striking force of the Sixth Army ordered to stand still and still still in their tens and tens of thousands.

In the end, the only prizes remaining to him who called himself an insatiable conqueror were Eva and Germany, both dead to the touch. And the listed names of the Jews who had waited in line for train and shower, believing like everyone else that Hitler would surely pursue gain. Why bother to ship and kill ordinary people? Anytime even just once in five full years all it could all have been different with one chance meeting. Next we invent that meeting.

PART THREE

ALTERNATIVES

Prologue to Part Three

Hitler begs for a remedy. The horror of a human juggernaut
bound for destruction since adolescence offends the western
belief in the possibility of salvation. There must have been a
way to spot him and head him off. We investigate each train
wreck to see how it could have been prevented--would have
been prevented, had everyone done his or her job. We demand
economic and moral progress as the rewards for honest toil,
truthfulness and faith. It is agony to hear that a man was born
who went bad and got steadily worse until he had dragged the
whole world into the flames of his rage. There must have been
some way to save him, or at least to save ourselves from him.
It cannot be that mankind is like a heap of dry kindling, needing
only a spark to become an inferno of self-destruction once
again. It would be impossible to live and build in a world so
slippery and uncertain. Life cannot be an endless cycle of
construction and destruction. Without hope for a future of
peace, love and harmony, we may as well eat each other like
savages, mat our hair with feces, twigs and dirt and throw
ourselves into the sea.

Chapter Fourteen

HITLER MEETS FREUD

Prologue.

History has its moments of crisis and opportunity when everything hangs in the balance; all is not the heedless elaboration of overwhelmingly powerful tides and trends as told by the ancient Greeks. However, some of these critical moments pass unobserved. A window closes, time moves on, and no one is the wiser.

Throughout five years, Hitler and Freud were neighbors. In this century, two world-shaking revolutions originated in Vienna, one built on the darkest evil of the human spirit, the other built on its endless capacity for growth and expansion. The originators of these revolutions, the Christ and the Anti-Christ, were both country boys dazzled by the capital city of the vast Hapsburg Empire. However, they both claimed to hate city life and often hiked in the mountains. Sigmund Freud had arrived in Vienna in 1860, at the age of four; Adolf Hitler, at eighteen, in 1907. Hitler tramped its streets daily from 1908 to 1913. Freud, who still lived there, was by then gathering fame and students, but each day after lunch he strode briskly forty minutes through town around the circular Ringstrasse. It is a wonder they did not meet. In fact, they may well have met without making note of the event. Freud would be unlikely to remember an austere, dejected young man of twenty selling hand-painted postcards. The card vendor would be unlikely to recall an austere, dejected man in his fifties striding past at a steady clip. They were two very serious men focussed on their own thoughts, too busy to notice each other. When they met again, thirty years later, on the same streets, again they were too busy to talk. In the spring of 1938 Hitler made a brief triumphal tour of the great city he had just conquered and annexed without a shot. Freud was packing to leave. He had not maintained any religious practices but, "having remained a Jew," as he put it, Freud was fleeing to England at the age of eighty-two. It took the influence of a Greek princess and a sizable ransom to escape the new régime. The four sisters Freud left behind would all be murdered. Freud had sent them a huge sum once he reached England, enough to buy twenty new cars, or to get out--if they got the money. The mouth cancer from his cigars also gnawed at him. When Hitler overran Poland with no opposition from the major powers, Freud committed suicide. It was Yom Kippur, the Jewish Day of Atonement.

Hitler, for his part, had publicly burned Freud's books among others by Jews. Hitler then installed a Christian, the Swiss minister's son, Carl Jung, as the head of Freud's psychoanalytic institute in Berlin. Freud had done no less, twenty years before, installing Jung as President of the International Psychoanalytic Association so that it would not become "a Jewish national affair." Freud sought to evade the anti-Semitism of Vienna. That city did not even mark his house until 1979. Vienna itself is mired in hate, but the connection between the two giants--the monster and the genius--could have been otherwise.

The Meeting of Freud and Hitler.

During 1908, the year they lived together in tiny apartment 17 at No. 29 Stumpergasse, August "Gustl" Kubizek had become alarmed by his friend's depression. Hitler "wallowed deeper and deeper in self-criticism" and became so upset over his rejection by the Academy of Art that he declared them: *"a lot of fossilized civil servants....the whole Academy ought to be blown up!"* Gustl was proud of being Adolf's only confidant, but he might have felt overwhelmed.

Suppose Gustl had heard at the Academy of Music, where he studied, or from other students, that a doctor lived around at 19 Berggasse, and offered an unusual new treatment for mental confusion and distress. Of course, he would have heard that established physicians still thought that psycho-analysis was "pornography," and not medical at all, because it emphasized discussion of sex. But Gustl and Dolfi were eager young men searching for new ideas. It could not hurt to try something new, and the walk over to the north side of the Ring would be no more than four kilometers. However, Gustl knew Adolf, like so many others, "would have suffered starvation and misery rather than have appeared to be in need of help."

Perhaps Hitler could bring himself to approach Freud as a fellow observer of Viennese sexual habits. Gustl knew Dolfi liked to tour the red-light district, even if he "grew angry at the prostitutes' tricks of seduction." Adolf was a "woman hater.... [with a] strict moral attitude. His conceptions of love and marriage were definitely not those of his [promiscuous] father ....In Vienna...this was an exception indeed!...[Adolf also] turn[ed] with disgust and repugnance from [homosexuality and] refrained from masturbation."

Freud too assigned negative values to homosexuality and masturbation, and held back on philandering, so these two social commentators might get along well if they compared notes. Certainly there would be no difficulty getting Adolf to talk, only in getting him to Freud's office. The fee would be a problem, but Freud might well refer the young man to one of his junior colleagues. Perhaps the brilliant young analyst Jan Nelken from the Weimar conference could accept a student at a reduced fee, even a self-taught student such as Adolf. On the other hand, seeing the intensity and energy of the young radical bubbling with hates, Freud might want to keep the case himself.

One can imagine there would be the usual wandering discussions that psychoanalytic interviews encourage. As he did so often with Gustl, Hitler would begin on the evils of society and fume with rage. In time, he might recall earlier episodes of indignation at the unfairness of his father's beatings. At first, he would leave out his own measured provocations and the whole orchestrated, ritual quality of the encounters, but this would emerge gradually. In time, he might touch on his father's made-up name, then on the secret ancestry and the incessant fear of being found out, part Jewish, with an illegitimate father. Of course, he would insist on his profound respect for his father for being strong and unmoved no matter what, and for keeping his family secure and prosperous through his steady habits.

Eventually there would come a tearful catharsis when Adolf realized he had never had a chance to square things with his father, having lost him so early. He would regret egging the old man on to fury every day. At last Adolf would recognize how much he had needed his father to help him grow up and become a man. The beatings would first be forgiven as reasonable and even helpful. Later, they would come to seem at least understandable and predictable, if not forgivable.

Secret regrets would emerge about being twenty years old and unable to enjoy anything in life, not women, not work, not school, not even liquor, only the moments of fantasy in the dark of the opera house, or in the few times when, hiking far enough from the city, he had been able to convince himself that he would some day mean something to the masses of people who lived there--he could care about them, from a safe distance.

In time he would weep to realize that he was so driven that he had nothing left for himself. He would see he had been unable to have any real life in the present, being so obsessed with creating somehow a future greatness. He would rage at his father for leaving him with no guide to a more realistic life. Later he would recall that he had steadfastly opposed every effort the old man made to guide him, had in fact opposed and mocked everything about his father: civil service, uniforms, the drinking and the women.

By then it might be safe for Freud to ask if Adolf had any thoughts about his mother, a subject too intense for either of them to touch on until they were well acquainted. Freud might begin wittily by asking Adolf if he *had* a mother, nothing having been said on that side of the equation. Adolf never spoke of her to anyone. Caught off-guard, he would show surprise, then anger, then fear. He would gradually recall the ways that his mother had encouraged his impertinence and his scorn for his father. He had accepted what he understood to be her assignments out of fear of losing her--and lost her anyway, lost them both, was orphaned and alone with only a numbskull music student for company in the miserable existence left to him. One brother a runaway, the other dead; one sister married to a busybody, the other young and useless.

His head thundering like a hammered gong, he would blurt out the stunning eruptions of feeling about his mother: attachment, dependency, love, hate, fear, suffocation, loss and panic. Above all, fear, fear of losing her and fear of getting her--fear of the crushing burden of having been her sole emotional support and fear at having been left alone in the world with no one close. Only later would he recognize that he continuously maintained his life that way, because his fear was stronger than his pain and yearning. He was a woman hater because he was a woman lover; he knew about nothing except women, how to get close and how to stay close and how much it cost to have a constant anxiety over closeness running his life. He was nothing without her. Always he had lived in fear of losing her and would never oppose or criticize her openly. She seemed, in her way, so cold and rejecting, with her scoldings and her washings.

When pressed by the doctor, Adolf would recognize that he was in fact surviving without his mother and that the demands of life were actually fairly simple. His mother had given him a sense of inadequacy and undermined his confidence in the outside world, to keep him home. She had battered him into submission with her fears, while also insisting he would be her avenger and her savior. But how to conquer the world without leaving home?

As his time with the doctor lengthened without damage, Adolf might recognize that, like the doctor, many women were less needy, demanding and intrusive than his mother had been. Of course, he would see the danger: the women who stirred him most deeply were just those who most resembled her. The bleakness of compromises would disappoint a young man raised in the expectation of being his mother's savior and winning her endless gratitude, and winning also the warmth and admiration she had never provided.

The demands of becoming a savior were overwhelming, just as they were vague and inconsistent. There was neither text nor school. One could only study the lives of the great in search of some common thread or experience, yet such study was hopeless; there was no way to recognize the golden fleece even should one find it. Meanwhile, life went on--for everyone else. And yet, the aura of greatness and the high hopes were intoxicating. The road to fame was no more possible to give up than to find. Its shape and dimensions were unknown, but it shone brightly in the mind.

Yet young Adolf might by stages let go of his dreams; his nightmares would ease accordingly. To die in battle on the ramparts is, after all, still a death and just as still as any. To be or not to be: not to be mother's hero would mean not having to be father's enemy. His late mother, being beyond help, would no longer care; even when she had lived, there had not really been any way to help her marriage--the rescue effort was in between a hoax and a delusion, Klara's hoax and Adolf's delusion.

Klara, his mother, had wanted to hold onto her surviving son as the first man she could trust and command. Grooming him as the captain of a mythical battalion on a splendid mission served to keep his interest. No matter what it cost her son, the fantasy lightened her own thoroughly bleak existence. She had told Gustl her marriage did not meet her expectations, but that simply confirmed that she was a dreamer who had always waited to be rescued by some outside power.

In this way Adolf would understand that he and his mother had inevitably separate lives and goals, no matter what their hopes or fears of merging. He could furl his lofty banner as the scrap of cloth it really was, once he admitted it had never been graced by the serious allegiance of anyone. Gradually, reluctantly, gratefully, he could consign himself to merely an ordinary life, and he might then begin to taste the pleasures that are also ordinary enough.

It might be some time before he could seek someone with whom to share his life, or to believe that another woman might not demand from him everything his mother had. He might remain a bachelor rather than risk being plunged again into the maelstrom. But Adolf could not avoid the unspoken lesson in Freud's method. The meetings go on so long that the schedule and the fee become second nature and the hours seem to run together, and always the analyst waits, watching and listening. The respect shown the patient, almost certainly for the first time in his or her life, is like water in the desert. It awakens new growth and thought and provides a new model of what human contact can be like.

There is no magic in this kind of work. Pain and grief are not banished, the past remains irretrievably marred, and the hard choices of daily life have still to be made. The difficulties of human life are inescapable, but Freud's way can ease the isolation and rigidity that stifle growth. What we survive become lessons, if we are free to observe and react.

Freud's interviews can also instill the habit of examining life and thought. This second life, as an observer of one's own life, is a specially protected one. At least in prospect, the observing self can find nearly equal interest and instruction from watching either successes or disasters that befall the active self. This change in viewpoint is modeled on the attitude of the analyst. The new way of keeping score confers the huge benefit of serenity. The contrast is very clear with the desperate misery in which Adolf was mired by having impossible goals and at the same time having to ward off the stream of signals from the real world that the goals were indeed impossible.

The Other Road Is Taken.

Kubizek failed to get Hitler into Freud's office. Left to himself, Hitler's method of dealing with his painful beginnings was to lose himself in bootless projects. At such times, says Kubizek, Hitler was: "oblivious of his surroundings, he never tired, he never slept. He ate nothing, he hardly drank." Yet he produced nothing of value: an imitation Wagnerian opera, a few poems to a girl he refused to meet, watercolor postcards, some drawings of buildings (never people). Later came the autobahn, the jet plane, the V-2 rocket (ballistic missile), but none of these were in themselves his projects, just props for his boomerang scheme of war-making.

The Second World War was a Hitler project. In its last year, as it reached fruition, he hardly slept, and was sustained on injections of vitamins and amphetamine stimulants--just as with the small projects of his youth. Still his faithful entourage clung to him and obeyed for, as Kubizek saw: "there was an incredible earnestness in him, a thoroughness, a true passionate in-

terest in everything that happened and, most important, an un-failing devotion to the beauty, majesty and grandeur of art."
Hitler's performances convinced even himself. However, when there was a tangible goal against which to measure the perform-ance, a different conclusion was drawn. Even the mesmerized Kubizek saw: "The more tenaciously he repeated his own slo-gan, *'I want to become an architect,'* the more nebulous did this goal become in reality."

And so it would be with *"National Socialism"* and fanatic German nationalism. These too were goals or wishes of a man too conflicted by internal struggles to achieve anything but the destruction of all that existed--always in the name of making way for something wonderful. He insisted Jews caused all his problems and frustrated his efforts; he set out to destroy the obstacle. Kubizek recalls Hitler's rejection by the Academies of Art and of Architecture. Already paranoid at twenty: "He spoke of *the trip-wires which had been cunningly laid*--I remem-ber his very words--*for the sole purpose of ruining his career."*
All problems were someone else's fault.

Hitler was an impostor from first to last. He had not been allowed to draw breath on his own, and never developed a life of his own. He simply took on whatever camouflage he thought suited the occasion. He borrowed the appearance of living. He liked best the image of the dedicated genius; it guaranteed isola-tion and reverence that together put him beyond confrontation. Meanwhile, he began a war against Germany. He began with an elaborate seduction, then arranged a horrible punishment for her, for listening.

The last word is rightly Kubizek's, for Gustl was Adolf's first victim of seduction and punishment. After living with Adolf for a year in Vienna, Kubizek went back to Linz for a visit, only to return to an empty apartment. He would have had no word from Hitler ever again, except that, twenty-five years later, Kubizek wrote the newly installed Chancellor to ask if he was the same man. As if he was speaking for all of Germany, Kubizek concludes:

> Naturally, I meant far less to Adolf than he did to me....He had learnt to appreciate me as an eager audience. He could not wish for a better public as, because of his overwhelming gift of persuasion, I agreed with him even when in my heart I held a completely different opinion.

Now consider what manner of man we have been dealing with.

Chapter Fifteen

THE ENCAPSULATED
ELDEST SON
SYNDROME

As Sophocles pointed out with the legend of Oedipus, the romance between a mother and her son cannot succeed. The best a boy can hope for is ordinary disappointment. Even that poor fruit is won only by a prudent middle course, guided by the child's needs, between the agony of abandonment and the terror of engulfment. These opposite errors both leave the child unfit to enjoy other people--unfit for love. Abandonment makes for a heart of stone. Excessive intimacy blinded Oedipus to the world. In effect, the same befell Adolf Hitler.

Adolf's entanglement with his mother was the most intense experience of his life. His few statements about her indicate that he idolized her, in his conscious thoughts. But she produced conflicts in him noticed in adolescence by Kubizek, who also remembered the intimacy between the adolescent Adolf and his mother, their isolation from the world and Klara's struggle for dominance over her son. With mother constantly on his mind (and her picture hanging over his bed), Adolf carefully avoided new romantic entanglements. In this sense, he was as blind to the world as Oedipus. Or is it that the ancient tale of Oedipus--he stabbed out his eyes because of having sex with his mother--was a metaphor implying just the kind of blindness Adolf suffered from.

Sophocles saw this problem twenty-four centuries ago. Human nature has not changed. Many families fall into the trap of usurping the life of a child, betraying the child's trust and neediness by imposing a program designed to meet instead the needs of a parent. In this way, the parent makes a slave or servant of the child, instead of building strength and confidence of self-expression.

Although guided by other forces as well, Hitler illustrates the encapsulated eldest son syndrome (EESS), a common source of pain and suffering. The well known "Oedipus complex" describes only the son's part when, in fact, the whole family joins in creating the EESS. Father abandons mother: he dies, leaves, drinks, or has interests elsewhere. Even simpler, mother and father may jointly conspire to evade and avert emotional intimacy. Lacking a husband who responds to her feelings, mother recruits her first son for the purpose.

A child starts out weak, small and totally dependent; a child cannot say, No. Indeed, the EESS son feels greatly honored, privileged and important. However, he is overwhelmed. A boy cannot be a man, even if everyone wants him to be. He cannot match his mother's maneuvers as an emotional equal and companion. Worse yet, by overriding what the boy himself needs, the family robs him of the chance to be a boy. To all outward appearances, they may treat him very well, but they deny his feelings, wishes and interests. They offer every inducement except respect.

His own self put aside, shut away and ignored, the son becomes bitter and hateful. Next he worries; he feels danger because of the depth of his own rage: *surely they will see how murderous I feel and strike me down!* The tension produced by this fear leads to preemptive attacks. Although initiating the conflict, these are excused on pretexts of vengeful vigilance. The Oedipus legend gives this aspect full play. There the father ordered his newborn son killed after being told that the boy would one day kill him; later, the two battle to the death. Both were out for blood. When a son's natural urges for mastery and achievement are forced back within the family, the family is in peril. If the urges are not softened by filial affection--father being remote or cruel--so much the worse. Such encapsulation results from continuous effort to draw the son back and contain him within the family. Oedipus shows the legendary extreme of this--he even had his children with his mother.

Sigmund Freud interpreted and popularized the urges felt by Oedipus. But the urges had been accommodated or encouraged by the family. As discreetly told by Sophocles, the legend proposes a series of unwitting accidents to bring mother and son together. In real life, the whole family may cooperate to promote the doomed romance.

The condition is often hard to treat: the family reinforces the problem, even while asking for help. Often what they want is help to continue in the face of outside criticism or complaints. EESS cripples the eldest son emotionally, Hitler being one example. Outsiders become upset; they judge the child by how he functions in the world. They overlook the special emotional tasks he performs within the family. In Hitler's youth, his schoolteachers flunked him and Kubizek found him strangely depressed and enraged. Yet Adolf and his family saw no problem with his loafing around the house for years, nursing huge aspirations. They explained his condition as an interest in the arts.

Focusing on another aspect of EESS, Helm Stierlin calls the son "bound and delegated" to represent his mother (see Chapter Thirteen). But at an earlier stage, the problem is the isolation and desperation of a mother caught in an empty marriage. She chose the marriage to avoid a more intense encounter, but the result is that she is caught and needy. In EESS, her solution is to conscript and train her son to become her savior, with the burden and honor that implies.

Case A. H.

Adolf Hitler formed a relationship with his parents that bede-viled him all his life--long after their physical deaths. In that sense, he never completed childhood, he never emerged from its coils. Whatever his effects on others, his course was pri-marily a struggle to resolve, symbolically, the conflicts of his childhood home.

In the Hitler family, the father was twice the mother's age, and she was his third wife. Following the wedding ceremony, he went back to his office to finish the day. In effect, he came home only to beat his sons. Alois gave full expression to the role of an EESS father. Mother told Kubizek how disappointed she was by the marriage. She turned to her son. She indulged Adolf, excusing herself by calling him sickly. He was the lone survivor of her first five children. When he asked, she bought him a piano. He studied just a few months; actual playing of the piano did not interest mother or son. The purchase showed their attitudes: Adolf protested his isolation and entrapment with outrageous demands; his mother soothed him by granting them. Learning to play would have reduced the piano trans-action to a musical event. By refusing to play, Adolf rejected his mother's gift, and kept the right to take vengeance later. He could ask anything of her--except separation. Klara convinced Adolf he was too weak to mingle with other boys. She would call him crazy for wanting to see Vienna, a two-hour train ride away. The results: Adolf and his father had an Oedipal battle every day. And when Adolf did nonetheless go off to Vienna, his mother fell terminally ill.

Outrageous demands, incessant battles, demonstrations of vigor, insistence on blind loyalty and obedience: Adolf's temperament drew upon the early experiences with his family. Unaccustomed as he was to pursuing his own personal inspira-tions, he could not afford to listen to advice from anyone. His solutions had to be rapid and final. He suffered bitter confusion and conflict in choosing his path; delay in executing a decision would permit renewed misgivings. Worse yet, inaction would threaten Adolf's thin hope that he had emerged from his mother's shadow and could manage on his own. Inaction seemed too much like the passivity of his over-indulged, yet suppressed, childhood. Equally, each decision was a gift he withheld until the moment suited him, or until the hue and cry of those awaiting the decision became intolerable.

He focused on rage and revenge to evade having a personal life; he had seen enough intimacy. He kept conspicuously distant from women, and had only formal relationships with men. He did not trust himself to get involved and, nonetheless, stay whole. His experience was with a mother who proposed to do his thinking for him. She invested great effort and concern in him. She therefore felt entitled to his eternal gratitude and loyalty, although he had never made any such agreement.

Her investment in Adolf gave him great vigor and a sense of importance. However, the intensity of his rage signalled a struggle very early in his life, a time when he would have felt impotent and immobile, dependent and helpless, because, as an infant, his life was at stake. Caged or encapsulated and deprived of any means of expressing his horror, he slid it beneath the surface of his mind, to lie dormant until later.

Adolf was never able to surmount his German problem, the one created by the demands of his Germanic mother. He tried to bury his confusion under shouts of ultra-nationalism, but these only led to more rage, since the nation failed as the family had failed--failed to live up to Adolf's exaggerated expectations. His mother's solicitude exceeded his needs. He would feel scorn from her denial of his capabilities, despite her mask of concern. But he also feared to part from her and go on his own. In reality, he survived her. In his war, Hitler's solution was to bring about their joint suicide, with his mother represented by Germany, and by Eva Braun.

As the world discovered, Adolf really had very little concern over what happened to anyone, be they German, Jew or otherwise. This coldness on a global scale echoed the global coldness shown him in infancy, when he was served according to the needs of his parents, virtually to the exclusion of his own needs and wishes. Father needed someone to punish for the sinfulness he could not acknowledge in himself. Adolf's bereaved and captive mother had great need of an emotional connection to allay her fear and rage stemming from a sad marriage and the loss of her first three children.

Adolf survived physically; his minimal needs for nutrition and protection were met. Emotionally, he presents a ravaged countenance; he was condemned to a bleak and friendless life. However much we may feel he deserved the tortures of the damned, in his case, the tortures came before his vicious deeds, not after. Grief for his lost childhood was a major cause for his disposition.

The monolithic figure of his father towered over him always, its image split by Hitler into positive and negative aspects, one to be courted and the other, despised. As Führer, Adolf draped the qualities of his parents on whole peoples: stern, orderly England and seductive, exploitative Jewry. The English he did not like he called *"Jewish or part Jewish."* He did not discuss individual Jewish people--except the one, his mother's last doctor, he sent to safety. Having been drawn into the power struggle between his parents as his mother's proxy, he punished the father-Jews for their intrigues and *"race-pollution."* But the qualities he ascribed to them--the seduction and exploitation-- derived from his experience of his mother.

Adolf served his long-dead mother once again, as her rescuer, by getting rid of the Jews who had darkened her life. He adopted her view that misfortunes are caused by others, over whom one is powerless--the perspective of a victim. He must have seen himself as a victim when Evian closed the door on his fellow Jews, and unexpected (and unwanted) victories put six million in his hands in the two years that followed. This gave him twenty-four times the number he had been trying to get rid of. The joke was on him. He decided on murder; the next Jew to cross his path would die.

That was the prologue to the Russian invasion. The invasion had the additional EESS function of making a hollow-eyed fool of his Motherland, overwhelmed and blown to bits in her monstrous arrogance, and he saw to it she was. Once he had won her loyalty, her demand for his leadership made Germany another oppressor, and a target for his rage.

In EESS, the boy feels smothered and oppressed from constant concern, anxiety and interference. Their ruinous mutual devotion embittered Adolf Hitler and his mother. Repeated interference is harsh no matter how quietly delivered nor whether done in the name of love, protection, education, religion or any other excuse for sadistic harassment. Alice Miller has been quoted earlier:

> All the biographers agree that Klara Hitler loved her son very much and spoiled him....a contradiction in terms if we take love to mean that the mother is open and sensitive to her child's true needs....[Adolf's] relationships with women, his perversions, and his whole aloof and basically cold relationships with people in general reveal that he never received love from any quarter....
> His mother was not capable of love but only of meticulously fulfilling her duties.

The war was Hitler's two-edged protest, uniting him with Germany and also, in striking her down, cleaving her from him. His emotional life never got past a struggle between trying to separate and trying to belong, a struggle he resolved as noted by Langer:

> *We may be destroyed, but if we are, we shall drag a world with us--a world in flames.*

The Steerforth/Leonardo Syndrome.
Dickens published in 1850 the novel *David Copperfield* in which a major character was the impetuous young man named Steerforth, his mother's much prized only child. Steerforth's mother: "was a widow, and rich, and would do almost anything, it was said, that he asked her."

Dickens saw Steerforth as defiant, being too aloof and too cynical for ordinary work or ordinary virtues, yet charming and bright enough to get away with it. After Steerforth collects the violent end he has earned, his grieving mother is berated by her female companion: "Is your pride appeased, you madwoman? *Now* he has made atonement to you--with his life!" The woman shows her disfiguring scar and describes an EESS family: "In your pampering of his pride and passion, he did this [scar].... [You] stunted what he should have been!....You were exacting, proud, punctilious, selfish. [Even] show[ing] the ardor that I felt in all he did, [I was] dropped, and taken up, and trifled with, as the inconstant humor took him."

Sigmund Freud in 1909 published one of his favorite essays, *Leonardo da Vinci.* [Hitler lived only a mile away, but was still an unknown.] Like Dickens before him, Freud saw EESS: "Like all unsatisfied mothers, [Leonardo's] took her little son in place of her husband, and by the too early maturing of his erotism robbed him of a part of his masculinity." Freud found that "the small human's long-drawn-out helplessness" and over-involvement with his mother resulted in "a stunted adult sexual life." Like Hitler, Leonardo was not known to have had sexual involvement with anyone. Freud found the confusion of mother-son enmeshment recorded in the *Mona Lisa*, whose "smile contained the promise of unbounded tenderness and at the same time sinister menace."

Freud's own family background bore many aspects of EESS. His father was twice his mother's age. She was his third wife, and younger than his children. Freud particularly remembered his father yelling that Sigmund would amount to nothing. Freud's tyrannical mother possessively called Freud, "My golden little Siggy," when he was past sixty. He was her only son for many years. She told him he was bound for greatness. Sigmund was even asked to name his baby brother; he offered a conqueror's name. Under his mother's wing, Sigmund led an isolated life of study. The reverse of Hitler, Freud demanded his mother get rid of the family piano; she did. No doubt all this conditioned him to find so much meaning in the *Mona Lisa* smile. He insisted that women were consumed with envy for men, but his mother had worn the pants in his home.

Famous EESS Men.

Beethoven was his mother's first child and never married. The most intimate relationship he ever had with a woman came when he successfully sued his brother's widow for custody of a nephew, only to return the boy when it appeared the younger Beethoven had no interest in becoming the image of his famous uncle. Ludwig had pleaded his love to certain women, but only those unavailable for marriage. He lived as a hermit. If it helped his music, it was still a thin life.

Picasso was his mother's first son. She marveled that she could not stop looking at him. His way of chopping up women in his paintings created the "cubist" school of art. Four children were biologically derived from him by his various mistresses, but he stayed faithful to canvas and clay. The son of an artist, Pablo dropped his father's name, Ruiz, in favor of his mother's. His own first son drank himself to death by forty.

Wanting twins, Ernest Hemingway's mother decided to raise him as a girl, like his sister. Not until her son started school did he put away his dresses and tea set. His novels were about the struggle to prove manliness. He married four times and produced three sons before shooting himself. Once an opera singer, mother had pursued fame; her son won it for her.

President Lyndon Johnson slept with his mother the nights his father was away, and brushed her long hair. Daytime found him "playing games with her that only the two of us could play." As a senator, he would phone his mother for advice. His two daughters married in the White House, all good and proper, but when women challenged his manhood, he answered. When Vietnam acted up, again he had to act bold.

The price of fame is diligence, single-minded pursuit of a goal. The world might say that the music, art, writing and politics of these masters was worth the price of EESS. But they themselves had no choice about their lopsided lives.

Not at all Feminine.

The EESS man is never sure he is one; because of the exclusiveness and the overwhelming strength of his ties to his mother, he is never sure he is not female, or at least feminine, like her, and not really a man at all. Accordingly, the EESS son works twice as hard to prove he is a man.

Any child growing up starts with the image of mother, the adult present most of the time and therefore the teacher, the one to imitate. Daughters can spend their whole lives imitating their mothers; they never have to break away. But a son is told to be different.

For the EESS man, held by his mother and estranged from his father, the burden is double. To prove himself a man, when he has very little of that name to imitate, becomes a painful challenge. Father is distant, alien or alienated, one way or another.

The compulsion to add new proofs of manliness is a hallmark of EESS. Correspondingly, access to "feminine" outlooks and aspects is easy for these men, and may surprise those who know only the sternness they present in their official capacities. The photograph of "Hitler unmasked" in the front of this book catches a moment when the world-destroyer lapsed into spontaneous imitation of the giggling schoolgirls he was visiting. This was not mockery or manners, this was Hitler literally for-getting himself--forgetting the self he was otherwise careful to show the world--and instead reacting with a piece of his mother's friskiness. Klara was twenty-nine when Adolf was born; he was raised by a woman still young. As the murdering dictator of Greater Germany, he was still just a girl at heart.

Conclusion.

It is either a harsh shock or a welcome reassurance to think that Adolf Hitler had a common malady that could have been relieved, had he put himself in expert hands. Freud, Dickens, Stierlin, Mahler (cited in Chapter Twelve), Miller and others have described pieces of what is better dealt with as a family pattern, the encapsulated eldest son syndrome. In order to produce lasting change, the entire system should be confronted and shifted. In favorable cases one individual may recognize his or her part in EESS and withdraw participation to a signifi-cant degree, but the most effective approach is to get the whole family into one room and provide all of them with an under-standing of how they have tied themselves down by knotting up the family. EESS keeps all their lives in a rut.

While the syndrome has been discussed as a three-person partnership between mother, father and the eldest son, the most important family members to include in therapy will be those ignored by the system, since they will have the most to gain by any change. The sister or brother who has been left by the wayside, relegated to watching the drama unfold, will be the best ally of the therapist for remembering and interpreting how the EESS portrait fits the family. (Paula Hitler gave a remarkable portrait of EESS at work between her brother and her parents.)

In order to produce acknowledgement of EESS by the three principals, it is often necessary to bring in even more remote outsiders, such as the grandparents forced to watch the corruption of the new generation. Aunts and uncles, friends and neighbors may serve in this capacity as well. (Kubizek would have been invaluable.) The therapist should go farther and farther afield, as necessary, until enough pressure is brought to bear on the family to get them to see what they are doing. Carl Whitaker showed that outsiders could be introduced into the privacy of therapy by having the therapist ask for help and more help in trying to understand what is going on. In effect, the therapist models for the family the humble attitude they need in order to admit confusion, and the questing attitude they need in order to escape their habitual patterns.

When Hitler did get to a psychiatrist in 1918, he was twenty-nine. Like Oedipus, Hitler insisted he had lost the use of his eyes. His parents were dead; he could not look at an abdicated Kaiser and a Germany that had surrendered to end her struggle. At the moment when he faced the end of the only employment he could stand--war--the doctor thought he was crazy, a hysteric. He was, by his behavior. However, as the world would learn, he was also EESS. EESS is more complicated, a family disorder, but unlike hysteria, EESS can be fixed.

THE END

—

N O T E S

Quotations are listed below by page number. The source for each quote is given [in brackets]. The initials [in brackets] refer to an entry in the Bibliography. The number following the initials is the page in the source text. Sources are also listed for certain statements.

Page

8   "A Lesson": Hitler quotations (respectively) BR 169, note 5; FG xxx; TJ 620; SH 104; SW 1102.
9   "A Plea": Associated Press, 6/26/95 (printed in *New Haven Register*, 6/27/95, p. C6).

Introduction.

22   "At her own request...." [TJ 996]
22   "My only bride...." [BR 22]
22   Eisenhower's actions and reactions, per his grandson. [ED 762-3]
22   "Still having trouble...." [ED 763]
23   "To prove its mettle...." [SW 1102]
25   "The past cannot be pushed...." NYT 12/16/94:A18, quoting Rita Süssmuth.
25   "Germany for the...." Nazi slogan.
25   "We have to decide...." [NYT 12/6/92:3]
25   "To believe that nonsense...." [NYT 12/6/92:8]

Chapter One: Winning by Losing.

30   "[Hitler had] no personal experience...." [BA 144]
31   "The November criminals...." [BR 169]
31   "I follow my course with...." [LW 29]
32   "The German people...will make every sacrifice...." [WW 493]
32   "Centuries will go by...." [SW 1124]
32   "Don't you think I'm fighting...." [GH 412]
34   "I want them to write...." [TJ 1002]

Chapter Two: Starting the Dying.

Chapter Three: Pursued by Victory.

Page

Chapter Four: Into the Abyss.

Page

Chapter Five: Stalingrad and Suicide.

Chapter Six: The Downward Trail.

Chapter Eight: An End Is Made (1945).

Page
116 "Do you think the English...." [SW 1098]
116 "They certainly didn't...." [SW 1098]
116 "The war is lost...." [SW 1103]
    NB: Speer claims Guderian stated this Jan. 24, 1945. [SAb 423]
116 "All he wants is to tell...." [GH 407]
116 Secret negotiations aimed at surrender. [TJ 962-965]
116 "Tried and trusted officers...." [GH 407, 409]
117 "[It is] to defend the capital...." [GH 412-3]
117 "How dare you speak...." [GH 412-3]
117 "This caused a new outburst...." [GH 412-3]
117 "We can't wait." [GH 413]
117 "I don't permit you to accuse...." [GH 413]
117 "I don't permit you to tell...." [GH 414-5]
117 "[Hitler's] fists raised, his cheeks...." [GH 414-5]
117 "The General Staff has won...." [GH 414-5]
118 "Hitler raved and...five officers...." [GH 419-420]
118 "At the beginning of March 1945...." [WW 497]
118 "If the war is lost, the people...." [TJ 967]
118 "The commanders have handled this...." [WW 508]
119 "All right for [removing] the...." [WW 508-509]
119 "Now that fate has removed...." [WW 513]
113 "The army has betrayed me...." [TJ 983]
113 "I'll stop the war at once...." [TJ 984]
113 "Here again is striking...." [TJ 987]
120 "In the final analysis...." [GT xi]
120 "The Führer has made so many decisions...." [TJ 997]
120 "If he did not deceive us...." [TJ 1011]
121 "Irrevocable decision to solve...." [GT 10]

Chapter Nine: The Holocaust as Strategy.

122 "[Hitler had] no personal experience...." [BA 144]
123 "What does it matter...." [HE 80]
124 New York newspapers report shooting of Jews. [WDS 20]
124 "Destruction of Jewry." [NJ 1136]
125 "The Holocaust is the central...." [NY 2/1/93:58-71]
125 "Die Lebenslüge" [NY 2/1/93:58-71]
125 "[The Holocaust is] a trauma...." [NY 2/1/93:58-71]
125 "How can we express remorse for...." [NY 2/1/93:58-71]
125 "[Germans] struggle with contradictory...." [NY 2/1/93:58-71]
125 "They came as innocents...." [NY 2/1/93:58-71]
126 "Germany ceased to be...." [NY 4/22/96:50]
126 "It is impossible to exaggerate...." [NYT 8/2/87:A14]
126 "Centuries will go by, but...." [SW 1124]
126 "Those ultimately responsible...." [SW 1124]
126 "A crime whose immensity...." [NYT 1/20/92:A10]

Page

Page

138 Anti-Semitism among Roosevelt's circle. [BRK 245]
138 "Slamming the[ir] doors...." [WDSb 50]
138 "The ultimate aim of Germany's Jewish...." [TJ 597]
138 Central Office for Jewish Emigration [NJ 567]
138 "If the international Jewish...." [TJ 598]
138 "It is a shameful example...." [HR 259]
138 "Force our hand on the refugee problem." [BRK 239]
139 "The expulsion and exclusion...." [HR 3, 260]
139 Wyman agrees. [WDSb viii, 35-36]
139 Jews murdered 1933-1938. [GM 57]
139 "[Leaving] all their cash and jewels...." [SW 236]
139 Development of Auschwitz. [HR 565-6]
139 "Thereafter, Hitler spoke with somber...." [FG 174]
142 "With the precision and...." [LW 29]

PART TWO.

Prologue.

144 "All happy families...." *Anna Karenina*, opening lines.
145 "There are no...." speech at Univ. of Connecticut School of Medicine, 1988.

Chapter Ten: Father, the Jewish Problem.

147 "The German sovereign." [GG 70]
147 "He got us into this...." [GG 70]
147 "How carefully I always kept...." [TJ 257-8]
148 Race law of 1935 [NJ 535-6]
148 "I do not remember hearing...." [HAa 62]
148 Adolf passed off his father's race. [KA 40]
150 Gestapo repeatedly looked. [WR 149]
150 "Adolf spoke but rarely...." [KA 11, 31]
152 "Whoever wants to understand...." [WR 118]
152 "It was especially my brother...." [TJ 13]
152 "Then barely eleven years...." [HAa 8-10]
153 "When Adolf was about eleven...." [SH 24]
153 "Very strict, exacting and...." [TJ 8]
153 "Iron energy and industry...." [HAa 22, 23]
153 "I resolved not to make...." [MA 156]
153 "Hard and determined as my father...." [HAa 8-10]
153 "Our poor father cannot...." [KA 30]
153 "Whenever [Adolf] heard the word...." [KA 15]
153 "Hearing him speak of his father...." [KA 19, 38]

Page
167 "There is only one thing...." [KA 107]
167 "It was the most impressive hour...." [KA 98-101]
168 "If the German people were...." [SW 1102]
169 "I have therefore decided to remain...." [SW 1125-27]
169 "In that hour it began." [KA 101]
169 "We may be destroyed...." [LW 163]

Chapter Twelve: The Messiah of Death.

171 "In that hour it began." [KA 101]
172 Hitler chronology. [TJ 6-78]
172 "Too few heads" [SW 16]
175 "Hard and determined as my father...." [HAb 23, 24]
175 "The so-called wisdom of age...." [HAb 36]
175 "Adolf spoke but rarely of his family...." [KA 11, 31]
175 "[Some find] in nihilism their final...." [SH 93]
176 "His brain was a sort of...." [HE 265-66, 123]
176 "He even kept his senior...." [HE 181]
176 "Adolf hated sentimentality...." [KA 255]
176 "It's crazy how fond...." [TJ 69]
177 "When I think about it...." [WR 44]
177 "There was in his nature...." [KA 35]
177 "Do his thinking for him." [WO 294-296]
178 "Even more than from hunger...." [KA 160]
178 "Extremely robust boys." [HAa 20-23]
179 "Crazy trip...." [KA 114]
179 "Blind loyalty...." [HAb 689]
179 "On the one hand is the toddler's...." [MM 222-223]
180 "I am Germany and Germany...." [SH 80]
180 "Young lads belong with...." [WO 294]
180 "A mother's love...." [WO 294]
180 "Anything but good." [HAa 20-23]
180 "[In] mystifying the child about...." [SH 52, 51, 33]
181 "Becoming newly bound-up...." [SH 80]
186 "This is a sensible government...." Assoc. Press 6/26/95
190 "When he died so did...." [TJ 1005]
191 "The baffling problem about...." [BAb 209]
191 "[Hitler as egotist:] It was when...." [BAb 209]
191 "As soon as the interests...." [BAb 214]
191 "The man [Hitler] destroys himself...." [NY 5/1/95:68]
191 "Hitler wasn't a madman...." [NY 5/1/95:66-7]
191 "The more I learn about Adolf Hitler...." [NY 5/1/95:50]
191 "His character remains elusive...." [NY 5/1/95:50]
191 "Even when he was dead...." [NY 5/1/95:60-3]
192 "Hitler was never confused...." [NY 5/1/95:60-3]
192 "To a great many staid and...." [HE 98]

Chapter Thirteen: Other Views.

Page
207 "The awestruck admiring child," [MA 175]
207 "In Hitler's view, the Jews...." [MA 178]
207 "The savage fanaticism of Hitler's...." [MA 189]
207 "In symbolic terms...the liberation...." [MA 189]
207 "If the path to experiencing...." [MA 197, 191]
208 "How can we explain that these...." [FE 374]
208 "A real self-made man...." [FE 373-4]
208 "Hitler's hatred of life" [FE 374]
208 "Hitler's fixation to his mother...." [FE 377-8]
208 "[Adolf could] live in a kind of...." [FE 386-7]
208 "A kind and concerned mother...." [FE 372]
209 "[Hitler became] a withdrawn, drifting boy...." [FE 386, 393, 397, 425]
209 "Everything depended now on wiping out...." [FE 391]
209 "Poor contact with reality...." [FE 427-430]
209 "Hitler stoked the fire, closed...." [FE 427, 430]
209 "[Hitler] stopped eating meat after...." [FE 404-5]
210 "Hitler was no genius, and his...." [FE 433]
210 "Hitler was a Jew-hater...." [FE 401]
210 "His high energy level, his passion...." [SH 20]
210 "Bound and delegated...to absorb her...." [SH 99]
210 "[In] mystifying the child about...." [SH 52, 51, 33]
211 "Becoming newly bound-up...." [SH 80]
211 "The tides of war turned." [SH 104]
211 "For the greater a man's works...." [HAa 212-213]
211 "[Hitler's] defiant loneliness...." [SH 80-82]
211 "[The war] was a sure recipe for...." [SH 84, 85]
211 "Strategy of grandiose perdition...." [SH 84, 85]
211 "Self-destruction in the...." [SH 84, 85]
212 "[Adolf showed] precariously ambivalent...." [SH 65]
212 "[Hitler] grappled with conflicts his family...." [SH 18]
212 "Hitler hated not only Jews but also...." [BN 272]
212 "The great frustration in Adolf...." [BN 234-5, 241-2, 233]
212 "Power was his sole program...." [BN 318]
213 "[Hitler's] excessively solicitous...." [BN 215, 277, 285]
213 "[Hitler experienced] a displacement...." [BN 285]
213 "In his great shame, [Hitler]...." [BN 291]
213 "He recreated his infantile situation...." [BR 57]
214 "[Hitler] is the loud-speaker...." [BR 53]
214 "Hitler took to remarking that for...." [BR 34-35]
214 "There was no attempt that failed...." [BR 44]

Chapter Fourteen: Hitler Meets Freud.

220 "Having remained a Jew" [FSc]
220 "A Jewish national affair." [JE 261]
220 "Wallowed deeper and deeper...." [KA 155, 157]

Page
221 "A lot of fossilized civil servants...." [KA 155, 157]
221 "Would have suffered starvation...." [KA 132]
221 "Grew angry at the prostitutes'...." [KA 236]
221 "Woman hater....[with a] strict...." [KA 152, 231-2, 237]
226 "Oblivious of his surroundings...." [KA 200]
226 "There was an incredible earnestness...." [KA 202]
227 "The more tenaciously he repeated...." [KA 182]
227 "He spoke of *the trip-wires*...." [KA 176]
228 "Naturally, I meant far less...." [KA 255]

Chapter 15: Encapsulated Eldest Son Syndrome.

234 "Jewish or part Jewish." [TJ 852]
235 "All the biographers agree...." [MA 180-1, 185]
235 "We may be destroyed, but...." [LW 163]
236 "Was a widow, and rich, and...." [DC 154]
236 "Is your pride appeased...." [DC 870-872]
236 "In your pampering of...." [DC 870-872]
236 "Like all unsatisfied mothers...." [FSb 59-135]
236 "The small human's long-drawn-out...." [FSb 59-135]
236 "A stunted adult sexual life." [FSb 59-135]
236 "Smile contained the promise...." [FSb 59-135]
237 Beethoven history [MG]
237 Picasso history [HAS]
238 "Playing games with her...." [KD]

END OF NOTES

BIBLIOGRAPHY

Source references [in brackets] in the preceding NOTES section indicate page numbers from the following works:

BC: Bekker, Cajus: *The Luftwaffe War Diaries.*
(Trans. Frank Ziegler)
Doubleday & Co., Garden City NY, 1968,
BR: Binion, Rudolf: *Hitler among the Germans.*
Elsevier, NY, 1979 (2nd printing).
BRK: Breitman, Richard and Alan Kraut: *American Refugee Policy and European Jewry, 1939-1945.* Indiana Univ. Press, Bloomington IN, 1987.
BN: Bromberg, Norbert and Verna Volz Small: *Hitler's Psychopathology.* International Universities Press, NY, 1983.
BA: Bullock, Alan Lord: *Hitler and Stalin.* Alfred A. Knopf, NY, 1992.
BAb: Bullock, Alan Lord: *Hitler: A Study in Tyranny* (abridged). Harper & Row, NY, 1971.
CW: Churchill, Winston: *The Second World War* (6 vols.). Houghton Mifflin, Boston, 1950.
CA: Clark, Alan: *Barbarossa: the Russian-German Conflict, 1941-45.* William Morrow, NY, 1985.
DC: Dickens, Charles: *David Copperfield.* Penguin, Harmondsworth, Middlesex, UK, 1987.
ED: Eisenhower, David: *Eisenhower: At War 1943-45.* Vintage, NY, 1987.
EE: Erikson, Erik: *Childhood and Society.* (2nd ed.) W.W. Norton, NY, 1963.

FJ: Fest, Joachim: *Hitler*. (Trans. Richard and Clara Winston), Harcourt Brace Jovanovich, NY, 1974.

FG: Fleming, Gerald: *Hitler and the Final Solution*. Univ. Calif. Press, Berkeley, 1984.

FS: Freud, Sigmund: "Psycho-Analytic Notes on an Autobiographical Account of a Case of Paranoia," *Standard Edition*, XII:3, Hogarth Press, London, 1953-74.

FSb: Freud, Sigmund: "Leonardo da Vinci," *Standard Edition*, XI:59, Hogarth Press, London, 1953-74.

FSc: Freud, Sigmund: "An Autobiographical Study," *Standard Edition*, XX:3, Hogarth Press, London, 1953-74.

FP: Friedman, Philip: *Roads to Extinction*. Conf. on Jewish Social Studies, Jewish Pub. Soc of America, NY, 1980.

FE: Fromm, Erich: *Anatomy of Human Destructiveness*. Holt, Rinehart & Winston, NY, 1973.

GG: Gilbert, G. M.: *Nuremberg Diary*. Da Capo Press (Plenum), NY, 1995 (orig. pub. 1947).

GM: Gilbert, Martin: *The Holocaust*. Holt, Rinehart & Winston, NY, 1985.

GDJ: Goldhagen, Daniel Jonah: *Hitler's Willing Executioners*. Random House, NY, 1996.

GT: Griess, Thomas, Series Editor:
The Second World War: Europe and the Mediterranean
The West Point Military History Series
United States Military Academy, West Point, NY,
Avery Publishing Group, Inc., Wayne, NJ, 1984.

GH: Guderian, Heinz: *Panzer Leader*. E. P. Dutton & Co., NY, 1952,

HF: Halder, Franz: *The Halder War Diary 1939-1942*. Ed. Charles Burdick and Hans-Adolf Jacobsen Presidio Press, Novato CA, 1988 [trans. from *Kriegstagebuch*, 3 vol., 1962-64]

HE: Hanfstaengl, Ernst: *Hitler, The Missing Years*. Arcade Publishing, NY, 1994.

HR: Hilberg, Raul: *The Destruction of the European Jews.*
Harper & Row, NY, 1979.

HAa: Hitler, Adolf [with Rudolf Hess]: *Mein Kampf.*
Houghton-Mifflin, Boston, 1943.

HAb: Hitler, Adolf: *My New Order.* Ed. Raoul de Rousy de
Sales. Reynal & Hitchcock, NY, 1941.

HAS: Huffington, A. S.: *Picasso, Creator and Destroyer.*
Simon & Schuster, NY, 1988.

JE: Jones, Ernest: *The Life and Work of Sigmund Freud.*
(3 vols.) Basic Books, NY, 1953-57.

KD: Kearns, Dorothy: *Lyndon Johnson and the American
Dream.* Harper & Row, NY 1976.

KJ: Keegan, John: *The Second World War.*
Viking, NY, 1989.

KA: Kubizek, August: *The Young Hitler I Knew.*
Houghton Mifflin, Boston, 1955.

LW: Langer, Walter: *The Mind of Adolf Hitler:
The Secret Wartime Report.*
Basic Books, NY, 1972.

MM: Margaret Mahler: *The Psychological Birth of the
Human Infant.* Basic Books, NY, 1975.

ME: Manstein, Erich von: *Lost Victories.*
Chicago: Henry Regnery, 1958.

MG: Marek, George Richard: *Beethoven, Biography of a
Genius.* Funk & Wagnalls, NY, 1969.

MI: Melchior, Ib and Frank Brandenburg: *Quest.*
Presidio, Novato CA, 1990.

MS: Milgram, Stanley: *Obedience to Authority: An
Experimental View.* Harper & Row, NY, 1974.

MA: Miller, Alice: *For Your Own Good:
Hidden Cruelty in Child-Rearing and the Roots of Violence.* Farrar, Straus & Giroux, NY, 1983.

NY: *The New Yorker.* [Dates and pages as noted.]

NYT: *New York Times.* [Dates and pages as noted.]

NJ: Noakes, J. and G. Pridham, eds.: *Nazism 1919-1945: A History in Documents and Eyewitness Accounts.* Schocken Books, NY, 1988.

SM: Schatzman, Morton: *Soul Murder: Persecution in the Family.* Random House, NY, 1973.

SP: Schmidt, Paul: *Hitler's Interpreter.* Macmillan, NY, 1951.

SW: Shirer, William: *The Rise and Fall of the Third Reich.* Simon and Shuster, NY, 1960.

SWC: Simon Weisenthal Center, Los Angeles, *Response.*

SA: Speer, Albert: *Playboy,* June 1971.

SAb: Speer, Albert: *Inside the Third Reich.* Macmillan, NY, 1970.

SH: Stierlin, Helm: *Adolf Hitler: A Family Perspective.* Psychohistory Press, NY, 1976.

TA: Taylor, A. J. P.: *The Origins of the Second World War,* 2nd ed. Fawcett World Library, NY, 1965.

TF: Taylor, Fred: *The Goebbels Diaries 1939-1941.* G. P. Putnam's Sons, NY, 1983.

TJ: Toland, John: *Adolf Hitler.* Doubleday & Co., Garden City NY, 1976.

WO: Wagener, Otto: *Hitler--Memoirs of a Confidant.* Henry Turner, ed. Yale Univ. Press, New Haven CT, 1985.

WR: Waite, Robert: *The Psychopathic God Adolf Hitler.* Basic Books, NY, 1977.

WW: Warlimont, Walter: *Inside Hitler's Headquarters.* (Trans. R. H. Barry.) Praeger, NY, 1964.

WDC: Watt, Donald Cameron: *How War Came, The Immediate Origins of the Second World War, 1938-1939.* Pantheon, NY, 1989.

WE: Wiesel, Elie: *Night.* Bantam, NY, 1986.

WRS: Wistrich, Robert S.: *Antisemitism: The Longest Hatred.* Pantheon Books, NY, 1991

WDS: Wyman, David S.: *Abandonment of the Jews: America and the Holocaust 1941-1945.* Pantheon, NY, 1984.

WDSb:Wyman, David S.: *Paper Walls: America and the Refugee Crisis, 1938-1941.* Pantheon, NY, 1985.

INDEX

About the Author

Michael Nelken earned his medical degree in twenty-one months at Washington University in St. Louis, then trained in child psychiatry at the guidance clinic directed by E. James Anthony, before taking a fellowship in psychiatry under Jules V. Coleman at Yale University. Informed as well by Carl Whitaker, Nelken taught family therapy in the psychiatry department of the University of Connecticut for many years, and now serves on the medical staff of the Hospital of St. Raphael in New Haven. A psychiatric associate of the American Academy of Psychoanalysis and a member of the Human Behavior and Evolution Society, he is certified as a specialist in psychiatry by the American Board of Psychiatry and Neurology, and consults to the courts of Connecticut on child protection issues, hospital commitment and other matters. Before following his father, grandfather, uncles and aunts into the practice of medicine, he first graduated from Reed College in physics and created computer systems in San Francisco. He has been the medical director of a number of clinics and hospital units, and has lectured in the United States, Canada and Mexico. He now is in private practice in child and family psychiatry in Connecticut, where he lives with his wife and the younger of his six children.

Please tear out this order form --

HITLER UNMASKED
The Romance of
Racism and Suicide

Michael Nelken, M.D.

For orders or educational discounts,

write: **Darkside Press**
P.O. Box 306
Glastonbury CT 06033

or call: 1-800-**DYG-DARK**

Price	$ 24.50
Shipping	3.50
	$ 28.00

[In CT, add $1.47 sales tax]